CW00520968

Discovery Guide to

JORDAN

and the Holy Land

by Diana Darke

IMMEL
Publishing

To my mother

The author wishes to thank Nasri Atallah for his help in making the
preparation of this book possible.

Discovery Guide to Jordan, first edition

Published by Immel Publishing Ltd,
20 Berkeley St, London W1X 5AE
tel: 071 491 1799; fax: 071 493 5524

Text copyright © Diana Darke 1993
   All rights reserved

Layout and cover design by Jane Stark
Typesetting by Icon Publications Ltd

Printed at The Bath Press, Bath, UK

A CIP catalogue record for this book
is available from the British Library

ISBN 0 907151 701

To help with the next edition, the reader is asked to send information and comments to
the General Editor, *Discovery Guide to Jordan,* Immel Publishing Ltd, 20 Berkeley St,
London W1X 5AE

CONTENTS

Introduction   7

Section 1: JORDAN – Background Information

Travel Facts   11
   Travelling to Jordan   11
   Travelling within Jordan   12
   Car Hire   13
   Accommodation   13
   Food and Drink   14
   Money   15
   Appreciation of Services Rendered   15
   Budgeting   15
   Visas   16
   Time   16
   Electricity   16
   Communications   16
   Media   16
   Vaccinations and Health   16
   Climate   17
   Clothing   17
   Opening Hours   18
   Security and Safety   18
   What to Buy   18
   Weights and Measures   19
   Useful Items to Take   20
   Tourism   20
   Watersports   20
   Where to go for Information   20
   Itineraries   22
   Crossing to the West Bank   23
   Calendar of Festivals and Public Holidays   24

Country File
   Cultural Heritage   25
   Geography   26
   Chronology of Historical Events   27
   Population and Religion   32
   The Government and the King   37
   Economy   40
   Education   40
   The Arabic Language   41
   Flora and Fauna   43

Section 2: **AROUND JORDAN**

Amman   **46**
   Amman Facts   46
   The City   52
   Environs of Amman   63
   Iraq el-Amir   64
   Qasr el-Mushatta   67

North from Amman   **68**
   Northern Jordan Facts   68
   Salt   70
   The Jordan Valley   72
   Pella   75
   El-Himmeh and Mukheibeh   77
   Umm Qais   79
   Irbid   82
   Capitolias and Abila   83
   Ajlun   85
   Jerash   88
   Umm el-Jimal   99
   The Desert Umayyad Palaces   102

South from Amman   **115**
   Southern Jordan Facts   115
   The Dead Sea   119
   The King's Highway   120
   Petra   140
   The Pilgrim Trail   172
   Wadi Rum   173
   Aqaba   176
   The Desert Road   180

Section 3: **THE HOLY LAND**

Introduction   **183**

Travel Facts   **183**
   Crossing from Jordan   183
   Flights   184
   Car Hire   184
   Food   184
   Money   185
   Visas   185
   Vaccinations and Health   185
   Climate and Seasons   185
   Clothing   186
   Where to go for Information   186

The Intifada   186
Touring the Holy Land   186

Jerusalem   **187**
Jerusalem Facts   187
History   188
Itinerary   189
Inside the Walls   191
Outside the Walls   205

The Southern Circuit   **210**
Southern Circuit Facts   210
Qumran   211
Massada   212
A Detour to Sodom   213
Hebron   214
The Herodium   214
Bethlehem   215

The Northern Circuit   **217**
Northern Circuit Facts   217
The Road North   218
Sebastea   218
Nazareth   219
The Sea of Galilee   219
The Jordan Valley   221
Hisham's Palace   221
Jericho   222

APPENDIX

Useful Arabic Words and Phrases   **224**

Further Reading   **227**

INDEX   **228**

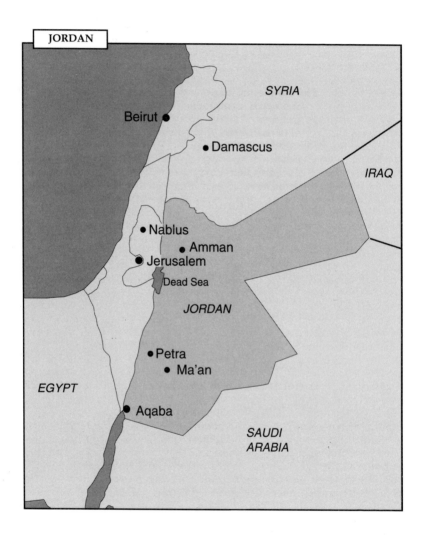

SYRIA

IRAQ

Beirut

Damascus

Nablus

Amman

Jerusalem

Dead Sea

JORDAN

Petra

Ma'an

EGYPT

Aqaba

SAUDI
ARABIA

INTRODUCTION

Jordan, a tiny kingdom whose borders were dictated by the vagaries of British policy after the First World War, can boast dramatic contrasts. In landscape it ranges from the forested highlands in the north to the sub-tropical Jordan Valley; from the eerie eroded mountains of Petra and Wadi Rum to the flat basalt deserts of its eastern reaches. In population it encompasses some of the few remaining nomadic Bedouin left in the Arab world, along with some of the region's most highly educated and sophisticated workforce, resident largely in Amman, its capital. In terms of sightseeing, the variety it offers is greater even than that of Egypt. Visitors can, in the space of a few days, walk along the intact streets of Roman Jerash, discover exquisite Arab palaces in the desert, visit wildlife reserves, marvel at Christian mosaics and Crusader castles, go on horseback through the narrow defile of Petra to be confronted with the Treasury, one of the most spectacular sights in the world, ride a camel through the haunting moonscapes of Wadi Rum, and complete the experience with the superb beaches and marine life of the Red Sea at Aqaba.

The country has seen some dramatic changes since 1988. As so often in its short history as a modern state, Jordan is facing a period of uncertainty. King Hussein's historic decision on 30 July 1988 to abandon the kingdom's 40 year-old claim to the West Bank was a watershed in Jordanian politics, but it was overshadowed towards the end of the year by a sharp fall in the value of the dinar and the introduction of wide-ranging austerity measures. A ban was announced on the import of many luxury goods.

The Gulf War of 1991, moreover, was a disaster for the country. Because of its attempt to stay neutral and its refusal to condemn Iraq, it isolated itself within the Arab world and disappointed the USA and Europe. The result was the cessation of Arab, especially Gulf, aid, and an influx of 300,000 Palestinians who had been working in Kuwait and the rest of Gulf. This was equivalent to a 10 per cent increase in population in less than a year, and the only assistance Jordan received in trying to cope was small amounts from Japan and Western Europe.

Looking ahead to the next ten years, what will be the impact of the severe economic recession on its internal stability? How will the future of the Jordanian-Palestinian relationship be defined? Will the Palestinians, who now form 60 per cent of Jordan's population invite the king to reclaim sovereignty over the West Bank which he renounced in 1988, or will they prefer a Jordanian Palestinian confederation? How will Jordan cope with its increasingly active Islamic factions?

These questions will generally be of concern to the tourist only in so far as they impinge on the stability of the regime; and indeed, the remarkable thing about Jordan is that, against all the odds, the king has maintained his popularity and the stability of his government. A beneficial effect for the visitor of Jordan's economic crisis and the devaluation of its currency is that, from being one of the most expensive countries in the region, it has now become one of the cheapest; cheaper indeed than Egypt, and unquestionably better value for money.

The procedures for tourists crossing to the West Bank and back again have remained unaltered despite all other changes, and the majority of visitors, if they have not previously visited Jerusalem, will want to include it and the other holy sites in their trip to Jordan, since they are geographically so close. It therefore makes sense, for the forseeable future, to keep this last section as part of the guide. The Palestinian uprising, or Intifada, which began in the Occupied Territories in November 1987, does not normally affect tourists. Disturbances tend to occur in particular areas, close to refugee camps, and mainly after dark, and no tourist has yet been caught up in any fighting or suffered any injury. Of course, as long as the Intifada continues, it obviously makes sense to enquire from local tourist offices about any possible no-go areas, but on the whole, as long as you behave sensibly and confine your sightseeing to the usual places, you are unlikely to find yourself in any danger or difficulty. Indeed, there can even be advantages: whereas Jerusalem at Christmas used to be extremely busy and crowded, it is now pleasantly deserted, hotels are half empty and service excellent.

This Discovery Guide to Jordan is divided into three sections in order to make the information readily accessible to the traveller. Section 1 provides basic information about Jordan. Around Jordan is divided into three parts – Amman and the regions north and south of Amman – and serves as a guide to the country. The third section is a guide to the Holy Land.

Section 1: JORDAN BACKGROUND INFORMATION

Travel Facts

Country File

Jordan

The headquarters of Royal Jordanian in the Shmeisani district of Amman (Vine)

TRAVEL FACTS

Travelling to Jordan

By Air

Air France flies from London to Amman via Paris three times a week, with a stopover at Damascus. ALIA, the Royal Jordanian Airline (*177 Regent Street, London W1R 7FB, tel: 071-734 2557*) flies from London direct daily except Mondays.

Security at Amman airport is tight, with frisking and body searches. Baggage is generally searched twice.

For non-package tour travellers wanting flights only, two of the best companies offering **discounted fares** are:*Trailfinders, 42/48 Earls Court Road, London W8 6EJ, tel: 071-938 3366*, and *STA, Priory House, Wrights Lane, Hight St, Kensington, London W8 6TA, tel: 071-937 9962*. The cheapest return fare is from £322 with Turkish Airlines flying via Istanbul twice a week.

By Land

From Syria. The only border crossing between Syria and Jordan is at Ar-Ramtha. If you are travelling in your own car you must have a *carnet de passage*, obtainable in advance from the AA, and an international driving licence. Third party insurance can be bought at the border. The procedures at the border generally take an hour, and tend to be a bit chaotic. Exercise patience. The **JETT** (*Jordan Express Tourist Transport Co, tel: Amman 664146*) buses run twice a day between Damascus and Amman, and take seven hours, including the border crossing. As they are the easiest way to make the crossing, places fill up quickly and should be reserved at least two days in advance. Service taxis also make the trip but are less comfortable.

From Egypt. JETT buses operate a daily service from Cairo.

From Iraq. JETT buses run daily from Baghdad.

From Saudi Arabia. The crossing south of Aqaba is open. There are no JETT buses, so local buses or taxis must be used.

From Israel and the West Bank. See the section on the Holy Land for full details on how to make this crossing. The permit you obtain from the Jordanian Ministry of the Interior allows for a one month stay and you can return to Jordan as long as your visa is still valid and your passport has no Israeli stamp. The Israelis are used to this and issue you with a card which is stamped instead. In 1980 60,000 tourists a year made the crossing.

By Sea

From Egypt. Car ferries run twice daily between Aqaba and Nuweiba in Sinai. The journey takes three to four hours, and the ferries leave Aqaba around 11.00 am and 5.30 pm, and Nuweiba at 10.00 am and 4.00 pm each day. In practice, the timings are theoretical and the boats usually end up leaving later. It is best to check timings locally. Car fares are charged according to the number of cylinders, since the ferries are used principally by lorries and freight traffic. The fare one way is currently approximately £10 per passenger and £20 per car. There is no return fare. One boat is Egyptian, the other Jordanian. Both are somewhat below the standards of European ferries, but hot food is served from a restaurant and self-service cafeteria.

There is no need to book in advance and tickets can be bought at a number of travel agents in Aqaba, or at the port office itself in Nuweiba. Border procedures are tedious and you are asked to be present an hour before sailing as a foot passenger, or one and a half hours before if taking your own car. Essential documentation to have is the *carnet de passage* (triptyche), international driving licence, car tax and insurance. If you are travelling from Egypt, a recent bank receipt must be produced showing exchange of sufficient foreign currency at a bank to cover the cost of the ticket purchase.

Car ferries also run between Suez and Aqaba, though less frequently than from Nuweiba, and involve one night on the boat. Since the boats are of a fairly basic standard, this service is not really to be recommended. Approximate costs are currently £25 per person including cabin, plus £65 for the car one way.

Travelling within Jordan
By Air
There are daily flights (45 minutes) from Amman to Aqaba by Alia, the national airline.

By Rail
The only passenger railway, from Amman north to Damascus, was part of the original Hejaz railway built at the beginning of the century by Turkish soldiers to take pilgrims from Damascus to Mecca. It only ran the full length to Mecca for six years, until 1914, when it was heavily bombed, but it cut down the pilgrims' journey time from 50 days in a camel caravan to a mere three days on the train. The section south from Amman to Aqaba is used only for the transport of goods, mainly phosphate.

By Bus
Buses link Amman (from the main bus station at Abdali – see Amman map for location) to most major towns in Jordan, as well as to Damascus. The bus tour company, **JETT**, runs efficient, comfortable, air-conditioned buses (blue and white) on specific routes within the country, and to the West Bank crossing point, at very reasonable prices. They run five times a day to Aqaba, taking five hours.

By Taxi
Service taxis follow a fixed route between two points, be it within Amman and its suburbs, or in the country at large. Generally they are Peugeot 504 station wagons or Mercedes sedans. They leave when they are full (seven passengers) and the fare is fixed. They can be recognised by a white square on the front door and a white light on the roof. The service route number and destination are written in Arabic in the square.

Ordinary taxis have a green square on the front door and a yellow light on the roof, and the fare is set by meters. Taxi drivers do not expect tips.

There are also limousine taxis which operate from the four- and five-star hotels and have fixed but expensive rates. They are generally cleaner than ordinary taxis and more luxurious, with air-conditioning.

A reasonable **fixed-price taxi service** runs from Queen Alia International airport to any part of Amman, and you should buy a ticket from the kiosk after you emerge from customs into the arrival hall. The journey takes between 30 and 45 minutes.

By Private Car
You can take your own car into Jordan, provided you have obtained a *carnet de passage* from the AA or the automobile club of your country of residence. This permits temporary import into the country for a period of up to three months. Insurance (third party) is bought at the border, though it is wise to buy comprehensive cover, either at the border or in your country of residence.

Petrol is cheap, costing about half what it does in the UK and Europe, and petrol stations are plentiful all over the country. Ordinary and super are the two types available, along with diesel. Unleaded is unheard of. An international driving licence is advisable but not essential, as your own national licence will also be recognized.

The road network in Jordan is excellent, one of the best in the Middle East. All secondary roads , even those to smaller towns, are surfaced. Traffic is generally lighter and better behaved than in any other Middle Eastern country, not least because the driving test is stiff – it is not a mere formality with the price for passing a matter to be settled by bargaining rather than ability (as is the case in some Middle Eastern countries!). Even more remarkable is that Jordan stipulates an eye test when your driving licence comes up for renewal every ten years. Traffic drives on the right. The Ministry of Tourism issues a good road map gratis. Women drivers are much in evidence.

Car Hire
There are many companies in Amman offering car hire, often of Japanese cars like Nissan and Toyota. The major companies are Avis and Budget; the other, smaller ones tend to be cheaper, but not necessarily so reliable. Prices range from JD80 to JD 100 per week for unlimited mileage. The larger companies accept credit cards. A few companies also offer car hire in Aqaba. Hire vehicles have green number plates, private ones white, and government ones red.

Accommodation
Hotels range from five-star to one-star. Outside Amman, the best hotels are in Petra and Aqaba. Jordan is one of the most hygienic Middle Eastern countries and even modest hotels are generally clean and free of smells. There is a *YWCA* in Jebel Amman (*tel: 621488, P.O. Box 5014, Amman*). Camping is possible at Petra, Wadi Rum, the Dead Sea and Aqaba. There is very little – indeed often no – accommodation at all in smaller towns such as Madaba, for example, and you should bear this in mind when planning your itinerary. Apart from Amman, Petra and Aqaba, adequate accommodation can be found at Irbid, Ajlun, Azraq, the Dead Sea, Zerqa Ma'in, Kerak and Wadi Rum (this last is self-catering only).

Five-star hotels are up to full international standard and prices range from JD65 to JD75 per double room. Four-star hotels are also quite luxurious and prices range from JD55 to JD65. Three-star hotels are perfectly acceptable for most travellers, with clean rooms and your own bathroom/WC. Prices range from JD15 to JD40 per double room. One- and two-star hotels are also fine for those who do not mind slightly spartan surroundings. Prices for these range from JD7 to JD14 per double room.

Food and Drink
Food is central to every celebration in Islam. To break food with someone is to seal a friendship, it is almost a ritual. Eating for eating's sake is considered a private affair, to be done with relaxation in the intimacy of one's own home. For this reason it was regarded as bad form until recently to eat out in restaurants.

Lunch is generally served in Amman restaurants from 1.00 till 3.00 pm and dinner after 8.00 pm. Outside the capital, times are more flexible. Much of the food is bland international-style cuisine, but some of the Middle Eastern and Jordanian dishes you may come across are listed below:

Mansaf. Jordan's national dish, unflatteringly but quite accurately nick-named 'mutton grab'. It is eaten traditionally with the right hand from a large communal platter whilst sitting on the floor. The meat, usually mutton but occasionally camel, is boiled, cut into chunks and then poured over a huge bed of rice. Sometimes pine nuts and spices are added to enhance the flavour, and a sauce of beaten yogurt and mutton fat may also be poured over to keep it moist. This is the traditional Bedouin feast, prepared for weddings or religious holidays. Do not be surprised if conversation over this type of food is sparse. An Arabic proverb says: '*When the food is served, the conversation stops*'.

Musakhan. A West bank speciality, chicken steamed in olive oil, onions and *sumak*, then baked on special bread and covered in onions.

Maqlouba. A Jerusalem speciality, meat on rice with stewed vegeatables, usually aubergine or cauliflower.

Daoud Pasha. Meatball stew with onions, pine nuts and tomatoes on rice.

Mulukhia. Meat, usually lamb, stewed with a spinach-like vegeatable. It is sometimes available in the resthouses along the desert highway. Originally more of an Egyptian speciality.

Mezze. A selection of starters, some hot, some cold, offering tremendous variety and often good value as a main course. The Lebanese do the best *mezze*, but the Jordanian ones are often a close second. Some of the standard cold dishes within the *mezze* are: *hummus* (chickpea dip); *baba ghanouj* or *mutabbal* (aubergine dip); *tahineh* (sesame dip); *tabbouleh* (chopped tomato, mint and cracked wheat); *labneh* (creamy yogurt) with walnuts. The hot dishes include: *kibbeh* (minced meat in cone shapes stuffed with pine kernels, onion and cracked wheat (*burghul*)); *fataayir* (thin triangular-shaped pastries filled with cheese or spinach); *falaafil* (chickpea balls fried in oil). *Falaafil* served in pitta bread with a little salad inside is a standard cheap snack in Israel and the West Bank.

Shawarma. The Turkish *doner kebab*, also served in pitta bread with salad.

Bottled, still **mineral water** is available everywhere and, apart from in the luxury hotels, should be drunk in preference to the tap water, which, though drinkable when first pumped out of the treatment works, may be contaminated in storage tanks on the roof of the hotel. There are several types depending on what region you are in: Al-Kawthar, Safa and Ghadeer. The latter, from the Petra area, has the softest taste.

The **wines** are drinkable, non-vintage, red, white and rosé. Latroun, from a monastery of the same name in the West Bank, is one of the most widely available. Other types are Cremisan and Chateau St Catherine, both from the West Bank. The local beer is Amstel and relatively expensive. Araq is the national drink, as in all of the Levant. It is 40 per cent proof, white, aniseed-flavoured and smoother than ouzo, its Greek counterpart. It is drunk with ice and water, and is an excellent accompaniment to lamb and other greasy dishes. Alcohol is on sale in shops and supermarkets.

Juice stalls, selling freshly squeezed orange, banana, pomegranate and strawberry juice can be found in Downtown Amman and in Jerusalem, as well as some regional towns, and make a very refreshing stop in summer.

Money
The Jordanian dinar is divided into 1000 fils. Notes range from $^1/_2$ dinar to 20 dinars. Coins are profuse, large and heavy, so bear this in mind when choosing your purse or wallet. Occasionally you will come across a piastre or girsh, which is worth 10 fils. JD1 therefore consists of 100 piastres or girsh.

Hotels give a slightly lower exchange rate than banks, but commission is included. The difference between the bank and the hotel rate is about JD1 per JD100 changed. There is very little difference between the exchange rates in Jordan and the UK, so there is no reason why you should not change some money in advance.

Banks are open from 9.30 am to 1.30 pm daily except Friday. Travellers' cheques are accepted by all banks and by some hotels. Major **credit cards** are accepted in most hotels of three-stars or more and at some restaurants. Visa is more widely accepted than Access Mastercard.

Appreciation of Services Rendered
A service charge of 10 or 12 per cent is usually added to hotels and restaurants, but it is normal to leave a small amount extra for the waiter (about 5 per cent). Taxi drivers are not generally tipped.

Budgeting
Jordan used to be one of the priciest countries in the Middle East, but in November 1988 there was a partial flotation of the dinar prompted by the economic changes resulting from the ending of Jordan's links with the West

Bank. Costs for visiting foreigners have therefore dropped considerably, and it is now cheaper than most Middle Eastern countries, including Egypt. Once you have paid your air fare and car hire, a reasonable daily budget for two including accommodation in a two- or three-star hotel, meals, drinks, entry fees and 200km of petrol is around £35.

Visas
All foreigners entering Jordan need a visa. Tourist visas are usually valid for three months, and can be obtained in advance at the Jordanian Embassy (*6 Upper Phillimore Gardens, London W8 7HB, tel: 071-937 3685*) or issued on arrival. An Israeli stamp in your passport will disqualify you from entry into Jordan, or indeed into any Arab country. If you are staying in Jordan longer than 14 days you need to report to a police station to register, otherwise you will be fined JD5 at the airport, a lengthy administrative procedure which can make you miss your flight if you are caught unawares.

Time
Jordan is two hours ahead of GMT in winter and three hours ahead in summer. It is seven hours ahead of US Eastern Standard Time.

Electricity
All of Jordan is on 220–40 volts, 50 Hz. Supply is reliable and power cuts are very rare. Plugs are of the two-pin continental style.

Communications
The postal service from Europe to Amman is efficient, usually taking less than a week. From Jordan abroad, however, it is less good, usually taking a fortnight. Letters and postcards should never be put in postboxes. They are liable to stay there forever. You should either hand them in at your hotel for delivery to a post office, or take them there yourself. Stamps can be bought at all the big hotels.

There are no postal street addresses in Amman – all letters are sent to post office boxes and collected from there, never delivered to houses. No one knows the street names and houses have no numbers.

Most of Jordan has automatic international dialling.

Media
The Jordanian press has a fairly free rein and censorship, which is common in most other Arab countries, is unusual here. There is an English-language daily, the *Jordan Times*, and a weekly, the *Jerusalem Star*. Jordanian TV broadcasts in Arabic, English, French and Hebrew. Radio Jordan's English service also broadcasts from 7.00 am till midnight on 350.9M, 855 Khz MW and on VHF FM Stereo 99 MHz.

Vaccinations and Health
No vaccinations are compulsory, unless you are arriving from a country or area where diseases such as cholera and yellow fever are endemic. Polio, typhoid and tetanus innoculations are advisable however. Cholera and

Gamma Globulin vaccinations (against hepatitis) are both short lived and of debatable efficacy anyway. The risk of malaria is very small and does not warrant taking anti-malarial pills.

Tap water in hotels with four stars or more is generally safe to drink, since they have their own filtering systems. The bottled mineral waters (Kawthar from Azraq springs, Safa, and Ghadeer from Petra) are all very good and cheap and available everywhere. They come in 1.5 litre plastic bottles or smaller.

Jordan is probably the cleanest country in the Middle East and is generally dust-free. The usual precautions apply about washing bought fruit and vegetables carefully (or peeling them), and in hotels and restaurants it is safest, as a new arrival, to avoid salads and raw foods, especially if they look at all 'tired'. Yogurt is often good for mild stomach upsets. Alternatively, a day of starvation, just drinking Coca Cola or fizzy lemonade every hour, can be very effective. Lomotil, the best anti-diarrhea tablets, can be bought over the counter at any chemist. It might be a wise precaution to bring a broad spectrum antibiotic (having checked with your doctor first on the best type), in case of persistent illness. Unlike other Middle Eastern countries, antibiotics are not sold over the counter in Jordan and are very expensive.

Climate

Jordan tends to be hot and dry in summer and cooler and wetter in winter – January and February are the wettest months. The most popular times to visit are spring, specifically March, April and May; autumn, specifically September, October and the first half of November; Christmas and New Year. At such times it is essential to book accommodation, especially in places where it is limited, such as at Petra.

The monthly average temperatures in Fahrenheit and Celsius are as follows:

Amman

Jan	Feb	Mar	Apr	May	Jun	Jul	Aug	Sept	Oct	Nov	Dec
46	48	53	60	69	74	77	78	73	69	59	50 °F
8	9	12	16	21	23	25	26	23	21	15	10 °C

Aqaba

Jan	Feb	Mar	Apr	May	Jun	Jul	Aug	Sept	Oct	Nov	Dec
60	62	68	75	82	89	89	91	86	80	71	62 °F
16	17	20	24	28	32	32	33	30	27	22	17 °C

Clothing

As in any Muslim country, clothing for both sexes should not be too revealing. Bare arms and legs are all right, but avoid displaying cleavages, backs, and too much upper thigh in shorts or miniskirts. For your own comfort as well as modesty, avoid clothes that are too tight. The basic rule is not to dress in a way that draws attention to yourself, especially in rural areas or in Downtown Amman. In winter thick warm clothing will be essential, especially when it gets dark, at around 5.30 pm, and the evenings are long. Comfortable shoes are essential for walking on the uneven stony ground of Petra.

Opening Hours
Friday is the weekly Muslim holiday, when banks, offices, businesses and most shops are closed. Other opening hours are:

Banks: 9.30 am–1.30 pm
Businesses: 9.00 am–1.00 pm and 3.00 am–7.00 pm
Government Offices: 8.00 am–2.00 pm
Museums: 8.00 am–4.00 pm or 5.00 pm. Closed Tuesdays.

Most shops keep longer hours, from 9.00 am to 8.00 pm. The souq in Downtown Amman is open every day, including Friday which in fact tends to be the busiest day.

Security and Safety
As one of the confrontation states with Israel, with more than twice the length of borders to defend than any of Israel's other neighbours, Jordan's defence expenditure has historically been very high, and nearly 20 per cent of the country's working population is in the armed forces (including conscripts). That said, the military keeps a low profile and unlike its counterpart in Egypt, for example, is not obsessed with security; the traveller will not be continually stopped at checkpoints and asked for documents.

Most Jordanians have a certain dignity, and theft is rare. Women are pestered less than in most Arab countries; indeed harrassment of foreigners in general, whether male or female is a relatively unusual occurence. By and large Jordanians allow all visitors to walk about unmolested. They will however, always be happy to help if asked.

What to Buy
The large hotel shops all offer the gold and silver jewellery, alabaster, mother of pearl and leather goods that are common in most Middle Eastern countries. Specific to Jordan are Madaba and Beni Hamida rugs, carved olivewood, Palestinian pottery, Hebron glass and cross-stitch embroidery. One of the best places to shop if you have the time is the **Craft Shop** in Jebel Amman (see Amman map for exact location), which sells a variety of fairly priced hand-made objects, including embroidery and stitching on tablecloths or napkins by Palestinian women refugees. Old copper implements from the Amman souq can be a good buy if you bargain well. Bargaining is normal where prices are not marked. Aim for $1/2 - 2/3$ of the first price given.

Another good place to shop is the **Kan Zaman Village** about 12km outside Amman on the Madaba/airport road. It is a nineteenth century village restored as a craft centre, with stone-flagged streets lined with shops and boutiques selling high quality goods. You can also watch the goods being made – like glass being blown, rugs and jewellery being made. In the village there are cafés and restaurants supplied with constant fresh bread from the traditional oven next door, and a Bedouin tent with Arab coffee served by waiters in

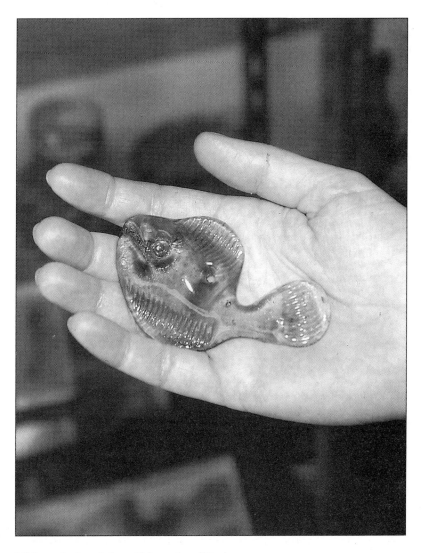

A fish pendant made from Hebron glass (Vine).

authentic costumes. Loosely translated, Kan Zaman means 'how it used to be', and the village is meant to show visitors a slice of life from the past. It is popular with tourists and Jordanians alike.

Weights and Measures
Jordan employs the metric system.

Useful Items to Take
In summer: sunglasses and a water bottle on a shoulder strap.
In winter: warm pullovers and windproof jacket.
All seasons: comfortable walking shoes; torch; penknife; universal plug for hotel washbasins (often no plug is provided); mosquito repellent tablets and electric plate which can be bought in local pharmacies to ensure undisturbed nights; toilet paper; small knapsack for transporting water, torch, books, camera etc. to allow you to walk freely and unencumbered.

Tourism
Tourism once provided 18 per cent of Jordan's gross national product, but has been declining since 1980 and dropped to virtually zero during the Gulf War of 1991. Numbers are picking up again now. British, Germans and Americans feature highest on the list of Western visitors, with French and Italians trailing.

Most visitors are struck by the friendliness and relaxed atmosphere, contrary to any expectations of instability stemming from Jordan's shared borders with Israel, the occupied West Bank, Syria and Iraq.

The current Director General of the Jordan Tourism Authority is committed to a gradual revolution in Jordan's tourist facilities, encouraging more visitors to stay longer, rather than just to stop off a night or two to see Petra and Jerash, before crossing to Israel, as 90 per cent of Western tourists, most of them on Christian pilgrimage tours, currently do. Recent legislation has exempted groups of five and more from visa and departure taxes if they travel on the national carrier, Royal Jordanian, or via an approved travel agency.

Watersports
Extensive watersports facilities are available at Aqaba, Jordan's only outlet to the sea, including waterskiing, pedaloes, windsurfing, glass-bottomed boats and snorkelling. Aqualung diving is also on offer, with tuition and courses. See **Aqaba** in Section 2 for further details.

Where to go for Information
In Amman you can call on the Ministry of Tourism and Antiquities (see map in Amman section for location) to collect a map and some glossy pamphlets and fact sheets which will give you basic information about the country. In London the office of **Royal Jordanian Airlines**, *211 Regent Street, London W1R 7DD, tel: 071-437 9465*, doubles as Tourist Office, and will gladly send pamphlets and maps. The recently opened **Jordan Information Bureau**, *6 Upper Phillimore Gardens, London W8 7HB, tel: 071-630 9277* (the same premises as the embassy) is always willing to help with any statistical information.

The following tour operators offer holidays to Jordan from the UK:

Abercrombie and Kent,
Sloane Square House, Holbein Place, London SW1W 8NS. Tel: 071-730 9600

Aquatours, 7 Cranes Drive, Surbiton, Surrey KT5 8AJ. Tel: 081-399 6953

Bales Tours,
  Bales House, Junction Road, Dorking, Surrey RH4 3EJ. Tel: 0306 885991

British Museum Tours,
  46 Bloomsbury Street, London WC1B 3QQ. Tel: 071-323 8895

Creative Holidays, 34/38 Evershott Street, London NW1 1DA. Tel: 071 383 4243

Explore Worldwide Ltd,
  1 Fredrick Street, Aldershot, Hants GU11 1LQ. Tel: 0252 319448

Flights of Fantasy,
  Concorde House, Stour Street, Canterbury, Kent CT1 2NZ. Tel: 0227 763336

Fellowship Tours, South Chard, Somerset TA20 2PR. Tel: 0460 20540

Hann Overland, 2 Ivy Mill Lane, Godstone, Surrey RH9 8NH. Tel: 0883 744705

Highway Holidays, 63 Gray's Inn Road, London WC1X 8TL. Tel: 071-405 1368

The Imaginative Traveller,
  59 Chepstow Road, London W2 5BP. Tel: 071-730 9841

Insight International,
  Insight International Building, 26/28 Paradise Road, Richmond, Surrey
  TW9 1SE. Tel: 081-332 2400

Interchurch Travel,
  The Saga Building, Middelburg Square, Folkstone, Kent CT20 1AZ.
  Tel: 0303 47000

Jasmin Tours,
  High Street, Cookham, Maidenhead, Berks. SL6 9SR. Tel: 06285-31121

McCabe Travel, 53-55 Balham Hill, London SW12 9DR. Tel: 081-675 6828

Maranatha Tours,
  Trafalgar House, Grenville Place, Mill Hill, London NW7 3SA.
  Tel: 081-959 5303

Martin Randall Travel,
  10 Barley Mow Passage, London W4 4PH. Tel: 081-994 6477

Noble Caledonia, 11 Charles Street, London WC1X 7HB. Tel: 071-491 4752

Orient Tours/Classic Tours,
  87 Regent Street, London W1R 8LS. Tel: 071-734 7971

Peltours, Sovereign House,
  11/19 Ballards Lane, London N3 1UX. Tel: 081-346 9144

Prospect Art Tours Ltd,
  454/458 Chiswick High Road, London W4 5TT. Tel: 081-995 2151.

Ramblers Holidays,
  Longcroft House, Fretherne Road, Welwyn Garden City, Herts AL8 6PQ.
  Tel: 0707 331133

Raymond Cook Holidays,
Bedfordia Street, Prebend Street, Bedford MK40 1QC. Tel: 0234 49512

Regal Diving,
Station Road, Sutton in the Isle, Ely, Cambs C36 2RL. Tel: 0353 778096

Saga Holidays,
The Saga Building, Middleburg Square, Folkstone, Kent CT20 1AZ.
Tel: 0303 857000

Speedbird,
Atlantic House, Hazelwick Avenue, Crawley, West Sussex RH10 1NP.
Tel: 01-741 8041

Special Pilgrimages,
44 Sandleigh Road, Leigh On Sea, Essex SS9 1JU. Tel: 0702 711566

Serenissima Travel Ltd, 21 Dorset Street, London NW1 5PG. Tel: 071 730 9841

Swan Hellenic, 77 New Oxford Street, London WC1A 1PP. Tel: 071-831 1234

TEFS, 77 Fredrick Street, Loughborough, Leicester LE11 3TL. Tel:0 509 262745

Travelsphere,
Compass House, Coventry Road, Market Harborough, Leics LE16 9BZ .
Tel: 0858 410456

Temple World Travel, 13 The Avenue, Kew, Surrey TW9 2AL. Tel: 081 940 4114

Tour de Force,
Glen House, 200/208 Tottenham Court Road, London W1P 9LA .
Tel: 071-323 0747

Trust Travel,
Rotal London Buildings, 42 Baldwin Street, Bristol BS1 1PN.
Tel: 0272 273554

Twickers World,
22 Church Street, Twickenham, Middx TW1 3NW. Tel: 081-892 7606

Voyages Jules Verne, 21 Dorset Street, London NW1 5PG. Tel: 071-730 9841

Wind, Sand and Stars, 2 Arkwright Road, London NW3 6AD. Tel: 071-433 3684

Worldwide Christian Travel,
50 Coldharbour Road, Redland, Bristol BS6 7NA. Tel: 0272 731840

In Amman, a tour operator for that special occasion is *Wadi Tours and Travel, P.O. Box 927195, Amman, tel: 962-6-697480, fax: 962-6 686490.* They do one-off, tailor-made tours, like ballooning over Wadi Rum, camel caravans in the desert, banquets in a Crusader castle and four-wheel-drive vehicle desert racing.

Itineraries
Overnight stops are shown in brackets.

One Week
Arrive in Amman (Amman) • Amman, Jerash (Amman) • Circuit of Desert Palaces (Amman) • King's Highway, Madaba, Kerak (Petra) • Petra (Petra) • Petra, Wadi Rum (Aqaba) • Aqaba (Amman).

Two Weeks
Arrive in Amman (Amman) • Amman, apply for West Bank permit, Jerash (Ajlun) • Umm Qais, Pella, Salt (Amman) • Circuit of Desert Palaces (Amman) • King's Highway, Madaba, Kerak (Petra) • Petra (Petra) • Petra (Petra) • Wadi Rum (Aqaba) • Aqaba (Aqaba) • Aqaba (Amman) • Cross to West Bank (Jerusalem) • Jerusalem (Jerusalem) • Jerusalem, Bethlehem (Jerusalem) • Return to Amman, Iraq el-Amir (Amman).

Three Weeks
Arrive in Amman (Amman) • Amman, apply for West Bank Permit (Amman) • Salt, Deir Alla, Pella, Umm Qais (Irbid) • Irbid, Abila, Dibbeen, Ajlun, Jerash (Ajlun) • Umm al-Jimal, Amman, Dead Sea (Amman) • Circuit of Desert Palaces (Amman) • Madaba, Zerqa Ma'in, Herod's Palace (Kerak) • Kerak, Buseira, Sodom and Gomorrah, Shawbak (Amman) • Cross bridge to West Bank (Jerusalem) • Jerusalem (Jerusalem) • Jerusalem (Jerusalem) • Qumran, Massada, Hebron, Bethlehem (Jerusalem) • Samaria, Sea of Galilee (Tiberias) • Belvoir, Jericho, Hisham's Palace (Jerusalem) • Cross bridge to Amman, Iraq el-Amir (Amman) • Amman to Petra on desert road (Petra) • Petra (Petra) • Petra (Petra) • Wadi Rum (Wadi Rum) • Aqaba (Aqaba) • Aqaba (Aqaba) • Aqaba (Aqaba) • Return to Amman (Amman).

Crossing to the West Bank (Allenby Bridge)
This is a straightforward but time-consuming process, involving obtaining a permit from the Ministry of Interior. The permit takes two or three days to come through and is valid for a month. The sensible thing is to apply soon after arrival in Amman, wait a few days while you tour other places, then go back to collect your permit whenever it happens to fit in with your itinerary. The **Ministry of the Interior** is *open from Saturday to Wednesday 8.00 am–2.00 pm. The crossing is closed on Saturdays, the Israeli Sabbath, and closes at 1.00 pm on all other days.*

The procedure for obtaining the permit is as follows:

First visit: Take your passport, a photo and a pen. Buy the necessary stamps, 50 fils each, from the kiosk outside the ministry. Then go to Room 34 or the Foreigners' Department and collect two forms per application, which you fill in and leave behind. The total process takes about half an hour.

Second Visit: This should be at least 48 hours later. Go to Room 33 to collect your papers, then take them to Room 10, where you have a long wait (some 20–30 minutes) while they are typed up. You are fetched when they are ready, and you then go upstairs to Room 37, where the *Mudir* (Manager) sees people one by one: as one leaves, another goes in. The *Mudir* signs your papers and you then take them back down to Room 33 or the Foreigners' Department where one copy is filed and one is returned to you. The whole visit takes between 40 minutes and an hour.

Journey to the Bridge: No private or hired cars are allowed to cross the bridge, so if you want your own transport on the other side, you will have to hire a car or taxi to meet you there. Set off early, as the bridge opens from 7.00 am till 1.00 pm but sometimes closes sooner if the maximum allowable number of people have crossed before 1.00 pm. The drive from Amman to the bridge takes 40 minutes, and the best way to do it is by JETT bus, booked in advance, which takes you straight to the special foreigners' terminal, then drops you off further ahead at the bridge. If you travel independently, by taxi say, you have to wait for a special foreigners' bus to be sent to take you to the bridge, which can delay you unnecessarily.

Calender of Festivals and Public Holidays
The fixed public holidays in Jordan are as follows:
1 January, New Year's Day; 1 May, Labour Day; 25 May, Independence Day; 10 June, Great Arab Revolt/Army Day; 11 August, King Hussein's Accession; 14 November, King Hussein's Birthday, 25 December, Christmas Day.

The Muslim religious holidays are not fixed, as their timings are dictated by the **lunar calendar**, and therefore move backwards by about 11 days each year. The **Muslim calendar** starts from 622 AD, the date when Muhammad and his companions fled from Mecca to Medina, where they established the first mosque. That year is given as 1 AH (After Hegira, i.e. the Hegira being Muhammed's flight). Saudi Arabia is the only Arab country still to use this dating system in everyday affairs; the remainder all use the standard Gregorian system.

The approximate 1994 dates of the main religious holidays celebrated in Jordan are as follows:
Id al-Fitr, this is the second most important feast, to mark the end of Ramadan, the month of fasting, *13–15 March*; **Id al-Adha**, the major Muslim feast, to celebrate Abraham's willingness to sacrifice Isaac, *21–23 May*.

These two major *ids* or feasts are celebrated in all Arab countries with exchanges of visits between houses of family and friends, with sweets, coffee or meals being offered. Children always get new clothes, and often extra gifts too. In **Ramadan**, the 30 days of fasting, consumption of food is in fact higher than at any other time of the year, when everyone makes up for the day's abstinence by feasting after dark. Government offices and businesses have shortened hours during Ramadan, and efficiency is generally much impaired, not so much because of the fasting, but because of lack of sleep, since the night is used for eating and celebrating. The rough 1994 dates for Ramadan are 12 February–12 March. Alcohol is not generally available during Ramadan except in the hotels, and smaller restaurants will often not serve food till after sunset.

COUNTRY FILE

Cultural Heritage

Jordan is a small country, a tenth of the size of Egypt, and a fifth of the size of France. Its current borders bear no relation to a coherent political historical entity, owing their position to the whims of foreign – largely British – policies after the First World War. The Kingdom of Transjordan was created in 1921, but the Hashemite Kingdom of Jordan, to give it its full current name, only came into being officially in 1947. What is today one political unit was throughout thousands of years two disparate regions – the settled agricultural areas to the west with their trade routes, and the deserts to the east with their nomadic Bedouin. Only the Arabs managed to unite these two conflicting sides, first in the Nabatean period – the Nabateans being an Arabian tribe, with their capital at Petra – and later under the Umayyad caliphs, with their capital at Damascus and their series of desert palaces in which to escape from the worries of government. It is in Petra and in these palaces that Jordan's most novel and original cultural heritage is to be found.

From its position between the Mediterranean and the Arabian Peninsula, on the fringes of the Egyptian and Assyrian spheres of influence, on the edge of the Hellenised world and of the Byzantine Empire, the land that is now Jordan formed throughout history a natural corridor for traders and a transit route for armies, a defensive belt on the edge of the desert, the boundary of the civilised world. Having been a perpetual buffer zone, the land today, not surprisingly, bears the traces of an enormous variety of cultures. Statues, for example, discovered on the citadel in Amman and dated to about 800 BC, reveal signs of Phoenician, Egyptian and Assyrian, the three dominant forces in the area at that time. One of the most exciting facets of this archaeological wealth is that because the country in its present borders is scarcely 40 years old, research is still in its infancy and new sites are being discovered all the time. As Queen Nour put it in her uniquely American/Jordanian way: 'In Jordan it is almost impossible to sink a shovel into the ground without turning up some vestige of the past'.

Perpetual buffer zone

Geography

Despite its tiny size, Jordan offers surprising contrasts in landscape, and consequently in climate. The 1000m high plateau gives Amman cool breezes and cooler nights even

Climatic contrasts

25

A LOVE FOR THE DESERT

The 40 minute drive from the smart new Queen Alia International Airport into Amman leads along tarred highways through sparse hillsides. Set back in the fields are black Bedouin tents with Toyotas parked outside. In this essential contrast lies the fascination of Jordan: a small population of predominantly nomadic origins finding its way with commendable speed and capability into the twentieth century. The Bedouin have been given land by the Government to encourage them to settle, the deal being that they raise their standard of living through acquiring pumped water, electricity and cars in return for cultivating the land and selling the surplus produce. The gain is in practice largely on the Government's side, for whereas before, the Bedouin saw to their own needs alone, they are now helping to feed the cities. As the Arab proverb says: '*The fortunes of the Arabs who wear sandals have been eaten by the Arabs who wear slippers*'.

Many Jordanians, reflecting their origins, still nurture a deep love for the desert and its nomadic lifestyle. King Hussein, in the following passage from his autobiography *Uneasy Lies the Head*, expresses well the sentiments of his people:

"Jordan itself is a beautiful country. It is wild, with limitless deserts where the bedouin roam, but the mountains of the north are clothed in green forests, and, where the river flows, it is fertile in summer and winter. Jordan has a strange, haunting beauty and a sense of timelessness. Dotted with the ruins of empires once great, it is the last resort of yesterday in the world of tomorrow. I love every inch of it. I love Amman, where I was born, and which I have seen grow from a township. I am still awed and excited each time I set eyes on the ancient city of Petra, approached by a defile so narrow that a dozen Nabateans could hold an army at bay. Above all I feel at home in the tribal black tents in the desert."

in midsummer. The Jordan Valley, which is 400m below sea level, and Aqaba have a semi-tropical climate, while in the desert proper the typical extremes of very hot days and very cold nights are found.

It is a country of extremes in other ways too. Rural and city life are at opposite poles, accentuated by the difference between Jordanians and Palestians. The nomadic Bedouin who were the original inhabitants are dwindling now, but can still be found in the desert regions, especially south of Ma'an. The Palestinians who poured in after 1948 and 1967, and more recently after the Gulf War, tended to be traders and professional men rather than farmers.

The natural wealth of the country is small, with no oil or valuable mineral deposits: subsistence agriculture is therefore a major feature of the Jordanian economy. By placing great emphasis on education however, Jordan has succeeded in developing an important service sector, especially active in finance and banking.

City life has only existed since the 1920s when Amman became the capital and grew from a small village into a major metropolis. As a result, society is still based to a large extent on a patriarchal tribal background, with extended families sharing a house or living near to each other, and many customs are still centred on the family: practices such as arranged marriages continue, and entertainment consists largely of socialising and visiting each other's homes.

Physically, Jordan is 90 per cent steppe and desert, and is bissected by the northern reaches of the Great Rift Valley as it runs from Lake Tiberias through the Jordan Valley and the Dead Sea, down to the Gulf of Aqaba and on into East Africa. The fault line means that Jerusalem still has minor earthquakes from time to time, and the large quantites of lava that swelled up have covered large expanses of Syria and Jordan with black basalt desert. A shift in the Jordan Valley fault line was thought to have been the cause of the 1927 earthquake which led to extensive damage in Amman.

To the east of the Rift Valley lies a ridge of mountains formed by rock strata pushed upwards and folding over as the crack of the valley opened and sank. It was along this high ridge that many of the oldest towns flourished, favoured for settlement by the earliest inhabitants because of their cooler temperatures and natural defences. East of the mountain range is a wide high plateau, which makes Amman the second highest capital in the Arab world, after Sana'a in Yemen. Beyond the plateau, the rainfall stops and the remainder of the country eastwards towards Iraq and south to Saudi Arabia, is desert, inhabited only by nomadic or semi-nomadic Bedouin. Besides the mountains, the valley and the desert, Jordan has a number of mineral springs and areas of forest, especially in the northern hills.

Chronology of Historical Events

50,000–10,000 BC. Paleolithic and neolithic period. Hunting tools used by these earliest inhabitants of Jordan have been found in desert regions such as Wadi Rum and Azraq.

10,000–4000 BC. Neolithic period. First sedentary villages and beginnings of agriculture. Sites at Jericho, Beidha (near Petra), the Jerash region and, most recently, at Ain Ghazal in Downtown Amman.

4000–3100 BC. Chalcolithic period. First use of copper. Sites near Irbid and in the Jordan Valley.

3100–1550 BC. Early and middle bronze age. Jordan Valley fertile and densely populated. Major site, Bab el-Dhra, east of the Dead Sea.

C. 1900 BC. Abraham arrives in the land of Canaan.

Exodus

1550–1200 BC. Bronze age. Egypt's pharoahs of the 18th and 19th dynasties undertake campaigns in Palestine and Syria. The exodus of the Israelites from Egypt, led by Moses is generally set around **1250 BC** during the long reign of Rameses II. Joshua captures Jericho and divides Palestine among the 12 tribes of Israel.

1200–539 BC. Iron ages I and II. Kingdoms of Ammon, Moab and Edom east of the Jordan and the Wadi Araba in constant conflict with the Israelites.

1020 BC. Saul crowned king of all Israel.

1010 BC. King David makes his capital at Jerusalem.

970–930 BC. King Solomon builds his temple at Jerusalem. His conquests extended as far south as Sheba in North Yemen.

800–700 BC. Assyrians campaign against Jordan.

612 BC. Assyrian capital Nineveh captured by the Medes and the Babylonians.

587 BC. Babylonian conquests in Jordan under Nebuchadnezzar. Deportation of Ammonites and Jews to Babylonia.

539 BC. Babylon captured by Cyrus the Great. End of the neo Babylonian empire.

538 BC. Nabateans come to power in the south, establishing their capital at Petra. Cyrus issues an edict permitting the return of the Jews to Palestine.

490–480 BC. Wars between the Persians and the Greeks.

332 BC. Alexander the Great takes Palestine.

323 BC. Death of Alexander at Babylon.

313 BC. Roman emperor Constantine converts to Christianity.

320–160 BC. Palestine ruled by the Lagides of Egypt, then by the Seleucids of Syria.

Roman rule

63 BC. Conquest of Palestine and Jerusalem by the Romans under Pompey.

63 BC–106 AD. The Decapolis, a federation of 10 cities, is formed, attached to the Roman Province of Syria.

37 BC–4 AD. Herod the Great, of Edomite origins, but converted to Judaism, becomes king of the Jews under the Roman protectorate. He rebuilds the Temple at Jerusalem and builds palaces called Herodiums to the west and the east of the Dead Sea.

4 BC–30 AD. Birth and life of Jesus Christ, and his crucifixion by Pontius Pilate.

70 AD. Titus puts an end to the first Jewish revolt against Rome and destroys Jerusalem.

106 AD. Nabatean kingdom is conquered and joined to the Roman Province of Arabia.

132 AD. Second Jewish revolt, put down by Hadrian.

324 AD. Emperor Constantine establishes Christianity as the state religion of the Roman Empire.   **Christianity official**

614 AD. Sassanid invasion of Jordan and Palestine, massacres in Jerusalem.

629 AD. First battle between Christians and Muslims at Manta, south of Kerak. Muhammad takes Mecca.

636 AD. Battle of Yarmouk at which the Byzantines are defeated by the Arabs and forced to evacuate Jordan, Palestine and Syria. Jordan submits to Islam.

637 AD. Jerusalem taken by the caliph Umar.

639–642 AD. Arab conquest of Egypt.

661–750 AD. Umayyad dynasty of caliphs founded by Mu'awiya, with their capital at Damascus. Construction   **Desert palaces** of palaces in Jordanian desert.

750–1258 AD. Abbasid caliphate at Baghdad.

1095. First Crusade launched to recapture Jerusalem from the Muslims.

1099. Jerusalem captured by the Crusaders.

1100–1118. Baldwin I, the Frankish Crusader rules Jerusalem.

1171–1187. Saladin deposes the last Fatimid caliph in   **Saladin** Egypt and recaptures Palestine and Jerusalem from the Crusaders at the famous Battle of Hittin. His Ayyubid dynasty rules the region.

1263–1516. Mamlukes under Baybars of Egypt capture Crusader castles at Kerak and Shawbak.

1520–1566. Reign of Suleyman the Magnificent, extending the Ottoman Empire over all Arabia. For the next 400 years under the Turks, the land of Jordan becomes the route for Muslim pilgrims travelling between Turkey and Mecca, but otherwise unimportant and stagnating.

Lawrence and the Arab Revolt

1916. The Ottoman Empire sides with Germany in the First World War, and faces the Arab Revolt of the tribes seeking their independence, inspired by T.E. Lawrence.

1917. The Arabs take Aqaba, the Allies take Jerusalem.

1917–1918. General Allenby campaigns against the Turks in Palestine and Syria. End of Ottoman domination of Arab countries.

1920. Transjordan and Palestine placed under British mandate.

1923. Administration of the Emirate of Transjordan given to the Hashemite Emir Abdullah. The Arab Legion is formed with Glubb Pasha as leader.

1939. Jordanian Arab legions under the Emir Abdullah fight with the Allies in the Second World War.

1946, 25 May. Transjordan becomes an independent monarchy when Britain gives up its mandate.

Jordan created

1947. The UN General Assembly recommends the partition of Palestine. The Hashemite Kingdom of Jordan is created.

1948. Britain ends the Palestinian mandate and pulls out its troops. Israel declares itself an independent state.

1949. The West Bank and East Jerusalem are annexed by King Abdullah and become part of the Hashemite kingdom. Egypt captures the Gaza Strip.

1951, 20 July. King Abdullah is assassinated outside the Al-Aqsa Mosque in Jerusalem.

1952. Prince Hussein, aged 17, is proclaimed King of Jordan. In Egypt King Farouk is forced into exile by the military coup under Nasser.

1952. New constitution adopted.

1955. Jordan joins the United Nations.

1956. Glubb Pasha is dismissed as the head of the Arab Legion.

1967. The Six Day War. Israel seizes the West Bank and Jerusalem from Jordan, as well as the Gaza Strip and Sinai from Egypt. Influx of Palestinian refugees to Jordan. UN Resolution 242 calls for Israeli withdrawal from occupied Arab territories.

1969. Yasser Arafat becomes chairman of the PLO.

1973. Israel seizes the Golan Heights from Syria.

1976. Party political activity banned.

1978. Wedding of King Hussein and Queen Nour.

1980. Beginning of Iran/Iraq War, Jordan sides with Iraq. Aqaba port experiences a boom.

Iran/Iraq war

1984. Women vote for the first time.

1987. Start of Palestinian uprising or Intifada in December, in the West Bank and Gaza.

1988, 31 July. King Hussein announces his decision to renounce all administrative and legal claims to the West Bank.

Renouncing the West Bank

1988, August. End of the Iran/Iraq War.

1988, November. Jordanian dinar loses nearly half its official dollar value. In Algiers, PLO leader Yasser Arafat declares the independent state of Palestine, consisting of the pre-1967 borders of the West Bank and Gaza Strip, with Jerusalem as its capital. It is recognised by Arab countries and Turkey, more than 60 countries in all.

1989, April. Riots at Ma'an against IMF imposed price rises in fuel and food staples. Eleven killed.

1989, November. First free elections to a new parliament. The Muslim Brotherhood gains 22 of the 80 seats.

1990, August. Iraq invades Kuwait.

1991, January. US-led military attack with backing of Gulf states, Egypt and Syria to liberate Kuwait from Iraqi hands. Jordan isolates itself from the rest of the Arab world by refusing to condemn Saddam Hussein. Jordanian and Palestinian workers expelled from Gulf countries, who stop their aid. Having lost US and most foreign aid, Jordan relies heavily on Baghdad for oil and trade.

Gulf War

1991, July. Martial law lifted.

1992. Jordan accused by USA of breaking UN sanctions against Iraq.

1992, September. King Hussein has a kidney removed in the USA in his fight against cancer. Receives a tumultuous welcome on his return with nearly a third of the population pouring on to the streets to welcome him back.

1993. First multiparty elections.

Population and Religion

The population of Jordan is about four million. Ethnically, the Jordanians are similar to the desert people of Syria and Saudi Arabia, while the Palestinians of the Jordan Valley and the West Bank are ethnically different, often being a little taller and more heavily built. It has been suggested that they may have been descendants of the Canaanites, originally from the Zagros region of Iran, but they have at any rate been settled in the areas west of the Jordan for many thousands of years.

Canaanite descendants

Over 90 per cent of the population is Sunni (orthodox Muslims) and some 60 per cent of these are Palestinian refugees who fled to Jordan following the 1948 and 1967 wars against Israel and the 1991 Gulf War. Many of these, often highly educated and qualified people, have become powerful figures in the business and political world of Jordan.

Some 8 per cent of the population is Christian, mainly Greek Orthodox or Catholic. They tend to live in Amman, Madaba, Kerak, Ajlun and Salt, and their liturgical languages are Greek and Arabic. The remaining 2 per cent comprise: 25,000 Sunni Circassians, who settled in Jordan in 1878 around Wadi Seer and Na'ur; a few Baha'is in the north Jordan Valley; and (near the Syrian border) a few Druze, an obscure Islamic sect considered so far from the Sunni, orthodox Islam as to be a virtual heresy. Related to the Circassians, also from the Caucasus, are the Chechens, a small group of about 1,000, who are Shia rather than Sunni Muslims.

You will hear the call to prayer five times a day, as in all Muslim countries: at *fajr* (dawn), one hour before sunrise; *dhuhr* (noon); *'asr* (mid-afternoon); *maghreb* (sunset); and *isha* (one and a half hours after sunset). The words are always the same, except for the dawn prayer, when the phrase *'Prayer is better than sleep'* is added. The standard translation is as follows, and each sentence is repeated twice in the actual call to prayer: *'God is the most great. I testify that there is no God but God and Muhammad is the messenger of God. Come to prayer. Come to salvation. God is the most great. There is no God but God.'*

Call to prayer

SUNNI AND SHIA ISLAM

The Sunni/Shia split in Islam is similar in importance to the Catholic/Protestant divide in Christianity, and goes back to a dispute over the succession after Muhammad's death. The Prophet died unexpectedly in 632 aged about 62, leaving the question of the succession unresolved. The wealthy Meccan families of the Quraysh, Muhammad's tribe, elected Abu Bakr, father of Muhammad's favourite wife Aisha, to be his caliph (from the Arabic word for successor, *khalifa*). This election was never accepted by Ali, the Prophet's first cousin and son-in-law, who felt that his own claim to be caliph was stronger. This produced the split between the Sunni (meaning orthodox) Muslims who supported Abu Bakr and his successors, and between the Shia (meaning party or faction i.e. of Ali) who supported Ali and his successors, and who were called imams rather than caliphs. Shia sects subsequently split among themselves over the succession of later imams, but all regard Ali as divinely inspired and as a paradigm. Mainstream Shia see this divine spirit only in Ali, whereas the fringe sects like the Druze, even go so far as to worship Ali and the later imams as God. Shia sects are also characterised by great secrecy in beliefs and rites, adhered to because of the persecutions they suffered during the periods of Sunni orthodoxy under the Umayyad (Damascus) and Abbasid (Baghdad) caliphs. Today, major Shia populations are found in Iran, Iraq, Bahrain, Kuwait and Lebanon, but there are few in Jordan.

Muhammad's successor

It is rare today to have the muezzin himself calling from the top of the minaret: he has been replaced by a loudspeaker or a tape recorder. The one God referred to is the same as the God of Christianity and Judaism, but where the Muslims consider the Christians heretical is in their worship of Christ as the Son of God. Jesus is mentioned in the Quran as one of the series of prophets, of whom Muhammad was the last and the 'seal'. 'God', the Quran states, *'was neither born nor gave birth to anyone.'* The word Quran itself means 'recitation', because the text is believed to be the exact words spoken by God, using Muhammad as his mouthpiece. Muhammad used to go up to a mountain near Mecca where these divine revelations would take place and he would then come down and recite them to his fellow citizens. By oral tradition they were passed down through generations, and the final text was fixed and set down in 933, some three centuries after Muhammad's death.

One God

The Bedouin
In the Wadi Rum and roaming all the desert lands east of
the Amman-Aqaba desert highway, there are still eight
main nomadic tribes in Jordan, numbering some 40,000
people in all, having dwindled from about 220,000 in the
1950s. Many are now semi-nomadic, with a fixed base
where much of the tribe stays, while only a small group,
usually the young men, go off into the desert with the
camels in search of grazing.

**The true
nomadic life**

The totally nomadic Bedouin, however, will break
camp soon after dawn with a herd of say 60 camels, four
of which are used to carry the baggage and belongings.
They will travel approximately 20km before setting up
camp again in the evening. It is normal to stay at the
encampment a few days, moving on once the grazing
around it has expired.

The women, heads covered against the sun but always
unveiled, do the lion's share of the work in this, moving
with that timeless ease that comes early to those who live
in the desert. One woman can erect the family's huge tent
('house of hair' as they call it) on her own in just 30 minutes. All the holes are then sealed against snakes and the
tent inside is checked for eggs and spiders. The chicken
coop is carried from place to place on the back of one of
the camels, and there tends to be a collection of sheep,
goats and donkeys which also trot along. Middle Eastern
sheep are usually of the fat-tailed variety, and the fatness
of their tails shows how well-fed they are and whether
there has been adequate grazing for them. At milking
time the women bind them all together in two neat rows,
using just one piece of rope, cleverly tied in such a way
that when the milking is over, they just give one sharp tug
and the whole lot unravels in a trice like a piece of knit-
ting. The women collect dried camel dung and scrub for
fuel in cooking. The ritual of coffee-making, flavoured
with cardomum and prepared in a traditional brass pot, is
usually undertaken by the oldest male member of the
family.

Camel's milk is an essential part of the diet, and the
women make butter and cheese from it, curdled in a
camel-leather bag. Meat is generally only eaten on special
occasions like weddings and feast days. A few years ago I
was fortunate enough to spend some weeks living with a
Bedouin tribe south of Ma'an. It coincided with the Eid al-
Adha, the Feast of the Sacrifice, the major Muslim festival
of the year. After being woken at dawn to witness the ritual slaughter of the camels by bleeding them to death, the
rest of the day was spent in ceremonially moving from

**Feasts in the
desert**

tent to tent, from the most senior downwards, eating the boiled camel's meat from the communal platters of rice. A sauce made of camel's cheese (*jameed*) was poured over the dish to keep it moist. By the end of the day, some 15 platefuls of camel later, it was easy to appreciate why such feasts are restricted to annual events! Bedouin women are not permitted to sit in the tents with the men, but foreign women are treated as honorary men. '*God brings the guest*', is a common Arabic saying, and theirs is indeed a true hospitality.

Life in the desert without a camel is inconceivable: they enter every aspect of daily life. Using a thick comb, the Bedouin girls collect winter hair from the camel, and this is used for weaving. They spin and dye the wool themselves, and a ram's horn is then used to pull down and tighten the weave of the garment on the loom. Men can sometimes be seen spinning as well, but only as a pastime. Enormous care is taken of the camels: *Ata 'Allah*, 'the gift of God', is how they are often referred to. Riding camels are invariably female and are often adorned with charms around their necks. The interdependence between man and beast is close in the desert. A medieval Arabic proverb runs: '*Better than beauty is a camel*'.

The nomad's best friend

Camels live to about 20 years old. They mate for life when they are two, and camel calves are generally born in early autumn. They cost between JD300 and 500, so the sacrifice involved in slaughtering them is great. Poorer families who may not even own a camel of their own can obviously not afford to buy one to slaughter it, so the provision in the Quran is that each family must slaughter according to his means, be it a camel, a goat or a chicken. Each family brands its yearling camels on the cheek and on the hind quarters, applying yogurt to the burn to soothe it.

In the desert the Bedouin get occasional meat in the form of lizards, sometimes over a metre long, and even the odd hedgehog, after the children have played with them first. Visiting friends and relations may bring a gift, such as a freshly caught hare, when they call on each other, and they will then all sit together to eat, perhaps reciting poetry, for there are still many Bedouin poets in the oral tradition of the desert. Arabs have always loved the magical rhythm of words and the man who can compose or recite poetry at the fireside enjoys great prestige. Hunting with hawks continues to be a favourite sport, though hawks are becoming scarcer and therefore more expensive. The female hawk is generally preferred as it is easier to train.

Desert poetry

Intermarriage between tribes is rare. There are of course notable exceptions, such as the blonde Englishwoman who married one of the Bdul tribe in Petra and lived in a cave with him until the government resettled all Bdul outside the archaeological zone. Today, several children later, they run one of the refreshment stalls set in a cave at Petra. Bedouin, like all Arabs, have a deep love of children.

Marriage customs

Marriage is in general an expensive business in Jordan, as indeed it has become in most Arab countries. It is usual, but not compulsory, for the bride's family to host the wedding feast. The average husband has to pay around JD2000 for his wife. The price is agreed through bargaining by the parents of the two parties, and may drop lower in poorer rural areas. This money is not for the bride's father, but for the wife herself, to secure her position and to give her some money for jewellery and dresses, as well as a certain independence. This price also deters the husband from having too many wives, something he may be inclined to do if he drinks a lot of camel's milk and is from a rural part of the country. The wife is considered *kharban*, broken, for the man's enjoyment, once she has had children, and second wives are often very young, around 16, to ensure that they will be 'tight'. In rural and desert areas a woman is still married not for her beauty or intelligence, but for her ability to bear fine children. *'Two-thirds of the boy takes after his* khal *(maternal uncle)'* is the saying.

After the first sum is paid over at the kitaab or marriage

A new born camel with its mother (Vine).

contract, there is another contract where the husband agrees to pay the girl a further sum in gold in the event of divorce, for her security. No money changes hands: it will only become payable if he divorces her. The third stage is the wedding itself, the dukhla or entering, named after the first sexual encounter which ensues. The lavishness of this occasion is important, for appearances are all. As a result of these expenses, to say nothing of the cost of buying or renting a flat, many men cannot afford to marry until their late thirties. Marrying a foreign girl can therefore be an attractive alternative, since neither she nor her parents will make such demands. In the claustrophobically small Amman society, bridal settlements are avidly discussed and high society families vie with one another to have larger and more showy weddings.

Security money

The Government and the King

The Kingdom of Jordan is a constitutional monarchy with the throne passing through male descent from the Hashemite dynasty of King Abdullah (1882–1951), the son of Hussein, King of the Hejaz. The constitution itself dates from 1952, though the parliamentary tradition goes back to 1921 when Abdullah was first given charge of the Emirate of Transjordan. Following King Abdullah's assassination in Jerusalem in 1951 the throne passed to his son Talal (1909–1972), who abdicated after just one year in favour of his eldest son, Hussein, then just 17 years old. He can trace his ancestry back through the Hashemite tribe directly to the Prophet Muhammad.

Related to the prophet

The king is vested with extensive powers which he can exercise through his Prime Minister and his cabinet, called the Council of Ministers, whom he appoints. He approves and promulgates laws, orders the holding of elections, convenes or adjourns the House of Representatives. He is Commander-in-Chief of the armed forces. The Jordanian parliament consists of the upper house or Senate, whose members are all appointed by the king, and the lower house or House of Representatives whose members are elected. Jordan's new age of democracy started in November 1989 with the free election of a new parliament in which the Muslim Brotherhood gained a quarter of the seats in the lower house. The Senate members must be unrelated to the king and over 40 years old, and are generally chosen from past and present ministers. The members of the House of Representatives must be over 30 years old and must have no active business interests, and must not be closely related to the king. Women were allowed to vote for the first time in 1984.

King Hussein was born on 14 November 1935 and educated in Amman and then at Victoria College, Alexandria, Egypt, before going on to Harrow and Sandhurst, England. He was formally crowned on 2 May 1953, once he had come of age and finished his schooling, having been unexpectedly catapulted to the throne by his grandfather's assassination and his father's abdication. In his autobiography, published when he was only 27, he regrets the loss of his childhood:

The price I have had to pay for position is not the unending work that I love, not the bad health that has dogged me, but a price much higher. It is that I have gone through much of my life surrounded by people, hemmed in by them, talking to them, laughing with them, envious of their casual, happy relationships, while in my heart I have been as lonely as a castaway.

Lonely as a castaway

At the age of 20 he agreed to an arranged marriage to the daughter of Sherif Abdul Hamid Aoun of the Hejaz, a distant cousin, called Princess Dina. He had one daughter by her, Alia, after whom the national airline is named. Dina was a highly intelligent woman with an MA from Cambridge, and a few years his senior. He originally had high hopes for the marriage, but it did not work out. She returned to Cairo after 18 months and the marriage was officially dissolved after six years. The King then married a young Englishwoman, Antoinette Gardiner, daughter of a British army colonel living in Amman, and she became Princess Muna. She bore him two sons, the Princes Abdullah and Faisal, and twin daughters, the Princesses Zein and Aisha. Though initially happy, this marriage was also dissolved and then at the age of 37 he married Alia Toukan, a Jordanian, by whom he had one daughter, Princess Haya, and one son, Prince Ali. Queen Alia was tragically killed in a helicopter crash in 1977. One year later, aged 43, the King married the American Elizabeth Halaby, the present Queen Nour, 16 years his junior, by whom he has two sons, the Princes Hamza and Hashem.

Much loved rebel

Much loved by his people, the King has nevertheless always been something of a rebel, perhaps because, with his early accession to the throne, he never had the chance to let loose. He always loved driving, though he was expressly forbidden to do so. Flying was his other great release, and again he did his first solo flight in direct contravention of his orders: '*I circled the capital, looking down from my lonely cockpit on the city I loved so well*'.

Shortly after coming to the throne, he took to slipping out of the palace after dark in an overcoat and red *shimagh* (head-dress), driving an old palace car, and posing as a taxi driver for the evening. He would then ask his fares what they thought of the new King, and was gratified to find himself popular among his people. On one occasion an old Bedouin threatened to beat him black and blue for suggesting that the King was less than perfect. General Lunt's recent biography of King Hussein also portrays a man of such integrity, so excellent in all respects, that you are left wondering whether His Majesty has any faults at all. On being asked this question, one impartial expert paused for thought a while and ventured: 'Too many wives perhaps?'. He is the longest surviving ruler in the Middle East.

QUEEN NOUR

Queen Nour has become remarkably popular in her time as Jordan's queen, which says much both for the King's personal standing in the eyes of his subjects, and for the Queen's own dedication to the country and its problems. When they met, she was working as director of Alia's Design Centre in Jordan, having graduated in architecture and design from Princeton, New Jersey in 1974, and then worked in Australia and Iran. She has taken an active role in many social and cultural activities in the country, and has done pioneering work on behalf of Jordanian women and working mothers. She created the Royal Endowment for Education and Culture and a fund for sending Jordanians abroad to be trained and educated, and is also in charge of the committee for the Protection of the Environment. She was the initiator of the Jerash Festival which began in 1981.

Queen Nour's Achievements

Now sick with cancer and approaching 60, the King has hinted that he may soon have to hand over to his younger brother, Crown Prince Hassan, heir to the throne and the regent when the King is away. An intellectual man, educated at Harrow and at Christ Church, Oxford, Prince Hassan plays a major role in the scientific, agricultural, developmental and political matters of the kingdom. Despite Prince Hassan's undisputed stature, it is difficult to imagine Jordan without the King who has ruled throughout its many swings of fortune for more than 40 years.

Economy

Jordan's façade of prosperity and the smartness of Amman's modern suburbs belie serious economic problems. The Gulf War which resulted in the expulsion of all Jordanians and Palestinians from the Gulf states and Kuwait led to a massive influx of 300,000 among whom unemployment is around 80 per cent. The remittances of these former expatriate workers used to keep Jordan going, and at the same time Gulf aid has dried up. The loss of the fertile West Bank and of Jerusalem as a tourist attraction in the 1967 war, was also a major earlier blow to the economy. The West Bank had provided more than 30 per cent of its agricultural land. It has sought to recover through ambitious irrigation schemes in the Jordan Valley, and 20 per cent of the population is engaged in agriculture. The main crops are wheat, lentils, chick peas, fruit and vegetables. Fruit and vegetables are still shipped across to Jordan in large quantites from the West Bank and Gaza. The loss of groundwater reserves (known as aquifers) under the hills of the West Bank was also a severe blow, and these reservoirs are one of the key reasons for Israel's outright refusal to give up occupation: the reserves account for more than a third of Israel's water supply at a time when the aquifers in the heavily populated region of Tel Aviv are badly depleted and the water levels in the River Jordan and the Dead Sea are declining.

Key water reserves

Phosphate and copper are the major minerals, and both are exported. Oil has not yet been found in commercially viable quantities, though exploration continues and costs about 1 per cent of GNP. Jordan currently gets its oil supplies from Iraq at very favourable prices, but used to refine crude oil brought in by pipeline from Saudi Arabia. There are high hopes for recent natural gas discoveries. The budget and balance of payments deficit is big for a country of less than 4 million, and since the Jordanian dinar's sharp losses against the US dollar, the country has run very short of foreign currency reserves. Unemployment is officially around 30 per cent.

Education

Education has a high priority in Jordan and has dramatically expanded since the 1950s. The huge influx of refugees since 1967 put a lot of pressure on the state education system, and government schools have to operate a shift system to cope with teacher and classroom shortages. The first shift starts at 7.00 am and the second at noon. Some 10 per cent of children go to private schools,

The student affairs building at the University of Jordan (Vine).

most of which are in Amman. Jordan has three universities, all of a high standard. The University of Jordan in Amman opened in 1962 with 167 students of whom 18 were women. Today it has more than 12,000 students, 50 per cent of them women. Yarmouk University, set up in the 1970s, is in Irbid and now has some 14,000 students. The third one is the small Mu'tah University in Kerak, with around 750 students, all of whom are men and all of whom study military sciences in addition to their chosen course. After graduation they all enter the police or the armed forces. Jordan has one of the highest percentages of graduates to population in the world.

Abundant graduates

The Arabic Language

To many Westerners Arabic is a language that looks like an incomprehensible series of squiggles and dots and sounds like an equally incomprehensible series of gutturals and hisses. It is, however, actually a subtle and expressive language, beautiful in the way that French is widely regarded.

Camel hisses

Non-Arabic speakers are generally daunted above all by the script and the right-to-left flow of text. Yet the script is in fact the easiest thing about Arabic. The alphabet contains 29 characters and there are strict rules to

Start from the right

41

Jordan

determine which characters join on to which. And unlike most European languages, there are no exceptions to these rules. The characters change their shape according to their position within the word but always within the same rules. The process of learning the characters and their shapes is purely a memory exercise which can be done easily in three days and thereafter just requires practice. As for the right-to-left text alignment, it just takes a little time to adjust, rather like driving on the right instead of the left of the road.

Having mastered the script the task begins in earnest. The first conceptually difficult thing you now encounter is that only the consonants are written – you have to supply the vowels yourself. In that case, how do you know which vowels to put where? The answer is that you do not, or at least not until you have a thorough grasp of the intricacies of Arabic grammar and word structure, which takes a minimum of three or four months' study. For this reason all beginners' texts and children's schoolbooks are fully annotated with vowel signs added in the form of dashes and dots above and below the line. Getting a student to read an unvowelled text aloud is always an excellent way of assessing his level, as it instantly reveals the depth of his understanding of Arabic grammar.

Pronunciation is another area which is not as daunting as it may seem. Of the 29 consonants, 18 have direct phonetic equivalents in English, such as *b, d, t, l, m, s*. The rest have no direct equivalent and range from emphatic versions of *d, s,* and *t,* to a small handful of sounds which are genuinely difficult for westerners to pronounce. The gutteral stop, usually represented in transliteration as a reversed comma, is probably the one that gives most trouble.

Like Hebrew, Arabic is a Semitic language with a root system. The root of an idea or concept is represented by a simple verb, usually consisting of three consonants. These verbs are the very basis of the Arabic language, and all variations of meaning around the root idea are expressed by imposing different patterns on the basic verb root. Hence, in the simplest of examples, from the verb root *ktb* (*kataba* when vowelled) which means 'he wrote', you can make *maktab* meaning 'office', *maktaba* meaning 'library' and *kitaab* meaning 'book'. The verbs are fully conjugated, so *katabnaa* is 'we wrote', and *yaktabuuna* is 'they are writing'.

Beyond this, there is the complication that each verb root has up to ten additional forms, all of which change the basic meaning. So the second form *kattaba* means 'he

No vowels written

Root system

made someone write', and the eighth form *iktataba* means he 'subscribed to something'. The three root letters are always in there somewhere, except where you have irregular and so-called 'defective' verbs, where one or even two of the root letters disappear and it becomes increasingly difficult to identify the root. Arabic dictionaries list words under their root, so if you cannot identify the root, you cannot look up the word. Hunting for words in the dictionary is something the beginner spends a long time doing!

Hunting in the dictionary

This said, Arabic is, by the very nature of its structure, an extremely rich language, capable of expressing fine shades of meaning, and this is reflected in the wealth of Arabic literature, especially poetry. The average English tabloid reader is said to have a working vocablary of 3000 words, whereas the Arab equivalent is said to have about 10,000.

There are also many interesting features of the language which hint at the nature and attitudes of the Arab mind, notably the existence of only two tenses, perfect and imperfect: there is no future tense. In the Arab concept of time there is only one distinction to be drawn: has something been finished or is it still going on? There is also the curious point, to delight feminists, that the plural of inanimate objects is treated grammatically as feminine singular.

Concept of time

The written Arabic language together with Islam is one of the few unifying factors in the Arab world. It means that newspapers published in Egypt can be distributed and read from Morocco to Iraq and down to Yemen. In the spoken language however, the 22 countries of the Arab league all express their individuality, to the extent that a Moroccan and an Iraqi speaking their local dialects will understand each other only with difficulty. In order to communicate, therefore, they have to compromise and speak a form of modern classical Arabic which is understood by educated Arabs everywhere, and it is this middle Arabic which you generally speak to a foreigner.

Spoken variety

See the Appendix for useful words and phrases.

Flora and Fauna

Camels, goats and donkeys are the animals you will see most in Jordan, although in the desert there are also a few foxes, gazelle, sand rats, jerboa, hyenas, jackals, hedgehogs, porcupines and badgers. Lizards and snakes are common, but the only poisonous snakes are the horned viper and the Palestine viper. Of the many colourful insects, the only two dangerous to man are the black widow spider, recognisable by its shiny black body, and the scorpion. Of the latter the yellow type is the more common, but it is the larger, rarer, black variety that is the more poisonous.

Reintroduction of the oryx

Many natural habitats have been destroyed by hacking down forest to provide fuel and the sleepers for the Hejaz Railway earlier this century, and overgrazing by goats has destroyed much grassland. The last Arabian oryx with its unicorn-like appearance when seen in profile, was shot in 1950 but it is now the centre of a Worldwide Fund for Nature scheme to reintroduce it at the Shaumari Wildlife Reserve at Azraq. This oasis is also home to thousands of birds which migrate south from Europe to Africa. In spring and autumn over 280 different species can be identified, from warblers and wagtails to storks, herons and flamingoes. Birds of prey, like huge griffon vultures or smaller falcons, are common.

In the hills to the north are some wild pig, though their days are numbered, as hunting is still a popular sport. The last bear was seen in 1930 when it withdrew to Lebanon, and the last ostrich ran off to Saudi Arabia in 1932. Lions have been extinct for many years but were quite common in the Middle Ages, as can be seen by their frequent appearance in early sculptures and mosaics. The coral reefs off Aqaba in the Red Sea still support a huge variety of colourful tropical fish, as well as the occasional shark.

The lily of the field

From February to May the landscapes come alive with seas of red anemones, wild white and pink cyclamen, orange poppies, white daisies and yellow euphorbia. The distinctive black iris, Jordan's national flower, is not found at all in Europe, but can be seen flowering in profusion in the region of Madaba. The Fransciscan fathers felt that this was surely Solomon's 'lily of the field'. The mandrake or love apple, used for centuries for medical and aphrodisiac purposes, can be found, and also the curious Dead Sea fruit shrub, with its large green balloon-like fruit.

Section 2: AROUND JORDAN

Amman

North from Amman

South from Amman

AMMAN

Amman Facts

Airport
Queen Alia International Airport is 35km south of Amman and the drive to the city takes 30–45 minutes depending on traffic. It was over 20 years in the construction, and was finally completed in the early 1980s. Tickets for taxis to any part of town are sold at a fixed price from a kiosk in the arrivals hall. There are buses or service taxis for the more budget-conscious (though the taxi fare is reasonable anyway), and there are also car hire offices.

Altitude
Set at 850m on the Jordanian plateau, Amman enjoys cool evenings and unusually clean air for a capital city.

Hotels
Amman boasts the full range of hotels from five to no stars. Most are situated in the northern and western residential areas of town. See **Accommodation and Hotels** in *Section 1* for more general information and for price ranges. For the traveller who is content with clean simple rooms but likes private facilities, the three-star hotels listed are fine.

***** **Lux. Intercontinental Hotel** (*tel: 641361. fax: 645217*). Oldest of the five-star hotels built in 1962 but newly refurbished. 396 air-conditioned rooms. Outdoor pool, children's pool, tennis courts, rooftop restaurant, bar, café, disco. In-house video and colour TV. Shopping arcade with banks, post office, hairdresser, pharmacy, beauty salon and car hire. Located between the 2nd and 3rd circles.

***** **Lux. Amman Plaza Hotel**. (*tel: 665912. fax: 674261*). In Shmeisani. 303 rooms fully air-conditioned and centrally heated. In-house video and colour TV. Outdoor pool, health club and cinema club. Two restaurants, two bars and a café. Night club. Airline office, car hire, gift shops, business suite.

***** **Lux. Amman Marriott Hotel** (*tel: 660100. fax: 670100*). Excellent hotel with good service, in Jebel Amman. 296 rooms. Indoor and outdoor pool. Health club. Tennis. Two restaurants, bar and café. Shopping arcade with all the usual facilities including tourist and travel office, car hire and business services.

***** **Regency Palace Hotel** (*tel: 660000. fax: 660013*). In Shmeisani. 300 rooms. Roof-top pool with sun terrace, health club, sauna. Rooftop nightclub. Tennis, squash, mini-golf. Restaurant, nightclub and bar. Hairdresser, bookshop, souvenir and flower shop. In-house video, colour TV and minibar.

***** **Philadelphia International Hotel** (*tel: 663100. fax: 665160*). In Jabal Amman. 216 rooms with in-house video, colour TV and minibar. Swimming pool. Tennis courts. Four restaurants, one bar. Travel agency, airline office, car hire, baby-sitting, souvenir shop.

**** **Jerusalem International Melia Hotel** (*tel: 665121. fax: 689328*). On University Highway. 162 rooms. Sauna, indoor pool. Opulent decor. Colour TV, in-house video and minibar. Two restaurants, night club and bar. Car hire, boutique.

**** **Alia Gateway Hotel** (*tel: 51000. fax: 51029*). At the Queen Alia International Airport. 316 rooms. Outdoor pool. Tennis, mini-golf. Shuttle bus service four times daily to Amman. Colour TV, in-house video. Restaurant, coffee-shop and pool snacks. Hairdresser, baby-sitting, bookshop and souvenir shop.

**** **Amra Forum Hotel** (*tel: 815071. fax: 814072*). On the main road between the 6th and 7th circles. Air conditioned. TV, video, minibar. Good pool. Probably the best in this category for the traveller who prefers to be on the edge of town and wants a bit of luxury. Part of the International Forum Hotel chain. 274 rooms. Two restaurants, two bars and a coffee-shop. Shopping arcade with car hire, travel desk and business services.

*** **Ambassador Hotel** (*tel: 665161. fax: 681101*). In Shmeisani. 97 rooms with colour TV, in-house video and minibar. Much used by groups. Italian restaurant, snack café and bar. Travel agency, car hire, pharmacy and gift shop.

*** **Amman International Hotel** (*tel: 841712. fax: 895950*). Near Jordan University. 40 rooms with colour TV and minibar. Two restaurants, bar and nightclub. Swimming pool.

*** **Amman Crown Hotel** (*tel: 798181. fax: 648050*). Near Jordan TV and Radio 20 minutes from the airport. 75 rooms. Air conditioning and central heating. Colour TV and minibar. Olympic-sized pool. Squash and tennis, sauna and fitness room, pool table, table tennis. Oriental restaurant, 24 hour coffee shop.

*** **Commodore Hotel** (*tel:665185. fax: 668187*). In Shmeisani. 96 rooms with colour TV, in-house video and minibar. Restaurant, coffee-shop and bar. Shopping arcade with hairdresser and gift shop.

*** **Darotel Apartment Hotel** (*tel: 668193. fax: 602434*). In Shmeisani. 38 rooms with colour TV, in-house video, minibar and kitchenette. Restaurant, coffee-shop and bar. Baby-sitting, car hire, health club.

*** **Gondola Apartment Hotel** (*tel: 815556. fax: 828847*). Near the 5th circle in Jabal Amman. 56 rooms with kitchenette and air conditioning. One restaurant and bar.

*** **Grand Palace Hotel** (*tel: 661121. fax: 660013*). In Jabal Hussein. 150 rooms with colour TV and minibar. Restaurant and bar. Travel agency, car hire, souvenir shop.

*** **Hisham Hotel** (*tel: 642720. fax: 647540*). In Jabal Amman. 23 rooms with colour TV, in-house video and minibar. Restaurant, coffee shop and terrace barbeque. Car hire, business services.

*** **Middle East Hotel** (*tel: 667160. fax: 667422)*. In Shmeisani. 95 rooms with colour TV, in-house video and minibar. Outdoor pool. Restaurant and coffee-shop. Car hire, bank, travel agency and gift shop.

*** **Olympia Apartment Hotel** (*tel: 810150. fax: 827113*). Just off 5th circle, Jabal Amman. 36 suites tastefully furnished. Coffee-shop, bar.

*** **San Rock Hotel** (*tel: 813800*). In Jabal Amman. 100 rooms with colour TV, in-house video and minibar. Two restaurants, two bars and a coffee-shop. Disco. Book and souvenir shop, hairdresser, beauty salon.

*** **Tyche Hotel** (*tel: 661114*). In Shmeisani. 184 rooms with colour TV and minibar. Outdoor pool and health centre. Rooftop restaurant, three bars, disco. Tourist office, car rental, hairdresser, gift and book shop.

** **Ammoun Hotel** (*tel: 671133. fax: 671132*). In Jabal Amman. 55 rooms with colour TV and minibar. Swimming pool, children's pool, tennis court. Book/souvenir shop.

** **Al-Sabeel Hotel** (*tel: 630571. fax: 630572*) In Jabal Amman. 9 suites with colour TV. Restaurant.

** **Al-Qasr Hotel** (*tel: 666140*). In Shmeisani. 36 rooms with colour TV and minibar. Restaurant, bar and terrace. Car hire. Souvenir shop.

** **Babilon Tower Hotel** (*tel: 662949*). In Shmeisani. 28 rooms with private bathroom and heating.

** **Balqa Palace Hotel** (*tel: 843291. fax: 842662*). In Sweileh near Jordan University. 42 rooms with private bathroom and telephone. Restaurant.

** **Blue Marine Hotel** (*tel: 667165*). In Shmeisani. 13 rooms with private bath and central heating.

** **Cameo Hotel** (*tel: 644515. fax: 644579*). In Jabal Amman. 36 rooms with minibar and telephone. Restaurant, snack bar and summer terrace. Car hire.

** **Canary Hotel** (*tel: 638353. fax: 674676*). In Jabal Weibdeh, Downtown Amman, 21 rooms with private bath and telephone. Canary cages in the mini-garden.

** **Dove Hotel** (*tel: 697601. fax: 674676*). In Jabal Amman. 30 rooms with private bath, telephone and colour TV. Restaurant and bar.

** **Granada Hotel** (*tel: 622617*). Near the 1st Circle, Jabal Amman. 20 rooms with private bath and minibar. Restaurant and bar.

** **Hala Inn Hotel** (*tel:644642. fax: 612311*). In Jabal Amman. 55 rooms with minibar and colour TV. Restaurant, coffee-shop and bar.

** **Holy Land Hotel** (*tel: 841309*). Opposite Jordan University. 35 rooms with private bath, telephone and fridge.

** **Mamoura Hotel** (*tel: 778174*). In Al-Wehdat, Amman's business centre. 40 rooms with private bathroom and telephone. Oriental restaurant.

** **Manar Hotel** (*tel: 662186. fax: 684329*). In Shmeisani. 72 rooms with minibar and colour TV. Small outdoor pool. Restaurant, coffee-shop and bar.

A view of Amman from Citadel hill (Vine).

** **Merryland Hotel** (*tel: 630217. fax: 657392*). In Abdali. 56 rooms with colour TV and minibar. Restaurant, bar and nightclub.

** **National Hotel** (*tel: 676091*). Near Sports City. 36 rooms with private bath or shower.

** **New Park Hotel** (*tel: 648144*). In Downtown Amman. 35 rooms with private bath or shower.

** **Ramallah Hotel** (*tel: 636122. fax: 639551*). In Downtown Amman. 27 rooms with colour TV, phone and private bath.

** **Royal Hotel** (*tel: 843335*). On Jordan University Road. 47 rooms with private bath and telephone. Restaurant, bar and terrace.

** **Region Hotel** (*tel: 689071. fax: 689091*). Overlooking Sports City. 45 rooms with private bath, telephone and TV. Restaurant and bar.

** **Rum Hotel** (*tel: 623162*). In the city centre, Downtown Amman, 28 rooms with private bath and telephone. Bar, coffee shop.

** **Saladin Hotel** (*tel: 623518*). In Downtown Amman. 26 rooms with private bath, black and white TV and fridge. Coffee shop.

** **Select Hotel** (*tel: 637101*). In Jabal Weibdeh. 26 rooms with a coffee-shop and bar.

** **Seven Hotel** (*tel: 603578*). In Jabal Hussein. 18 rooms with private bath, kitchenette, telephone and TV. Coffee-shop for snacks.

** **Shepherd Hotel** (*tel: 639197*). In Jabal Amman. 30 rooms with private bath and telephone. Restaurant and bar. Car hire.

** **Sultan Hotel** (*tel: 639710*). In Downtown Amman. 28 rooms with private bath and telephone.

The grand old Philadelphia Hotel has, alas, now been destroyed to reveal Roman ruins underneath and to create an archaeological park.

The rock bottom hotels, as you might expect, are all to be found in Downtown Amman around the souq and the El-Hussein Mosque. Many are along King Faisal Street and prices range from JD1.500 to JD6.500, reflecting the lack of facilities.

Restaurants
Amman does not abound in good restaurants and some of the best food is to be found in the better hotels – 4-star and above.

New Orient Restaurant. Near 3rd circle. Very passable *mezze* in pleasant shady open terrace. Good service.

Omar Khayyam. Near Intercontinental Hotel, opposite Citibank. Good Middle Eastern cuisine, but quite high prices.

Istambouli. Between 1st and 2nd circles. Good Middle Eastern cuisine at moderate prices. In a private house with a garden.

Diplomat Restaurant and Coffee Shop. On 1st circle. Café style with pavement tables.

The following downtown restaurants are cheaper and offer largely Middle Eastern cuisine:

Jerusalem Restaurant. King Hussein Street.
Jordan Restaurant. Post Office Square.
Dar es-Sorour Restaurant. King Hussein Street.
Jabri Restaurant. King Hussein Street.

Fast food, pizza and hamburger joints abound throughout Amman, as well as Chinese and Indian restaurants, and even Greek and Turkish, and though you may turn your nose up at all these if you are looking for 'ethnic' cuisine, they can make a pleasant change after a spell outside the capital. Local cheap snacks come in the form of *falaafel* (fried balls of chickpea paste) and *shawarma* (doner kebabs on spits) stands, but beware of hygiene standards.

Car Hire
Hire cars have distinctive number plates of yellow on green. A refundable deposit of JD100 –150 is generally required. The minimum age is 25. An international driving licence is required. Rates do vary quite a lot from company to company (between JD70 and JD120 per week with unlimited mileage), so it is worth shopping around. **Avis** and **Budget** are the two major companies, but there are a host of cheaper ones. An up-to-date list with telephone numbers is given in the booklet *Your guide to Amman* which is distributed free at local travel agents and some hotels. Some cheaper companies to try are **Star Rent a Car**, **Firas Rent a Car**, **Dirani**, and **Amman Rent a Car**. Hire of four-wheel drive vehicles is generally from JD20 per day.

Petrol is comparable in price to the UK. Most saloon cars require super rather than normal petrol.

What to Buy
The large four- and five-star hotels all have souvenir shops, but prices are obviously higher than you may find in Downtown Amman. The Craft Shop (in Jebel Amman) is a good place for embroidery, place mats and other handmade objects, often the work of Palestinian refugees. Prices are fixed and labelled. Copper and brassware is best bought in Downtown Amman, after bargaining.

The Kan Zaman Village is also good for shopping, and is a 20-minute drive from the centre of Amman. It is a nineteenth century village restored and resuscitated with great taste and flair as a craft centre. The flag-stoned streets are lined with shops and boutiques selling goods of high quality, and you can also watch items like rugs and jewellery being made. There are cafés and restaurants constantly supplied with hot bread from traditional ovens. Most people take a taxi to the village.

The City

Anyone visiting Amman for the first time will be surprised above all by the hills. The mental image of a Middle Eastern capital set on a dusty plain must be discarded, for Amman lies on a high plateau of some 850m.

Hilly site

Built originally on seven hills, now spread on to 13 or 19 (depending on what you class as a hill, and what you regard as merely a mound), the city is dotted with a number of historic sites from the Stone Age to the Greek, Roman, Byzantine and Islamic eras. None is especially dramatic, but each has its own interest. Of the hills, or *jabals* as they are known in Arabic, it is the northern and western ones which boast the prosperous and fashionable areas known as Jabal Amman, Shmeisani, Jabal Hussein and Jabal Weibdeh. Here are to be found most of the ministries, embassies, international companies and quality hotels, along with the city's middle- and upper-class residents. In the centre lies the old core of the city, known as Downtown Amman, now one of the poorer areas, and to the east is the industrial sector, well located, since the prevailing winds carry the effluent away into the desert.

When the Emir Abdullah moved here in 1921 to administer the country under a British mandate, the town had a mere 3,000 inhabitants and was little more than a large village. The population of the country as a whole was 350,000, about the same as the island of Malta. In the short time since, and especially following independence in 1946 and under the benevolent rule of King Hussein, the country has made remarkable progress in the face of adversity. It has fought four wars, it has no oil and few natural resources, and it has had to assimilate hundreds of thousands of Palestinian refugees. Of the total 1072 km of Israeli Arab borders, Egypt has 288, Syria 72, Lebanon 80 and Jordan 640 to defend. It is hardly surprising therefore that military expenditure accounts for over half of the national budget.

Clean and well-maintained

As you arrive, the initial impression is of a modern city with smart limestone and concrete office blocks, well-maintained cars cruising wide streets, and predominantly western dress. The bustle, noise and squalor which accompany this western veneer in so many other Arab capitals like Cairo, Damascus and Baghdad, is not to be seen except in the small pocket of Downtown Amman, which was also the hub of life in ancient times.

With the orderly facelessness of its modern suburbs, Amman has been called 'the Purley of the Middle East' by one diplomat. One modern concrete block looks much like another, and because of this sameness and relative newness, no one has an address. Most streets do have names, but as in a large suburban estate, no one knows what they are, so they are known instead by their most prominent building, such as the Air France building or the Emir Cinema. In explaining your destination to the taxi driver, you must first give the district – Shmeisani, Sport City etc. – then the nearest landmark – opposite such and such a building, behind so and so company. Post is delivered only to post office boxes because of the lack of addresses, and an Amman resident's description of how to reach his house may run something like: 'At the 3rd circle, coming from the 4th circle, take the second exit and go down the hill passing three turnings on your left. Take the fourth and my block of flats is the sixth on your left, opposite the Disco Supermarket.' With the recent removal of most of the circles (i.e. roundabouts) in favour of traffic lights, one of the key landmark systems will be lost, making finding one's way around Amman ever more complex!

No addresses

The city's population today is close to two million, swelled by refugees from the 1948 Palestine conflict, the Six Day War in 1967, and the Gulf War in 1991, but even so, many Jordanians still refer to it as 'a big town'. Nearly half the population of Jordan lives in Amman.

Belying its modern appearance, Amman's origins go back a long way. Near what is now Downtown Amman, a 10,000-year-old neolithic site was discovered in the 1980s, called Ain Ghazal. It was found when the authorities were bulldozing through a hillside to build a new highway, and in 1982 an emergency dig began which revealed a neolithic village at least ten times the size of Jericho, the most famous of the neolithic sites in the region.

Neolithic origins

During the Iron Age Amman was the capital of the Ammonites, and it is referred to as Rabbath-Ammon in the Old Testament. Called by God to lead the children of Israel out from Egypt to *'possess the land which the Lord sware unto your fathers'* (Deuteronomy 1: 8), Moses led them northwards. God had commanded them not to fight with the people of Edom or Esau (the 'hairy man' of the Bible) in the area around what is now Petra, nor against the kingdom of Ammon, for they were the descendants of Lot, nephew of Abraham: *'And when thou comest nigh over against the children of Ammon, distress them not, nor meddle with them: for I will not give thee of the land of the children of Ammon, any possessions, because I have given it unto the children of Lot for a possession.'* (Deuteronomy 2: 19).

The Biblical Amman

The Bible, in the Books of Samuel, tells of many fights and wars which took place between the Israelites and the Ammonites. Perhaps the most gory were under King

David who captured and looted Rabbath Ammon. *'And the spoils of the city which were very great he carried away. And bringing forth the people thereof, he sawed them, and drove over them chariots with iron: and divided them with knives, and made them pass through brick-kilns. So did he to all the cities of the children of Ammon. And David returned with all the army to Jerusalem.'* (2 Samuel 12: 30–31). At the same battle he contrived the death of Uriah the Hittite, so that he could take his wife, the lovely Bathsheba.

Solomon's wives

Not all the links across the Jordan were hostile: many Israelites married Ammonites, and Solomon, the son whom Bathsheba bore David, had Ammonite wives in his royal harem. *'Did not Solomon king of Israel sin by these things? Yet among many nations was there no king like him, who was beloved of his God, and God made him king over all Israel: nevertheless even him did outlandish women cause to sin.'* (Nehemiah 13: 26).

Throughout history the land to the east and west of the Jordan river has been contested by rival powers, a situation which still exists today. After the demise of David and Solomon, the Assyrian period (859–612 BC) was again characterised by battles and revolts, especially between Egypt and Assyria, and the lands east and west of the Jordan were once more caught in the crossfire, now falling to one power, then rising up to unite with other tribes against another enemy. The mighty Assyrian king Tilgath-Pilneser (745–727 BC) crushed Egypt like a *'broken reed'* (Isaiah 36: 6) and abducted many of the people of the Jordan. The Assyrian kingdom finally ended in 612 BC with the fall of Nineveh to the Chaldeans or Neo-Babylonians. Their greatest king, Nebuchadnezzar (604–562 BC), from his capital at Babylon, used the people east of the Jordan to help him attack Jerusalem and the kingdom of Judah (2 Kings 24: 1–4), causing many Jews to flee to the regions of Moab and Edom, south of Ammon.

In the sixth century BC the Persians swept over the whole of the Fertile Crescent, Babylon and Egypt, but their rule was benevolent, and they left their conquered provinces much freedom in lifestyle and religion. The Persian reign continued until the advent of Alexander the Great, when the lands east and west of the Jordan, along with the whole of the rest of the Near East, were conquered in rapid succession. On Alexander's death, when the newly acquired territory was divided between his generals, Seleucus took Asia Minor and Syria, while Ptolemy, from his capital at Alexandria, took Jordan and Egypt.

In the wake of Alexander an influx of Greek ideas and culture coursed through the countries of the East. Greek became the lingua franca, Greek-style cities grew up, and Greek fashions, culture and religion became the norm. Ptolemy II Philadelphus (285–247 BC) completely rebuilt the city of Amman in the Hellenic style and named it Philadelphia after himself. The epithet Philadelphus means 'Friend of his Sister', a name he acquired by marrying his sister, Arsinoe, who was seven years his elder. It was a shocking act to the Greeks and Christians, though not to the Egyptians, for whom a precedent had been set by the god Osiris marrying his sister Isis. Ptolemy II and Arsinoe in turn pronounced themselves deified, along with all their offspring. In the following century the Seleucids captured Philadelphia from the Ptolemies, and around this time it became part of a confederation of cities known as the Decapolis, which originally, though not always, consisted of ten cities. Sometimes there were as many as 18, and all except one were east of the Jordan. Some were founded by Greek soldiers, others were existing communities converted to the Greek model.

Alexander's legacy

In Amman today there are almost no traces of this Greek city, for the Romans wiped out the previous Hellenistic structures in rebuilding the city themselves. Under Pompey, they conquered Syria, Palestine and all of the eastern Mediterranean. Amman was, however, occupied by the Arabian Nabateans from their capital at Petra, and they were in turn chased out by Herod the Great around 30 BC. When the Emperor Trajan annexed the Nabatean kingdom with the Decapolis cities to create the province of Arabia, Amman, situated as it was on the Roman caravan road from Bosra to Aqaba, became an important trade centre, specialising in horse trading. It prospered, and beautiful buildings arose to reflect this prosperity: a theatre, an odeum, temples and a forum. A few can still be seen today.

Roman trading centre

The first Arab invasion came in 633 AD, a year after the Prophet Muhammad's death, and the whole country was soon overrun. When the Umayyads under their first caliph Mu'awiya established their capital at Damascus, Jordan remained important as it lay on the Damscus –Mecca route. After the Umayyads were destroyed by the Abbasids in 750 AD, the capital of the Arab empire moved to Baghdad, and Jordan, no longer so well placed, became a largely forgotten backwater. It was referred to in the fifteenth century as 'a field of ruins'. Under the Ottoman Turks its importance lay again in its position on the pilgrim route, this time from Constantinople to Mecca.

En route to Mecca

Mixed population

The population of Jordan has always been very mixed, the inevitable result of a buffer zone position. According to the Bible the people were descended from Ammon, the product of a night of incest between Lot and his younger daughter in a cave after too much wine (Genesis 20: 35–38). Apart from the Greek, Roman and Arab elements which form the bulk of the population, the Ottoman Sultan Abdul Hamid II additionally settled groups of Chechens, a Muslim mountain tribe from Dagestan, at Zarqa, Sukhneh and Suweileh. When Russia conquered Dagestan in 1864 many Chechens emigrated to Turkey.

In 1878 Circassian Muslims who fled their country on the western slopes of the Caucasus along the coast of the Black Sea after Russia's invasion of the region in the Russo-Turkish war. They sought refuge in the Ottoman Empire from where they were sent off to be settled in various regions. The Circassians in Jordan are settled mainly in Wadi es-Sir, Jerash, Na'ur, Suweileh and Amman.

Two further small settlements exist: a Turcoman one at Er Rumman on the road to Jerash, and a Baha'i community at 'Adasiyeh in the Jordan valley.

The Arab Revolt

After the First World War most of present-day Jordan was taken by Arab armies under Faisal and Abdullah, the sons of King Hussein of the Hejaz, in what was known as the Arab Revolt. The original Arab demands were for the independence of Syria and Iraq, with Faisal and Abdullah as their kings, but this was in conflict with both French and Zionist aspirations in the region. In 1921 at a meeting in Cairo between Winston Churchill and Abdullah bin El-Hussein, it was recommended that a national Arab government be created in what was then called Transjordan, with its capital at Amman and Abdullah as its ruler. Despite much opposition from Zionists, Jordan in practice became separate from Palestine from that time on.

The modest little town of the 1920s has now become a large city. When the country was first created half a century ago, the boundaries of Amman scarcely reached the 2nd circle. Now it is well beyond the 8th circle and extending further in all directions.

Good base

So little remains today of Amman's history that most people find half a day is generally enough for a visit. Alternatively, since Amman makes the best base for a number of day trips to places such as Jerash, the Dead Sea, Madaba and the desert palaces, the city sights can be slotted into the odd spare hour here and there between excursions. Those with only one or two days to spend in Jordan should drop them altogether in favour of a visit to Jerash or a crash visit to Petra.

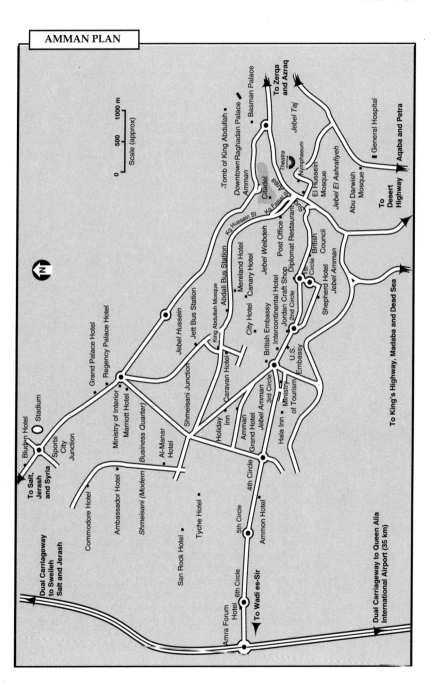

AMMAN PLAN

Tour of the City

A tour should begin at the **citadel**, which is now, as in ancient times, at the heart of the city, facing the Roman amphitheatre in the valley below. Most of the hills in Amman are steep, and the citadel hill is no exception: the best approach is therefore to ask a taxi for the *qal'a* (Arabic for citadel) and to get yourself dropped at the top near the small **Archaeological Museum** where the road ends. There is no refreshment stall on the citadel and it is worth bearing this in mind if visiting in the summer. The museum is open 9 am–4.30 pm in winter and 9 am–5.30 pm in summer (closed Tuesdays) and a tour will take 30–45 minutes. The whole excursion however will take at least three hours, because on leaving the museum, you should walk some 300m to reach the ruins of an Umayyad palace, recognisable by its broad tall arches, then visit the theatre in the valley below.

Start at the citadel

Besides the museum and the palace, the third reason you have come to the citadel is for the view, and for the sure-footed who don't mind getting a little dusty, the best way to appreciate this is by returning to the museum and plunging down the hillside towards the theatre below, a descent of some 20 minutes. Alternatively, you can ask the taxi to wait and then get it to take you down to the theatre.

Before entering the museum it is worth just standing a little while and pondering the history of the spot. This, as excavations by Italian archaeologists in the 1920s and 1930s revealed, is the site of the biblical city of Rabbath-Ammon, and it would almost certainly have been here that Amman's earliest exhibit, the bed of the giant King Og, was put out on display. As Moses said: *'For only Og king of Bashan remained of the remnant of the giants; behold his bedstead was a bedstead of iron; is it not in Rabbath of the children of Ammon? Nine cubits (4m) was the length thereof, and four cubits (1.8m) the breadth of it.'* (Deuteronomy 3: 11)

Giant King Og

The first exhibits in the museum, moving round from the right of the entrance, are the neolithic plastered skulls found in Jericho dating back to 6000–4000 BC. The skulls of forbears were kept in plaster to be worshipped by their descendants. Jericho was of course in Jordan pre–1967.

Citadel museum

Next comes a chalcolithic jar containing a child's skeleton. These jars were often buried under the living room floor to keep the dead person 'within the family' as it were. This whole series of funerary displays originated from Jericho.

After a group of wooden boxes elaborately decorated with bone inlay, you come to a cluster of bronze weapons and cylinder seals found at the 'Amman Airport Temple'. This unlikely name derives from the fact that the temple was found when the new airport was being constructed.

Next there is a selection of the famous Dead Sea Scrolls, discovered by chance in 1947 by a Bedouin shepherd in a cave near the north-western shore of the Dead Sea. The scrolls themselves, on copper, date from the first century BC and speak of 200 tons of gold and treasure hidden between Hebron and Nablus. Over 600 manuscripts were discovered, a third of them books of the Old Testament, but the treasure remains elusive.

From the Iron Age comes a curiously endearing statue of an Ammonite king. At only 75cm tall, he would have been no match for the mighty King Og. He shows an intriguing mix of Hittite, Egyptian and Phoenician, highly stylised, with his head and feet far too big for his body. From the same period (seventh century BC) is the limestone statue of a two-headed woman, also found on the citadel, and dressed in Assyrian style. The eyes are in black stone with ivory for the pupils.

Midget king

Nabatean art is represented in a Roman-style carving from Khirbet Tannur, a Nabatean temple on the summit of a mountain close to the King's Highway in Edomite territory.

On the left as you enter is a head of Tyche, resting on a purple velvet cloth. This, the goddess of Ammon and Philadelphia, was discovered when the gardens of the museum were being set out in 1957.

City goddess

Umayyad art is shown in the elaborately carved limestone lintel from Qasr et-Tuba, the most remote of the desert palaces. Later Islamic art, from the Mamluke and Ayyubid times (1174–1516) is represented by glazed bowls and turquoises with black-and-white geometric patterns.

From Pella, one of the Decapolis cities in the northern Jordan valley, comes an exquisite cedar, ebony and ivory box in the Egyptian style. It is in the shape of a shrine, and displays an unusually advanced level of craftsmanship for the late Bronze Age (1550–1200 BC). In a separate display case, on a garish orange cloth, are two lions raised up on their hind legs facing each other, their front paws resting on two entwined snakes. In the centre, on a purple velvet cloth, Roman and Byzantine gold jewellery with finely worked earrings and bracelets is displayed.

Turning right as you leave the museum, you follow a dusty track for some 200–300m, passing a fenced-in military camp, until you come to the distinctive shell of the Umayyad Palace. It is quite well preserved, its graceful arches reminiscent of Byzantine styles. Entering through a

Umayyad palace

monumental door you come to the grand hall where the public would have waited for audiences with the caliph. All around the walls on the inside, a decorated frieze of floral and geometric design runs round at a height of about 2m.

THE ISLAMICISATION OF AMMAN

When the Prophet Muhammad's troops overran Amman in the seventh century, the city's islamicisation followed without pressure or torture. Mu'awiya, the founder of the Umayyad dynasty, had the supreme Arab virtue of *hilm*, the use of peaceful measures wherever possible, only resorting to force when all else had failed. *'I apply not my sword,'* his Arab biographers report him as saying, *'where my lash suffices, nor my lash where my tongue is enough. And even if there be one hair binding me to my fellow men, I do not let it break: when they pull I loosen, and if they loosen, I pull.'* When Mu'awiya established the Umayyad capital at Damascus, Amman was made a coin-minting city. A coin found by the archeologists enabled the palace to be dated to the Caliph Hisham's reign, between 715 and 730.

Of the ancient biblical city of Rabbath-Ammon and the successive towns of the citadel, only shapeless mounds and ditches remain in which the trained eye can see ramparts, terraces and enclosures. A large cistern has been cut into the rock near the palace.

Directly opposite the museum where the road ends, are the foundations of a temple of Hercules of the second century AD. Beyond them, a loose slippery walk leads, sometimes on a path, sometimes not, down to cross a road at

Walk down to the theatre

right angles. From here a wide flight of steps descends to the **Roman theatre**. Today, as you gaze down on it, the steep slopes all around it are clustered with houses piled on top of each other, yet pictures drawn in 1880 of the view from the citadel show the theatre below in isolation on a bare hillside.

Built into the hill itself, the theatre is now meticulously restored and partially rebuilt, and opens out onto a large forum with Corinthian colonnaded porticos. Dating from the second century AD it could hold around 6000 specta-

Still performing

tors, and is still used for cultural performances. The fine old Philadelphia Hotel, built in 1925, which once stood opposite the theatre, has now been knocked down and the area turned into an archaeological park. The remains of a colonnaded walkway and a small odeum for musical performances can be seen in this area. It was next door to the Philadelphia Hotel that the Emir Abdullah (King

The Roman amphitheatre at the base of Amman's Citadel hill (Vine).

Hussein's grandfather) and the first government had their modest offices. The streets at that time were still unsurfaced and narrow, and fragmentary remains from the Roman and Byzantine eras could still be seen before they disappeared under the explosive population growth that resulted from the influx of Palestinian refugees in 1948–9.

The vaulted *paradoi* of the theatre have now been cleverly converted to house two attractive little museums. The **Folklore Museum**, the smaller and less interesting, contains Bedouin costume displays and scenes of Bedouin daily life, and the **Museum of Popular Traditions** also contains examples of Bedouin costumes. Among its most interesting exhibits is the Bedouin jewellery in gold, silver and even Red Sea coral, which they had access to. A woman acquired her jewellery at marriage as part of the price the bridegroom paid to her father, and it remained entirely her own property, as a kind of insurance in the event of divorce. This system continues in Jordan today, and indeed in most Arab countries.

Folklore and Costume Museum

Another interesting group of displays are the stones carried by the Bedouin to cure illnesses, in the belief that they had mysterious powers. They are worn smooth from contact with the body. One particularly fine pale green half domed stone was believed to help liver ailments. If all this pride in Bedouin ancestry seems misplaced in the

Cured by a stone

centre of a small modern capital, you must recall that Jordan's population was predominantly nomadic till relatively recently. King Abdullah, Jordan's first monarch, was always a Bedouin at heart and would erect tents in the grounds of his palace in Amman where he preferred to sit on the ground on carpets during balmy summer evenings. His grandson, the current King Hussein, still has this strong tie to the past: in his autobiography he writes, '*Above all I feel at home in the tribal black tents in the desert'*.

Mosaic displays

The museum also houses a fine display of fifth- and sixth-century Christian mosaics, mainly from Madaba but some from Jerash. Scenes of tigers chasing antelopes hint at the once abundant animal life.

Walking a little to the east of the theatre along the paved way, you come to the odeum, with its orchestra and scene building relatively well-preserved, though missing most of its 18 rows of seats.

To the west of the theatre you can stroll in the direction of the two Ottoman style minarets which belong to Amman's largest congregational mosque, the **El-Hussein Mosque**. Built in 1924, it is on the site of many earlier religious buildings including the cathedral of Philadelphia. In the vicinity of the mosque is the bustle of Downtown Amman's market area. The colourful shops sell all manner of goods from food to household wares and clothing. In the Arab tradition, they tend to be grouped together by type. Many fruit juice stands abound, selling orange, lemon and strawberry juices freshly squeezed while you wait – especially refreshing after a hot and dusty descent from the citadel.

Bustling market area

In a street behind the mosque (see map) the dedicated may discover another relic of Roman Philadelphia, a delapidated nymphaeum, whose front part is now occupied by shops, houses and cafés.

The animated character of this, the old centre of Amman, with its bustling narrow lanes, pavement cafés and colourful wares set in a dramatic landscape of escarpment and gorge, contrasts strongly with that of modern Amman. The orderly prosperous quarters from Jabal Amman through to the 7th circle have an air of suburban propriety, with wide streets and smart modern blocks testifying to the affluence of the new wealthy community of Amman, which has benefited since 1975 from the decline of Beirut as a financial centre. Here is the most 'Western' and orderly of Arab countries, its traffic congestion minimal by Arab standards. Jordan is also one of the most progressive countries in the area, and has recently even

Cleanest and most orderly of Arab countries

introduced a government-sponsored anti-smoking campaign and banned smoking on public transport and in public places. Littering is heavily discouraged by signs and the profuse distribution of bins, but changing the habits of a lifetime takes a little while.

The Arabs milling in the streets may be Muslim or Christian, Jordanian or Palestinian, and mixed in with them are also sprinklings of Kurds, Circassians, Armenians and Greeks. Other Arab capitals like Cairo, Damascus and Baghdad all have their Western sectors with supermarkets and luxury good shops, but you never need go far to find the bustling alleys of chaos and squalor which are an essential part of an oriental city. In Amman it is confined to the souq area of the El-Hussein Mosque, and many foreign residents find little cause to visit this Downtown sector since all their shopping requirements can be far more easily met from modern shops in the smarter residential areas.

Environs of Amman

European travellers of the last century found Amman a small town huddled round the tumbling ruins of the theatre. In the hillsides they found numerous graves and sarcophagi, but today these have been swallowed up beneath the mushrooming houses. Two Roman mausolea alone have escaped, one to the north and one to the south, both dated to the second or third century AD.

Roman mausolea

The first, **Al-Quweisme**, lies on the road out of Amman to the south, some 4km before the turn-off to Sahab. The monument still stands to its full height, built of fine blocks, its roof still largely in place. Set up on a cliff, three steps lead to its entrance and the exterior is virtually undecorated. Around the turn of the century travellers described nine sarcophagi inside, but today there are only four. Nearby are two ruined Byzantine churches with mosaic floors, dated to the eighth century.

To the north, **Al-Nuweijis** is on the Zarqa road out of Amman, as you head north from the Sport City junction past the monument to the Unknown Soldier on the right of the street. It is a Roman family tomb, well-built and attractive, the exterior decorated with a frieze.

Also in this area are the cliff tombs of **Al-Kahf** (also known by the name of Ar-Rakim), associated with the legend of the Seven Sleepers. They are Christian tombs, decorated with pillars and niches carved in rock. Throughout the Muslim world many cliff graves and caves were called *al-kahf* (Arabic for cave), as according to Islamic popular belief these places had special sanctity,

Cliff tombs

and many mosques are often found in the area around such caves. The eastern grave here in fact had a *qibla* (pointing towards Mecca) wall, and shows signs of conversion to a mosque.

The Church and Mosque of Swafiyeh
Swafiyeh is today a western suburb of Amman, to the south of the exit road to Wadi Es-Sir, in the height of the 6th circle. The mosaics were discovered in 1969 in the garden of a private house, and originally formed the floor of a small Byzantine church. It is still in good condition, covering an area of 9.5m by 5m, and the quality of the art testifies to a high cultural level.

Iraq el-Amir
There is an interesting and short excursion some 22km from Amman, which takes about two hours, to the intriguing second century BC palace at **Iraq el-Amir**. It is a unique monument, and the best preserved Hellenistic structure in the country. It can also be incorporated, say, at the end of a day's outing to Madaba or the Dead Sea, or on the way back from the King Hussein Bridge should you find yourself returning to Amman too early. In springtime especially, the Wadi es-Sir, where the monument lies, offers one of Jordan's most lush and attractive landscapes, blazing with flowers and greenery.

Intriguing palace

Following the road out of Amman west to Wadi es-Sir, you drive along a straight wide street lined with shops that leads down the hill into the town of Wadi es-Sir itself, today settled largely by Circassians. From here the way is marked in Arabic only. There is a battered signpost saying 10km to Iraq el-Amir, on a fork to the right at an angle of about 30° to the main road. The narrow tarmac road is badly potholed, and you follow it as it leaves the town and begins to wind down into a narrow fertile valley, the Wadi es-Sir itself, with irrigation channels feeding the lush vegetation. There is an unusual amount of water in the area, and this, together with its closeness to Amman and its abundance of trees and grass, makes it a favourite picnic spot on holidays and weekends. At other times it is pleasantly deserted.

Good picnic spot

Some 4km beyond Wadi es-Sir town, where the road crosses the river bed, you pass the remains of an aqueduct. To the left, above the valley floor, is a carved stone façade, called locally Ed-Deir, the Monastery, perhaps because it was used by hermits at some stage in its history. The interior houses hundreds of wall niches and the building was clearly an elaborate early dovecote.

Jordan's national flower, the black wild iris, can be seen growing along the roadside of Jordan's plateau-land (Vine).

With fertile soil and a sub-tropical climate, the Jordan valley springs to life when there is a supply of water (Vine).

Agricultural development in the Jordan valley (Vine).

The road arrives, after a further 7km, at Iraq el-Amir village and you continue straight on and beyond the village, forking left whenever there is a choice. Quite suddenly, you see the huge palace, built of colossal limestone blocks, set down on the flat ground of the valley. All around is a natural circle of cliffs, and archaeologists are now certain that the hollow where the palace stands was artificially constructed, and once held a lake that surrounded the building.

The site was first discovered in 1818, but until a joint French-Jordanian excavation project recommenced in 1976, it had puzzled archaeologists for the last two centuries. The remains of a water basin on the terrace close to the end of an aqueduct leading in from the north, together with the surrounding lake, suggested water connections, yet it was evidently never built for any protective or defensive reason. The stones used in the construction are vast, sometimes 6m long by 3m high, but they are only about half a metre thick.

A puzzle for archaeologists

Later travellers and archaeologists saw in it a Jewish/Hellenistic palace, an Ammonite or Hellenistic temple, or a Syrian-style sanctuary, or indeed a lake sanctuary in the Ptolemaic style. The size, and the constant use of the lion carvings as protectors on the outside walls, is also reminiscent of the Hittite art of eastern Turkey. It is known today by the sedentarised Bedouin who settled here at the beginning of the century as Qasr el-Abd, the Palace of the Servant.

Protective lions

Based on the archaeologists' evidence, historians are now generally agreed that the builders of the palace were from the family of Tobias, the administrator of Ammon for the Persian king Artaxerxes I in the fifth century BC. This Tobias is referred to in the Old Testament book of Nehemiah as 'the servant of Ammon', hence the palace's name. The last of the Tobiads, called Hyrkanus, quarrelled with the Jerusalem branch of the family, crossed to the east of the Jordan around 180 BC, and set up a small separate dynasty here, building the palace for himself, and remaining friendly with the Egyptian Ptolemies. When the powerful new Seleucid king Antiochus IV came to the throne in the north, and began moving threateningly south, the politically isolated Hyrkanus saw no future for his little kingdom and took his own life. Antiochus thereupon confiscated his domain. Archaeological remains for this period are extremely rare in the Near East, and this monument, with its curious mix of Egyptian concepts of scale and delicate Greek-oriental styles, is the only one of its kind known.

Unique mixture of styles

Lion fountain at Iraq el-Amir (Vine).

The joint French-Jordanian project to reconstruct the palace began in 1980 and a commemorative plaque states that the work was finished in June 1987. A vast crane was used to lift the colossal stone blocks, some of them weighing upwards of 40 tons. A barrier now prevents a car approaching right up to the site and iron railings, kept locked, have been installed across the main entrance.

Missing royal quarters?

The internal layout of the rooms was also a puzzle to the archaeologists, as the small series of rooms were far too modest to have been palace accommodation. The consensus of opinion now is that these rooms were stores for provisions, while the royal accommodation was on the upper floor, missing today, but reached by the wide stairway which can still be seen leading up from the colonnaded entrance hall.

Fine lions

The lions which now stand guarding the top of the walls were in fact originally at the floor level of this palatial accommodation. The lower animals are more like panthers, and one is in very fine condition, standing proudly, left paw raised, mouth open. Water fed from basins inside the palace would have run out in the water channels near his paws.

The best-preserved lion of all is on the furthest side of the palace from the barrier, high up on the wall. The other striking relief is that of a lioness with a cub suckling underneath. It was found on a block buried under heaps of rubble, and has been re-erected a few metres north-west of the palace.

Huge cracks in the stonework of the palace bear witness to the effects of earthquakes over the centuries. It was the fourth century earthquake which finally destroyed the building. Other blocks lie all around as if waiting to be re-erected, but the plaque suggests that work has finished, for the time being at any rate.

As you start climbing back out of the valley, you will see after about 1km, the steep cliff-face above the road cut out in various shapes. These caves can be entered just to the left of the road by a crag. Iraq el-Amir means Hollows of the Prince, and you will find a 300m long gallery cut into the rock, which you can walk along, partly in the shadow of an overhanging rock. Steps and passages lead into a whole network of 14 caves and hollows arranged in two rows one above the other. They are not particularly well-hewn and they bear no decoration except in two large caves at the lower level, which have proper doors. Where there are large inscriptions in a form of Aramaic which was in use in the second century BC, they say simply 'Tobias', and the caves are thought to have been tombs of the Tobias dynasty. The upper level of grottos are more like a little troglodyte village of refuge, but it is still not known whether they were built before or after the palace.

Cave network

Passing through the village of Iraq el-Amir on your way back you may notice the old houses, frequently built with ancient stones, gradually falling into disuse. The Bedouin tribe of Abbadi, a portion of whom settled here at the beginning of the century, are abandoning these, their original houses in favour of the concrete breeze block houses scattered on the hillside.

Qasr el-Mushatta

Another short trip in the environs of Amman is to the ruined Umayyad palace of Qasr el-Mushatta, just outside the perimeter fence of the airport. If you do not have time to visit the palaces in the desert east of Amman, you could perhaps leave for the airport early and at least have a glimpse of this remnant of desert life. A full description is given in the following section: 'North from Amman'.

NORTH FROM AMMAN

Northern Jordan Facts

Salt. Many humble places selling refreshments line the road that leads below the town through the valley to the Roman tombs.

Pella. There is a resthouse restaurant serving simple meals and refreshments.

Umm Qais. There is a simple restaurant at the site.

El-Himmeh. There is a resthouse by the hot springs with 10 rooms and six bungalows equipped with kitchenette, private bath and balcony. The accommadation is simple but adequate, and there is a restaurant serving hot meals and refreshments.

Irbid
There are two hotels in Irbid:
**** Hijazi Palace Hotel (*tel: 247267. fax: 279520*). 60 rooms with air-conditioning and colour TV. Two restaurants, bar, coffee shop and nightclub. Indoor pool and health centre, sauna, jaccuzzi. Shopping arcade.

*** Ar-Razi Hotel (*tel: 275515. fax: 275517*). Opposite Yarmuk University. 48 rooms. Adequate but rather institutional in atmosphere. Designed for visiting academics rather than tourists. Mediocre food. Pizza house, bar and coffee shop. Car hire.

Keys for the Roman tombs at Wadi Queilbeh and Beit Ras must be collected from the Department of Antiquities Office in Irbid.

Ajlun
Ajlun has two hotels:
** Ar-Rabad Castle Hotel (*tel: 04-462202*). A charming hotel opened in 1982, with an excellent location above the town, overlooking the castle. It has a delightful series of stepped terraces where you can eat or drink outside, with fine views and a small menagerie. The 18 rooms are spacious with private bathrooms and balconies and colour TV.

** Ajloun Hotel (*tel: 462524*). 13 rooms with private bath and colour TV. Restaurant, bar and small garden.

In the castle, a torch is useful to explore the darker corners and the dungeon. On the descent into the Ajlun valley, the Ajlun Park and Restaurant lies up a turning to the right.

Dibbeen
There is a restaurant and resthouse (*tel: 452413*) with chalets for overnight accommodation. All chalets have a telephone, TV, minibar and room service.
There are picnic places in the picturesque hilly forest setting of the park.

Jerash

Allow a minimum of two or three hours for a visit to this site, which is about 45 minutes to 1 hour's drive from Amman. **The Visitors' Centre** has souvenirs and bookshops, and guides can be hired at fixed rates. There is a resthouse offering hot meals and snacks but no accommodation. Camping is permitted in the vicinity of the resthouse, although no facilities are provided. From May to October there are nightly *son et lumière* performances beginning at sunset.

Just outside the town, on the left hand side of the road leading back to Amman, is the **Lebanese House Restaurant**, run by an old Lebanese lady, which serves much better food than the restaurant on the site. The trees and terraces also make the setting pleasant.

The Jerash Festival lasts for 2 weeks in July and August. Initiated by Queen Noor in 1981, it began as a six day festival, but was extended to 10 days, then to two weeks. The site closes at 3.00 pm during the Festival, to allow the police to check for bombs etc. Security is very heavy, with rigorous searches of people as well as bags. The programme always includes a heavy dose of folk dancing in costumes, Jordanian military bands with bagpipes, Arabic plays and often such excitements as gymnasts and trapeze artists. A scantily clad Western girl hanging upside down from a high trapeze watched by women totally shrouded in black can make interesting viewing. The eternal flame burns on top of the central pillar in the forum.

Azraq

A resthouse (*tel: 647611*) has recently been built with 24 rooms set round a large swimming pool with an extensive terrace. All rooms have airconditioning and private bathroom. There is also a smaller pool with hot sulphurous water from the local oasis springs. The restaurant is a little Spartan, but the food is fine. There is also the **2-star As-Sayyaad Hotel** (*tel: 647611*) on the left of the road about 1 km before the fort. Private hotel, more expensive and a little better fitted out than the resthouse, but with a smaller pool. 36 rooms.

The Roman Theatre at Jerash (Vine).

The Route North

Towards Salt and the Jordan Valley

Setting off early from Amman, it is possible, if you don't mind a long day, to head north up the Jordan Valley and end up for the night in Irbid, the only northern town with good accommodation. The route takes you via Salt to the Zai National Park (an excellent stopping place for refreshments and view), and then drops suddenly to the valley. In the valley itself you can stop off at the Bronze Age mound or 'tell' of Deir Allah, then continue north to Pella and Umm Qais which are, after Jerash, Jordan's two most important Roman cities, both finely situated on the eastern slopes with commanding views towards what is now Israel.

Exit road

You leave Amman by the eastern exit passing the traffic lights at what used to be the 6th and 7th circles, then turn north onto the main highway towards Suweileh, another of the Circassian villages established by the Sultan Abd el-Hamid in 1878. After some 8km of driving through hillsides still close enough to Amman to be partially developed, you leave the main road which continues north to Jerash, and fork left, to the west towards Salt and the Jordan valley. After a few more kilometres the road descends into the valley and the small town of Salt .

Salt

At the beginning of the century Salt and Amman were both small towns with governors of equal rank, but when in 1950 King Abdullah passed over Salt as his capital in favour of Amman, Salt was spared the ensuing population explosion, and still has only about 40,000 inhabitants. It therefore serves as a model of what Amman might have looked like had it not been proclaimed capital.

Handsome Ottoman buildings

Its name, properly Es-Salt, is thought to be derived either from 'sultana', the dried grape which was said to have originated here, or from the Latin *saltus*, a wooded valley. A number of handsome residential buildings remain, built from the local yellow sandstone in beautifully dressed blocks. They are only a little over a hundred years old, dating back to the Ottoman period, and their elegant arched windows reflect Turkish and Mediterranean influence rather than a particular local Arab style. Any attempt to recapture the old atmosphere in a photograph however, will be marred by copious power pylons and telegraph wires.

The town was inhabited throughout the Byzantine era and at the time of the Crusades a Muslim fort was built there and subsequently destroyed by the Mongols in 1260, only to be rebuilt a year later by the Mamluke Sultan

Baibars. For the eighteenth- and nineteenth-century Ottomans Salt was the most important town in Transjordan and they chose to build their barracks there; they are still on top of the hill.

Salt had the first Latin church in Transjordan, in 1866, and it still has a Christian minority with a Greek Orthodox church and a Rosary Sisters convent.

A short detour is to be recommended to visit the small group of Roman Christian rock tombs just outside the town. Taking a sharp left turn as the road approaches the bottom of the valley just 200m or so before the town, follow this road for about a kilometre as it passes through lush vegetation on either side of the road. At a yellow traffic police box, a passable dirt track leads down to the left into what appears to be a factory. It is in fact a fertiliser plant, and the smell can be rather strong. Entering the factory gates and then skirting round the left hand side of the fertiliser tanks, you come to a series of low buildings with pretty flower beds in front. Just to the left the tombs are cut into the rock, partly concealed behind bushes and shrubs. They date back to the third century AD and were discovered around 1974. The carved reliefs show crosses, and one has a figure known as King Salt.

Roman rock tombs

ZAI NATIONAL PARK

Some 8km north-east of Salt, at a large roundabout at the top of a hill, Zai is signposted to the right. From the main road it is another 9 or 10km to the resthouse at Zai (*Istiraha* Zai), an extensive and magnificently situated refreshments area that opened in spring 1987. It makes an excellent spot for lunch. The network of small surfaced roads that cover the National Park area can be a little confusing, but initially you follow the signs pointing straight on. You then fork left up towards the summit of a little hill, then go down the hill and past a small white hut and barrier for the last 500m.

The extensive open air terraces of the resthouse, laid out with attractive seating, command superb views east down into the Jordan valley. There are playground areas for children, quaint little wooden bridges crossing over water channels, and a large tented area used for parties and weddings. Being only 45km from Amman and about 45 minutes drive, the hope is that many families will be lured out here for celebrations or just for a relaxing day in the clear mountain air.

To continue the journey you can follow a different road that winds in sharp hairpin bends down the valley side to rejoin the main road after about 4km.

Fun for families

A brief tour of the town and the Roman tombs will take about an hour, after which you can return to the T-junction and turn left, north-east.

The Jordan Valley

Northern Rift Valley

You soon descend some 350m into the vast geological phenomenon which is the Great Rift Valley in its northern manifestation. This colossal crack in the earth's crust extends from northern Syria through the Beqa'a valley in Lebanon, into Lake Tiberias (the Sea of Galilee), then on through the Dead Sea, the Wadi Araba and the Gulf of Aqaba, all the way to East Africa, 5000km away. The valley between the Dead Sea and the Sea of Galilee is known as the **Ghor**. It is all below sea level and has been sinking in spasmodic jerks since its formation, each jerk causing an earthquake in the area. The most recent of these movements was in 1927, and the accompanying earthquake caused a lot of damage in Amman.

The climate of the Ghor is subtropical with meagre rainfall, high humidity and extremely high temperatures, especially in summer when it never drops below 38°C. The effect of this heat, closed in by the high sides of the valley, and combined with the fertile alluvial soil, is of an

Open air greenhouse

open-air greenhouse. Extensive government backing for agricultural schemes since 1958 has produced an impressive network of irrigation canals and dams to exploit the available water to the full. In the 1967 war Israeli bombardment of the irrigation installations set progress back considerably, and repairs did not begin until after the 1970 civil war. Some 100,000 people had lived in the valley before, but by 1970 it had dropped to a mere 3,000. With the loss of the West Bank, Jordan lost some 80 per cent of its fruit growing and 45 per cent of its vegetable growing area. Between the seventies and eighties the country also suffered a drift of around 8 per cent of its workforce away from agriculture into the cities and towns, with the result that only about 10 per cent of the total workforce is now employed in agriculture.

Despite all these setbacks, the government's persistence has been rewarded, and the development projects of the valley are now seeing real results, with excellent yields of tomatoes, cucumbers, bananas, melons and cit-

Early ripening

rus fruits. The greenhouse effect means that crops ripen at least two months earlier than elsewhere in the surrounding countries of the Middle East, and sometimes three crops a year can be produced. The surplus is exported, mainly to the Arabian peninsula. Jordan's eventual aim is to be self-sufficient in food by the 1990s, and by establishing new housing, schools and a complete social infrastructure, the government is hoping to lure skilled people back into the valley to help run the complex new water and electricity installations. Many items in the countrey's development programme have had to be cut back, however, owing to its economic problems, but plans for the construction of the Al-Wahdeh Dam, crucial to the further development of the valley, are well advanced and will continue.

The valley today, with its plastic greenhouses, concrete pipes and irrigation ditches, is a far cry from the Biblical version of the Jordan. In the Bible descriptions, its banks were heavily wooded, the vegetation lush and abundant, and wild animals prowled the forests. Paintings from as late as the nineteenth century also portray the lush vegetation that existed until relatively recently.

Biblical lushness

The acceleration in the agricultural and commercial development of the valley, together with the building of new roads and water installations, spurred into motion a joint project of the American Centre of Oriental Research and the Jordanian Department of Antiquities. They excavated and catalogued as many sites as possible before everything was submerged under the greenhouses. This study revealed 52 new sites and looked again at 54 that were previously known.

In spite of this enormous richness in archaeological remains, very few of the sites would repay the attention of the non-specialist, as they consist of neolithic or Bronze-Age settlements where little remains to be seen. The two which are most rewarding for the amateur are the Bronze-Age mounds or *tells* of Deir Allah and Tell es-Saidiyeh.

Deir Allah and Tell es-Saidiyeh

As you descend into the sweltering, dead-flat valley, you pass the sign marking sea level shortly before reaching the bottom. Turning north up the valley you pass the occasional check-point – where you are rarely stopped – and after a few minutes, you will pass through the sprawling town of **Deir Allah**. The huge mound itself, about 30m high, is not signposted at the time of writing, but it lies just 10m or so to the left of the road opposite a petrol station. Driving along a track round the side of it, you will come to the gate of the dig house, a modern building built in 1982, which houses a museum, pleasantly set in its own gardens. Before this, the dig team lived in tents.

A tour of the site and museum will generally take about an hour. From the gate of the dig house you can begin the ascent of the mound to reach the excavated

Mound and museum

**Scorching
ascent**

areas at the top. In temperatures of 42°C in the shade and with very high humidity, this requires more effort than you might think in the summer, and on the summit the scorching wind funnelled through the valley is like a blast from a furnace. The main building here, in the Middle and Late Bronze Age (1600–200 BC), was a large open sanctuary, hence the name Deir Allah, Arabic for 'House of God'. Houses and storerooms surrounded the temple, which seems to have been destroyed in about 1100 BC, possibly by an earthquake, after which it was abandoned.

Valley views

The view from the summit gives a fine impression of the cultivation in progress in the Jordan Valley. The river itself is not visible, as it lies some 5km to the west, but over to the north-west, further Bronze-Age mounds can be seen. Sometimes there are also the black tents of a few Bedouin, tucked apart from the houses.

The museum, which will usually be opened when you arrive, contains a meticulously laid out series of exhibits covering an enormous timespan, from ancient Egyptian scarabs and cylinder seals to loom-weights for weaving, and various later Islamic oddments dating from the Middle Ages when the site was used as a cemetery. In adjoining workrooms, jars are stuck together with glue and clothes pegs.

**Unknown
script**

The most significant finds here were some clay tablets inscribed in an unknown script resembling the Phoenician script of Byblos, and an Aramaic text dating back to the seventh century BC, which refers to a prophet called Bileam who is head of the sanctuary. This text is thought to confirm that Deir Allah is the only known example of a sanctuary independent of the ancient Hebrew religion, outside the influence of the kings of Judea.

Ten kilometres further on, the mound of **Tell es-Saidiyeh**, at 42m largest of the tells in the valley, rises on the left. It is set back about 1km from the road, near the village of Kureyma. To the layman it is more impressive than Deir Allah, not only for its height, but also for the 125 steps which lead from its northern side down to a spring.

**Highest and
largest**

Archaeologists have deduced that this staired walkway would originally have been covered by a wooden roof for its entire length and divided into separate uphill and downhill passages. Dated to the early Iron Age, it is perhaps the first known example of a one-way system. It is thought to have been destroyed around 924 BC by the Egyptian Pharoah Scheschonk I, who passed through Palestine with 1200 chariots and 60,000 chariot fighters, conquering almost everything in his path.

Pella
Continuing north for some 20km up the flat valley bed, you approach the turn-off for **Pella**, unsignposted at the time of writing. The main road becomes dual carriageway as it runs through a scattered town, and about 1km before the dual carriageway ends, you take a right-hand fork on a tarred road leading uphill for a further kilometre, until you see some tall columns rising to your left and a dirt track leading off to the right, over a hill. From the brow of this bare hillside, you can look down into the valley below, with its fine streams, to view the extensive ruins of Pella, one of the Decapolis cities, known locally as Tabaqat el-Fahl. A resthouse serving food and refreshments has now opened here.

The attractive site was chosen for its natural advantages. Tucked up a little side valley, the Wadi Jirm, it is spared the worst of the summer heat of the Jordan Valley proper, and is also sheltered from the sharp frosts and cold winter winds of the highland plateau. It has a spring, Ain el-Jirm, which has water even in the hottest summer months. Because of these factors, the site has been inhabited more or less continuously for 7000 years, starting in neolithic times. According to Egyptian papyri of 1250–1000 BC, Pella had around 5000 inhabitants, and produced the wooden spokes for the chariot-wheels of Pharoanic Egypt, a fact which shows that the bare hills you see today were not always so.

Well-watered site

It became a real city, as a Hellenistic foundation of Macedonian veterans of Alexander the Great's army who named it Pella after the town in Macedonia where Alexander was born. The Hellenistic town was destroyed in about 80 BC by Israelite troops because the inhabitants would not promise to adopt Jewish customs.

After the Roman conquest in 64 BC, Pella was rebuilt, and was one of the cities of the Decapolis league. In the Christian era it was a thriving town, and during the siege of Jerusalem by the Roman emperors Vespasian and Titus in 70 AD, Christians from Jerusalem took refuge in Pella. It was later absorbed into the Roman province of Palestine.

The town enjoyed its heyday in the Byzantine era and in the fourth century it was much visited as a spa. It had its own bishop, who sat on the Council of Ephesus in 449 and at Chalcedon in 451. Yet curiously, even as late as the sixth century, Christians were being buried with pagan objects, showing the continuing strength of the earlier oriental cultures. The most notable, nicknamed the Lady of Pella, is a figurine of a Syrian/Palestinian fertility goddess, and was found in a Christian grave of that period.

Popular Byzantine spa

During the fifth and sixth centuries Pella was heavily populated, and the slopes of the surrounding hills were all covered in houses, the remains of which can still be made out in parts. The most impressive monument of Pella also dates from that time – the colossal **Great Basilica** in the valley, once in the city centre, with a monumental stairway leading to the west towards the spring.

An important battle took place here in 635 between the Arabs and a strong Byzantine army, in which the Byzantines were roundly defeated and a staggering total of 80,000 Greeks were said to have been killed. It was known thereafter by the Arabs as the Battle of the Marsh

Name origin

(*Fahl*), as the Byzantines had broken the nearby dams and this is where it gets its current name, Tabaqat el-Fahl, Terraces of the Marsh. Despite the Arab victory, the town remained half Greek, half Arab, according to a ninth century Arab historian. The Arab element evidently stuck to its nomadic habits, as findings of the late seventh century show that animals and people lived under the same roof, and camel caravans continued to link them with the Arabian peninsula. With the gradual decline of Christianity, the churches fell into disrepair, and the side rooms of the basilica were put to use as stables.

There were three earthquakes, in 658, in 717, and a particularly severe one in 747, which destroyed most of the buildings and killed many of the inhabitants. Human bones were found under some of the collapsed blocks during the excavations.

Mamluke ceramics show that the town was inhabited again in the thirteenth and fourteenth centuries, and in the nineteenth century Arab farmers settled among the ruins,

Excavations continue

until they were relocated by the government in the 1960s to protect the ruins and facilitate excavations. Since 1967 there have been American, Australian and, most recently, Jordanian digs and reconstruction projects on the site, though with the outbreak of the Six Day War in 1967, excavations did not begin in earnest till 1974.

Most of this work has been concentrated in the valley, because the buildings by the road have lost many of their well-crafted blocks. The so-called West Basilica which was located here, served the local inhabitants well as a quarry. Three columns are still standing on their Attic bases and with Attic capitals. The three-naved basilica is thought to have been part of a monastery complex, and the central nave originally had a mosaic floor. Scattered column bases and pillars are strewn about what were once courtyards. East of the basilica a deep trench was dug through the hillside to reveal the layers of Hellenistic, Byzantine, Roman and Islamic occupation in these, the living quarters of Pella. The area is now fenced in.

From the end of this trench, there is a fine view down into the centre of Pella. When the ruins were first discovered by archaeologists in the nineteenth century, the blocks were scattered in such confusion that the main Great Basilica was mistaken for a Roman temple, and the Roman theatre was not seen at all. Extensive reconstruction work has made matters clearer now, though the theatre, the only remnant of the Roman city, is still only recognisable as a hollow in the hillside, missing most of its seats.

The Great Basilica was built in the fifth century using the stones and columns of the Roman city, and geometric mosaics decorated its floor. Rather than being an adaptation of an existing temple, it was built totally from scratch. The monumental stairway reused the seats of the Roman theatre and odeum.

Basilica

On a hill to the east of the centre, the columns of another large building have been re-erected. Until 1980 it was thought to be a temple, but it is now known to be a third Byzantine church, also built around the fifth or sixth century, again from the stone of the Roman city. Like the West Basilica, it is thought to have formed part of a monastic complex on the edge of the main town.

On the summit of **Mt Sartaba**, rising some 300m over the valley and about 2km away from the city centre as the crow flies, is a Hellenistic fort. From its vantage point you can see not only into the Jordan valley, but also east to the castle of Qala'at er Rabad, and west to Mt Carmel on the Mediterranean coast. It has been identified as a Seleucid construction, built in about 218 BC by Antiochus III as one of a string of forts east of the Jordan to ward off attacks by local Bedouin tribesmen.

If you drive carefully, ideally in a four-wheel-drive vehicle, you can descend the rough track and even ford the stream just by the spring. But without a vehicle, a comprehensive tour of the whole site would take some two hours at least, as the distance between the basilicas is quite long. In the summer the hills become gaunt and barren, with little or no shade, but in the winter some greenery starts to appear making the whole valley an attractive spot, which is often used by the locals for family picnics on Fridays and holidays.

El-Himmeh and Mukheibeh

Continuing north up the Jordan valley from Pella for a further 20km or so, you reach the settlement of Shuneh, where there is a fork right to Irbid, and a road block. (At each fork in this road there is a road-block to monitor traffic movement, but they rarely stop tourists and there is nothing to worry about if your documents are to hand; you should always carry your passport on you.)

Keeping straight ahead, i.e. north, at this junction, you pass a petrol station on your right. You then cross a roundabout and fork to the right to **Adasiyeh**. This small town has Jordan's major Baha'i community.

Baha'i community

THE BAHA'IS

The Baha'is are a sect founded by Baha Allah, 1817–1892. Born of noble family in Tehran, he was imprisoned in Palestine at Akka in 1868. When he was released in 1877 he settled close to this little town in Jordan. It is a curious faith, an independent religion, not an offshoot of any other. There are 800 communities scattered all over the world, following absolutely the teachings of the Prophet Baha Allah.

The complete text of the Baha'is' sacred works has not been translated, but the following is a fragment of its teachings, which advocates spiritual brotherhood and unity throughout the world:

> *The Tabernacle of Unity has been raised; regard ye not one another as strangers... Of one tree are ye all the fruit and of one bough the leaves... The world is but one country and mankind its citizens.*

Sir Flinders Petrie in a letter to the Daily Sketch, London, in 1932 wrote:

> *The Baha'i Movement of Persia should be a welcome adjunct to true Christianity; we must always remember how artificial the growth of Latin Christian ideas has been as compared with the wide and less defined beliefs native to early Christian faith.*

Besides Adasiyeh, other Baha'i communities in the region are to be found in Salt, Hebron, Akka, Jaffa and Majdal.

Beyond the town you will come to another road-block, this time with a barrier across the road, for you are now entering the sensitive border zone with the Golan Heights. Very little traffic is encountered beyond this point, though as a tourist you will have no difficulties.

Dramatic gorge

Immediately after the barrier, the road climbs up into the gorge of the Yarmuk river which forms the boundary with Syria. Here you can enjoy (but do **not** photograph) perhaps the most spectacular scenery to be found in Jordan outside Petra. The road is eerily empty, and a bombed and blackened bridge hangs across the gorge, a relic of the Six Day's War and a reminder not to linger too long in this fascinatingly different landscape. From the top of the gorge, the view now opens out and across the river a series of impressive-looking reservoirs testifies to the diligence of the Israelis in marshalling the water supplies they were so short of in their pre-1967 borders.

A few kilometres further on, you reach a junction: one road goes to El Himmeh 5km down the valley to the left, and the other goes uphill to the site of Umm Qais and then Irbid, 35km away.

The winding descent to the springs of **El-Himmeh** brings you to another barrier, which is raised as you approach. A little further on, you will see the resthouse on your right, perched on a hillock, and to the left, just in front of a sign to Mukheibeh, is a baths establishment, laid around a rather sordid, stagnant, litter-strewn pool, which smells of the hot sulphurous water for which the place is renowned. You can swim or wallow in this large outdoor pool, though its murky colour and surface litter are hardly enticing, but there are three other areas in which to bathe, all indoors and each entered by a separate door. Their temperatures range from 42° to 25°C. The smallest pool is the prettiest, with blue patterned tiles all the way up to the ceiling. The entry fee is 500 fils and the baths are used alternately by men and women, changing every hour.

Sulphurous pools

To soak up the atmosphere afterwards, you can sit and have fizzy drinks at the tables round the large open pool. At holidays and weekends, the whole area is crowded with day-trippers from Irbid. The resthouse, classed as three stars, has a few rooms and serves meals.

Following the road on down towards **Mukheibeh**, ask for the waterfall, *shelale*. You will be directed into a dead-end street in the mud-brick village, from where you should continue on foot to the edge of the gorge. A lush and pictureque track leads down into the gorge itself, with fine views over the river below, and ends after a few minutes in an area of subtropical vegetation with water cascading over a rocky outcrop, while you stand underneath in an earthy hollow. Below, the Yarmuk sweeps down, green and majestic, with abundant vegetation flanking the narrow banks before the cliffs rise sharply. This is closer to what most people expect of the river Jordan itself, which is, alas, disappointing in comparison. The Israelis began diverting the Jordan's headwaters from above the Sea of Galilee 30 years ago.

Waterfall grotto

Umm Qais

Returning up the hill to the junction, the road then winds on steeply, and just before the summit is another road-block, at which you will be waved on. Immediately after the barrier, a dirt road forks sharply to the right. Bumping along this for some 200m you arrive at the ruins of **Umm Qais** or **Gadara** to give it its correct name. It is another of the Decapolis cities, superbly sited on the crest of a hill, facing out towards the Sea of Galilee and the Golan Heights, both of which are visible on a clear day. Before 1977, when the extensive German excavations began, the view here was all there was to see, for the site itself consisted of a confused jumble of stones.

Some have speculated that it was here that Christ made himself unpopular by transferring the unclean spirits from two wild men to a herd of Gadarene swine, *'and, behold, the whole herd of swine ran violently down a steep place into the sea, and perished in the waters...'* And *'behold the whole city came out to meet Jesus: and when they saw him, they besought him that he would depart out of their coasts'*. (Mathew 8: 28). If this scene did indeed take place at Gadara, then the tombs you see on your left set down in a slight hollow just a few metres after turning off the main road, could be the very tombs from which the two men emerged. There are two of the same style, both remarkable for their colossal limestone doors, which still swing on stone hinges and are carved to resemble fortified metal and wooden doors. Greek inscriptions are carved into the stone above the lintels. When the first European visitors found the site in the nineteenth century, it was inhabited by just a few Bedouin families and the tombs were being used as goat pens. A resthouse serving food and refreshments has now been opened on the site.

Some 50m further on you can make out, again on your left, the contours of the East Theatre, originally the larger of Gadara's two theatres, Greek in its cliff position, Roman in its semicircular shape. Many of its seats are missing today – they have been used as convenient building blocks in the modern settlement. Immediately opposite, to the right of the road, is an ancient terrace whose strategic qualities were perceived by the Jordanian army and used as gun emplacements.

Just a few metres further on you arrive at the core of the ancient city, recognisable by the impressive octagon of black basalt Corinthian columns which the German team has re-erected, and which mark the main Byzantine church of the city. From the fourth to the seventh centuries the town was an episcopal seat of some importance. Its floor is finely decorated with marble and geometric-patterned tiles, and the whole is thought to date back to the early sixth century. It was destroyed by an earthquake in the eighth century, probably the one which inflicted so

Gaderene swine

Gigantic stone doors

Basalt basilica

much damage in neighbouring areas in 747. Above it on a rocky outcrop are the Turkish houses which the archaeologists restored to use as their own headquarters and accommodation. One of these has now been restored and opened as a museum. Scattered about are several fine carved blocks, notably a highly decorated architrave from a Byzantine sarcophagus and a block, realistically carved, scales and all, in the form of a thick coiled snake.

As a Graeco-Roman settlement, and one of the most important towns of the Decapolis, Gadara prided itself on its cultural life, and produced a succession of well-known philosophers and poets, the best known of whom was a second-century satirist and poet called Meleager. He was a Phoenician by origin and known especially for his epigrams:

Notable inhabitants

Island Tyre was my nurse, and Gadara, which is Attic, but lies in Syria, gave birth to me. From Eucrates I sprung, Meleager, who first by the help of the Muses ran abreast of the Grave of Menippus. If I am a Syrian, what wonder? Stranger, we dwell in one country, the world; One Chaos gave birth to all mortals.

Other notable inhabitants were the poet and philosopher Menippus, of the Cynic school, and the Epicurean philosopher Philodenus, born here in the first century BC.

Gadara was captured from the Seleucids by Pompey in the first century BC and rebuilt. It was at that time that it became one of the Decapolis cities. The Emperor Augustus later gave the city to the unpopular Herod the Great as a reward for the latter's support of Rome, but the dismayed Gadarenes tried to bring him into disfavour with the emperor. The plan misfired however, and *'they killed themselves for fear of torture, some with their own hand, some flung themselves into the valley or drowned themselves in the river'*. (Flavius Josephus).

Continuing some 50m beyond the basilica, you come to a superb door leading down into the basalt West Theatre, smaller than the eastern one, with a seating capacity of only about 3,000, but far better preserved. The vaulted tunnel in Roman style still runs intact around the semicircle under the seats.

In sharp contrast to the black blocks of basalt that form the seats, a larger-than-life-size statue of Tyche, goddess of drama, sits in the front row, carved out of white marble. Now headless and rather battered by earthquakes, she used to hold a horn of plenty. The theatre looks out westwards towards the sunset along the crest of the hill.

Black theatre, white statue

Returning by a different path that leads in front of the stage building level of the theatre back towards the octagonal church, you will notice, built into the terrace at a level beneath the church, a series of arcaded shops, once on the edge of the old Roman forum. A few metres further to the west, opposite the row of shops, are the heavily ruined remnants of a bath.

Two other structures of note lie some 250m away, to the other, northern or valley side of the approach road to the site. They are reached by forking off on a small path. The first is the badly ruined North Mausoleum, built from basalt blocks on a platform on the cliff edge, and the second, a little further on, is a late Roman bath, with very little remaining except a few marble basins and some fine mosaic floors in elaborate geometric patterns dating from the fourth to the sixth century. The mosaics are currently covered over with earth and protected by a surrounding wall. The plan is to display them once the villagers of Umm Qais have moved into a modern settlement lower down the valley. The Department of Antiquities has recently purchased the site to ensure its preservation.

The pleasures of the Roman lifestyle

As well as having their own baths the Romans of Gadara used to go down to El-Himmeh to take the spring waters. Strabo wrote :

To Gadara the pleasure-loving Romans, after having enjoyed the restorative effects of the hot springs down the valley, retired for refreshment, enjoying the cooler heights of the city and solacing their leisure with the plays performed in the theatres.

Elaborate grave

Returning to the dirt track and continuing west for some way, you reach a vast round water basin. Just beyond this is the remarkable West Mausoleum, approached by a flight of 17 steps leading down about 4m below the current ground level. The elaborate grave, with its columns and various rooms, was at this level for centuries, not even sinking when, in 1981, several Jordanian army tanks stood on its roof.

Irbid

A drive of 35km along a hilly and narrow tarmac road brings you to Irbid, the major town of the north. As Jordan's chief agricultural and industrial centre, it has one of the fastest-growing populations in the country. This growth has left Irbid itself a town of neither character nor charm, but of endless half-finished streets and buildings. In 1976 the new Yarmuk University was also set up here with Saudi money, and the vast campus on the edge of town is one of the few landmarks. This is useful, since the best hotel, the Ar-Razi, is situated directly opposite the university. A mediocre, colourless hotel with poorish

Charmless town

food, and a disconcertingly pervasive smell of disinfectant, it is nevertheless the most comfortable in town.

Irbid is the third largest city in Jordan with 200,000 inhabitants, after Amman and Zarqa. Signposts are a rarity, and in the dusty, dirty streets, continually stopping to ask the way is not a pleasant experience.

Irbid was originally an ancient settlement surrounded by a wall of ancient basalt blocks, and was identified as the Arbila of the Decapolis cities. Some historians have also linked it to the town of Beth-Arbel, referred to in Hosea, and there are still a number of Christian churches and schools in the town. The central mound, dating back to the Bronze Age, continued to be lived on until the nineteenth century, when the Turks built their palace on the summit. At that time, 1884, the town had 130 houses and a population of 700, but the accelerating sprawl of the modern town has obliterated most traces of earlier civilizations. Some Roman tombs and statues are implanted in the pavement on the eastern side of the prison.

In the centre of town there is the Department of Antiquities' small office, which announces itself with a sign at first floor level at one of the main crossroads. You must call here before visiting the Byzantine tombs of Abila and Capitolias – the officials hold the key and will be happy to act as guides. The little office, also at first-floor level, houses a small museum with finds from Pella and Gadara.

Capitolias and Abila

Spending the night at Irbid gives you the chance to visit the frescoed tombs of Abila and Capitolias in the morning, before driving on to Ajlun and Dibbeen to see the engaging little castle of Ar-Rabad and the forests of the Dibbeen National Park. A comfortable night can then be spent at Ajlun, leaving the whole of the next day free for the visit to Jerash.

From Irbid, retrace your route back on the Umm Qais road, and **Capitolias** is the first ancient settlement you reach, now set beside the village of Beit Ra's, some 5km north of Irbid. Scattered capitals and decorated blocks are to be seen in the village, sometimes in gardens and yards, sometimes built into the houses themselves. There are several rock-cut tombs with large basalt doors, as at Umm Qais, which, because of their proximity to the village, are now used as animal stabling and storerooms. A few discarded sarcophagi also make useful cow troughs. The major tomb, however, now lies under the playground of the village school. Thought to be late Roman or early Byzantine, it is decorated inside with frescoes.

Tomb under playground

The vineyards of the area were praised by pre-Islamic poets, and the Umayyad Caliph Yazid II, always fond of the grape, is said to have built a palace here, where he lived with his favourite wife.

Continuing some 2km beyond Beit Ra's on the Umm Qais road, you reach the turn-off, right, to Wadi el-Queilbeh and Horta. After heading north for some 7km on this narrow tarmac road, you cross at right angles a valley with a spring to the left of the road, where tractors are often to be seen filling up huge cylindrical water tanks. The valley cleft is very fertile and thickly vegetated, as even in high summer the water here is plentiful. This is the Wadi el-Queilbeh, in ancient times the necropolis of the Decapolis city of **Abila**. Of the city itself, very little remains to be seen, though the archaeologists may eventually transform the site once work has finished on the necropolis. It lies over the hill to the west of the wadi, reachable by a dirt track which brings you over the saddle of a hill, passing the remains of a basilica and then dropping down into the hollow, where the scattered blocks of the theatre can still be recognised. The spot is pleasantly deserted, save for the occasional grazing goat. One dignified old local here, dressed in fine baggy trousers and a white cummerbund, pronouced with great conviction that the city had been designed and founded by Alexander the Great. The current historical view however, is that the town was Seleucid, founded after Alexander's death.

Fertile valley

Returning to the wadi, you can visit the Roman tombs themselves, of which there are several hundred, some 20 with frescoes, all built into the cliffs on both sides of the valley. The most impressive cluster is always kept locked, following excavations by a joint French-Jordanian project from 1981, and to see inside them, you must be accompanied by the Antiquities Department official from Irbid, who holds the key. Before they were locked, the tombs were subject to the frequent attentions of pillagers, and the Antiquities Department is now anxious to protect them, both from further vandalism and from natural deterioration, which occurred rapidly once the tombs were opened to the elements. Salts began to form a whitish layer where micro organisms multiplied at alarming rates.

Frescoed Roman tomb

The tombs are reached by forking off the main road just by the spring, from where you will notice a path leading off into the vegetation by the gorge. A few minutes' walk brings you to the first of the deep channels dug out by the archaeologist, leading to an iron door. Inside, the main tombs are surprisingly roomy, with accommodation for up to 42 bodies, sometimes in neat little cubicles off the main chamber, sometimes in stone sarcophagi, and sometimes in dug trenches. The whole is hewn out of the rock, and coloured traces of frescoes remain, with delicate paintings of the heads of men and women, thought to be the occupiers of the graves. The ceiling of the tomb known as Q2 is especially fine, carved in octagonal patterns carrying a male or female face, or a leaping dolphin, all linked by elaborate crosses. The tombs have been dated by an inscription to 151–200 AD.

Delicate paintings

On the opposite side of the valley, the tombs are more difficult to reach, as they have to be approached from above. From the spring, the tarred main road continues across the wadi bed and winds up to the opposite cliff. When you judge that you are roughly opposite the tombs you have just visited, you drive or walk through the rough scrub to the cliff edge. Here, again cut into the rock, you will see a series of tombs which almost resemble troglodyte dwellings, with clusters of underground rooms and stairs. Again, the major tombs are locked, though a few minor ones are open from above and can be clambered into. It is remarkable that the archaeologists knew where to dig, for some of the tomb entrances could only have been reached by digging down at least 4m from the current ground level. The rock also has a natural tendency to crumble, which must have made digging even harder. From the cliffs there is a striking view, showing the stark contrast between the barren hillsides and the green lushness in the gorge.

Striking contrast

From Irbid, those heading for Syria will drive east to Ramtha, the town just before the only border crossing into Syria. Those continuing on a circuit within Jordan, however, would do best to head south some 32km on an attractive hilltop road to the town of Ajlun, where you can spend an enjoyable few hours exploring the castle and resting on the scenic terraces of the Ar-Rabad Castle Hotel.

Ajlun

The little **Ar-Rabad Castle** can be seen in solitary splendour on its hilltop from whichever direction you approach. And from its vantage point you can get an excellent view in all directions, especially to the west and the hills of distant Judea. Jerusalem is said to be visible on a clear day. A tarred road now takes you right up to an open parking area in front of the castle, where there are sometimes a few stalls selling fizzy drinks.

Hilltop castle

Despite its superb position, the slopes surrounding it are not especially steep, and so to protect it further from attack, a deep dry moat was dug. In the 1960s the entrance could only be reached by climbing up iron rungs embedded in the rock, but today, as would have been the case originally, a wooden drawbridge has been built to span the wide gully.

The castle was built in 1184 by the Ayyubid Emir Izz ed-Din Osama, a cousin of Saladin, both to safeguard this western border of Ayyubid territory, and to withstand the attacks of the French Crusaders. It is therefore one of the rare examples of a true Arab castle, the others being Marqab, Aintab, and Shayzar, all of which are in Syria. Osama, as one of Saladin's most able governors, was given the district as a fief, and his original thinking in building the castle was as a defence against the feuding local emirs. When these emirs queried his project, Osama pretended that he was building it as protection against the Frankish Crusaders who were already installed in their castles at Kerak and Shawbak. This satisfied them, and they even helped him build it. When it was finished, Osama invited the emirs to a celebratory banquet in the new castle, and after they had eaten their fill, he had them all locked up to try out the new dungeons.

Banquet trickery

A thirteenth century Arab writer said he was told by the local people that the castle had once been the site of a monastery and the founding monk had been called Ajlun. The upper part of the current town still has a Christian community with two churches, and the approach road to the castle also passes a mosque on the left, which, with its fine square thirteenth-century minaret, is thought to have been converted from a Byzantine church. The name Qal'at ar-Rabad means 'castle and its surroundings', and the ruins of some suburbs can indeed still be made out on the slopes around it.

The heavy stonework of Saladin's time

Most of the present castle dates from Saladin's time; the oldest parts are recognisable by the coarser heavier stonework and the narrower window or arrow slits. A few years after the Battle of Hittin and the fall of Jerusalem, when Saladin had inflicted such damage on the Frankish kingdom that the castle was no longer required for defence purposes, Osama also lost his authority, having become entangled in political struggles after Saladin's death. The castle was taken over by a certain Aybak, a Turkish slave who was the major-domo to the Sultan's son. In 1214 Aybak made some extensions to the castle, and these can be identified by their fine craftsmanship (Aybak was also the master builder at

AYBAK AND SHAGARA ED-DURR

Aybak's occupancy of the castle came early in his career, and later he was to rise to fame in military campaigns, becoming the commander-in chief of the army. When the last Ayyubid Caliph As-Salih, died, he left behind his widow, a former Turkish slave girl called Shagara ed-Durr. This bold lady declared herself Sultana and ruled Cairo for 80 days. The emirs, however, were scornful of such female dominance and chose Aybak as Sultan instead, whereupon the dauntless Shagara ed-Durr married him to ensure that she retained power.

Aybak was the first of the Mamluke sultans, and his reign began in 1250. Seven years later, when she heard he was contemplating another marriage, Shagara ed-Durr had him murdered in his bath in the royal palace on the Citadel of Cairo. She herself was thereupon beaten to death with wooden shoes by the slave women of Aybak's first wife, and her body was thrown to the dogs from a citadel tower.

Cairene drama

Azraq) and by the wider windows which reflected the castle's changed role to more of an administrative centre than a military fort.

In Mamluke times the castle of Ar-Rabad was one of a chain of points that linked Damascus to Cairo by pigeon post. By this highly developed means of communication, the Sultan could receive news in Cairo of what was happening on his northern borders the same day. The castle was unfortunate enough to be in the way of the Mongol hordes in 1260, but though they plundered it, they caused less damage to the structure than the earthquake of 1837, which left it collapsing and dangerous.

Pigeon post

Between 1927 and 1929 extensive repairs and rebuilding were carried out, and it is from that time that the current main entrance to the castle, which is reached across the wooden bridge, dates. From this bridge you can see to the left of the entrance a square cistern cut out of the rock. There were five other cisterns inside the castle itself, and some of them were being used until quite recently.

Inside, the stone-vaulted corridor kinks first right and then left to enter the castle proper through its original gate. Stairways, passages and doorways lead off tantalisingly in all directions to a multitude of different levels, usually ending up eventually on one of the towers, with their fine views. At regular intervals the authorities have thoughtfully erected orange waste bins lovingly inscribed with the Arabic proverb that equates to '*Cleanliness is next to Godliness*'. A walk round the exterior walls of the castle is also worthwhile to appreciate the full height of the walls and towers.

In high summer, when Jordan is popular with Gulf Arabs seeking escape from the blistering heat of the Arabian Peninsula, many of them make the trip to the castle. Their large cars pull up in the car park, the doors open, and members of the family pour out in an endless stream, all draped from head to toe, the women giggling nervously as they cross the slatted drawbridge in their high-heeled shoes.

From Ajlun to Jerash is only some 25km, well under half an hour's drive, making it an excellent base for a visit to there. The route itself is also picturesque, leading through the hills and forests of northern Jordan.

DIBBEEN

Forests of pine

Those with time to spare en route to Jeresh could incorporate a short diversion to the Dibbeen National Park, which, with its picnic places and restaurants, makes a pleasant stop for lunch. Established in 1972, the park is one of the great prides of Jordan, containing the country's most extensive forest. Most of the trees are Aleppo pines, but there are also old oaks, cypresses, acacias and wild pistachio trees. In spring the hillsides are prettily coloured with flowers. At weekends and on holidays the charm of the place can be marred by large and noisy family gatherings, liberally scattering their debris and litter.

Jerash

Jerash and Petra are Jordan's two major tourist attractions, receiving more visitors than any other place in the country. **Jerash**, the ancient **Gerasa**, is one of the three great Roman cities of the Near East, the others being Petra and Palmyra (in the Syrian desert). With its superb colonnaded streets, its exquisite oval forum, three theatres, two temples and 14 early Byzantine churches, it is more successful than its neighbours in recreating, as you stroll along its magnificent marble streets, the sense of a complete classical city. One twentieth century historian commented: '*Baalbek is more gigantesque, Palmyra more spacious, Petra more exotic, but none of them preserves more that is of*

Pompeii of the East

historical interest than Gerasa'. It has earned the epithet the 'Pompeii of the East'.

For all the excellent preservation of so many of Jerash's monuments, the one area where it cannot compete with its rivals is its setting. Sprawling in a shallow valley directly on the main Damascus–Amman road, there is no gasp of amazement here to rival that first glimpse of the Treasury at Petra, no romantic enchantment as you come, after miles of endless wild desert, to the graceful columns of Palmyra rising against the background of the Arab castle. The ruins of Gerasa, superbly preserved and renovated as they are, tumble into modern Jerash, and only in spring, when the colourful flowers help distract one from the ugly town, does the setting acquire a little magic. A visit at public holidays or best of all, at the annual Summer Festival, is to be recommended, as the crowds help to enhance the atmosphere of a once-bustling city.

When the first Western travellers stumbled on the place in the early nineteenth century they found the city picturesquely abandoned in its valley, the columns tumbled, the streets heavily grassed over. In 1878 Circassian Muslim refugees from Russia were settled in the valley by the Ottoman Sultan Abdul Hamid II and took advantage of the convenient supply of stones to build their houses. Some of the eastern part of Roman Jerash disappeared under what is now the modern town, but the Circassians, labelled as vandals by early Western archaeologists, later redeemed themselves to some extent by putting their stone skills to use in the subsequent restoration works. These have continued off and on for most of this century, carried out by the British, Germans, Americans, and the Jordanian Department of Antiquities. The Germans did especially well. In 1907 they found a superb Roman mosaic with mythological scenes under the house of the Mayor of Jerash, the finest mosaic ever found in Jordan. The German dig leader had it shipped to Berlin, where, after spending more than 50 years locked up in the storerooms, it is now on display in Berlin's Pergamum Museum.

Vandal stonemasons

The earliest signs of settlement in the Jerash valley go back to neolithic times, though it did not exist as a full blown city until the fourth or third century BC, when it was known as Antioch on the Chrysorhoas, or 'Golden River', a rather grand description of the little stream that still runs through the town, close to the main road. It is not known for certain who founded it; opinions vary between Alexander the Great, one of Alexander's generals, and Ptolemy II Philadelphus of Egypt, the founder of Amman. At any rate no Hellenistic remains are to be seen now at all, and everything extant in Jerash today dates from Roman times.

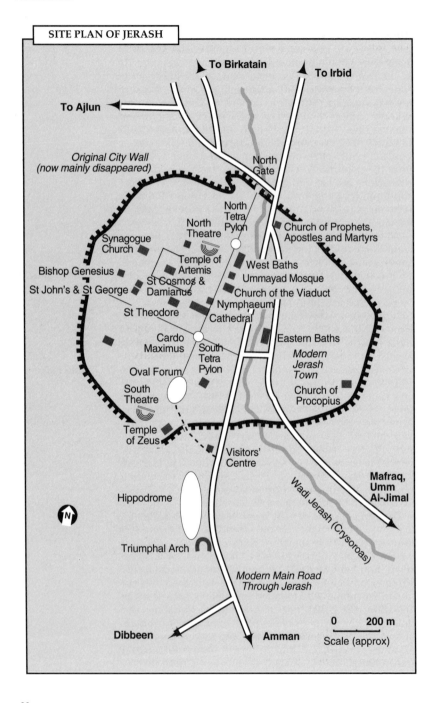

SITE PLAN OF JERASH

To Birkatain

To Irbid

To Ajlun

*Original City Wall
(now mainly disappeared)*

North
Gate

North
Tetra
Pylon

North
Theatre

Church of Prophets,
Apostles and Martyrs

Synagogue
Church

Temple of
Artemis

West Baths

Bishop Genesius

St Cosmos &
Damianus

Ummayad Mosque

St John's & St George

Church of the Viaduct

St Theodore

Nymphaeum

Cathedral

Cardo
Maximus

South
Tetra
Pylon

Eastern Baths

*Modern
Jerash
Town*

Oval Forum

South
Theatre

Church of
Procopius

Temple
of Zeus

Visitors'
Centre

Mafraq,
Umm
Al-Jimal

Hippodrome

Wadi Jerash (Crysoroas)

Triumphal Arch

*Modern Main Road
Through Jerash*

Dibbeen

Amman

0   200 m

Scale (approx)

Tour of the ruins
The following is a suggested tour of round the ruins, which takes a minimum of two hours.

Passing the triumphal arch immediately to the left of the road, drive past the Hippodrome to the car park, then walk to the Southern Gate in the city walls. This is also the entrance to the site, where tickets are bought. Enter the oval Forum, then climb up to the Temple of Zeus and the Southern Theatre. Return to the Forum.

At the main street junction, fork left to reach the complex of Byzantine churches, then return to the Cardo past the Cathedral. Pass the Nymphaeum, the Church of the Viaduct and an Umayyad Mosque. Then approach the colossal Temple of Artemis and the Synagogue Church behind it. Continue via the Isaiah Church to the North Theatre and North Tetrapylon and the Western Baths. The North Gate is closed, so you now return the length of the Cardo to the southern gate.

The splendid **Triumphal Arch** was built in 129 AD in honour of the emperor Hadrian's visit, and now stands to some 7m, half its original height. Its three vaulted passageways mark the beginning of the old road that led to the city's main gate in the south. The theatres, temples, forum and baths all date from this time, the time when the region benefited from the prosperity and stability of Rome.

Gerasa was captured by the Roman Empire in 84 BC, and Pompey, in carving up the territory into provinces, put it into the province of Syria. In practice, it governed itself to a large extent, and then joined the Decapolis, a league of ten free cities. These ten, apart from Gerasa, were Philadelphia (Amman), Pella (Tabaqat el Fahl), Gadara (Umm Qais) and Abila (Irbid), all in Jordan; Scythopolis (Beitsam) on the West Bank; and Dion, Hippus, Canatta and Damascus, all in Syria. Trade and agriculture flourished under the Pax Romana, and by the second century AD the city had amassed so much wealth that it was able virtually to rebuild itself. The place must have rung to the chiselling of stonemasons and sculptors for decades, and the result of their labours was the city we see today, built in attractive golden stone. Marble slabs from Asia Minor and granite columns from Aswan in Egypt were also brought to help embellish the buildings, and fragments of these can still be seen in various parts of the city.

The **Hippodrome** which lies just beyond the Triumphal Arch is little more now than a depression overgrown with vegetation, with just a few rows of seats

Polo and ship battles

remaining on the west to indicate its original function. A Polish team of excavators has discovered a row of shops in the eastern wall that would have flanked the main road. Another curious discovery inside the stadium was a set of goal posts for polo, which was introduced by the Persian Sassanids when they invaded in the seventh century. The game was originally played on foot as well as on horseback, and its first mention is in a Persian novel of the early seventh century, suggesting that the game had started life in Iran.

The English traveller Buckingham was convinced that the Hippodrome was also used for ship battles, the water being conducted by an aqueduct and controlled by sluice gates, both of which he claimed to have seen.

The car park is situated just next to the **Visitors' Centre**, a large stark building built in about 1980, with a restaurant and a display area where Jordanian crafts are on sale.

Entrance gateway

You now enter the site proper through the **South Gate**, which is a smaller version of Hadrian's arch in style. If you visit at the time of the Jerash Festival, the security checks here are more rigorous than at the airports, with separate body-check cabins for men and women. Items such as nail scissors will be confiscated from handbags as potentially lethal weapons.

This was always the major gate into the city walls, which are still traceable for most of their 3.5km length and enclose the city in a rough circle. The area thus enclosed has been estimated as containing a population of some 15,000, about right for a Roman provincial town. The walls were not thick enough to have been built for serious defensive purposes, but acted more as a deterrent to Bedouin raids from the desert.

The paved street beyond the gate brings you, after just a few steps, to the jewel of Jerash, the oval, colonnaded **Forum**. Looking at the superbly preserved and beautifully crafted stones and columns now, it is hard to imagine that, at the beginning of the century, the Forum and main street were covered in rubble. This debris in fact turned out to be collapsed huts and houses dating from Byzantine and early Arab times, when the forum was no longer used as a market or meeting place. By close examination, you can still detect the change in the colour of the stones, darker where they were buried and hence not exposed to sunlight.

Jewel of Jerash

The curiously pleasing shape of the Forum has led to speculation about whether it was indeed ever really the market place of the city or whether it was rather a place of sacrifice in front of the Temple of Zeus. The podium, of which only traces remain in the centre of the space, was originally thought to have borne a statue and a few benches, but the theory has now been ventured that it might have been a sacrificial altar.

In shape, the Forum is neither a perfect oval nor a perfect ellipse, but somewhere in between the two. The Ionic columns were thought originally to have been painted in reds, yellows, blues and greens, and the limestone paving stones are larger towards the outer edge, becoming smaller as they approach the central podium.

Curious shape

From the Forum a footpath leads up the hill to the **Temple of Zeus,** now quite ruined, but still with its monumental stairway and sacred chamber. It was in this

A view of Jerash (Vine).

Vaulted bookshop

chamber that Theodosus, 'tyrant' ruler of Philadelphia in the second century BC, kept his treasure for safekeeping, as the chamber was inviolable. The temple was originally surrounded by a colonnade, but earthquakes over the centuries have left only one column standing. The colossal vaults under the temple have been cleared and are used during the Festival as a novel book and map exhibition. The vantage point afforded from the terrace in front of the temple gives the best view to be had over the forum.

Set into the hill of the temple is the excellently preserved **South Theatre**, which is still used for performances, especially during the Festival. It was reconstructed in 1953 by the archaeologists Diana Kirkbride and Theo Samaan. Its capacity is 5000, with 32 rows of seats. The lower seats were numbered, presumably for booking purposes.

Cardo Maximus

You now return to the Forum and begin the walk up the **Cardo Maximus**, the wide main street of the city that runs for some 800m all the way to the North Gate. There were 260 Corinthian columns on each side of the street and the majority are still in place, which is all the more remarkable when you consider that in the nineteenth century, the German Schumader described how the newly settled Circassians were collapsing column after column with gunpowder charges, to find the exact size of drum

Bustling main street

they needed for their own houses. The street would originally have been lined with numerous boutiques and shops, giving an atmosphere which is to some extent revived today during the Festival, when street vendors with their stands and booths sell everything under the sun from cooked chickpeas to local craft rugs. The scene in Roman times may have been slightly different: the arcade was covered, so that wealthy shoppers could walk the length in all weathers, buying at leisure, dressed in their elegant finery.

Chariot ruts

Some 200m from the Forum, at the first major junction, stands the **South Tetrapylon**. In this area, chariot wheel ruts are especially noticeable, worn into the paved stone. The street to the right leads east to where a bridge used to cross the Chrysoroas river into the residential parts of town on the other bank. A few of its arches can still be seen beyond the modern main road, just in front of a small mosque.

Beyond the tetrapylon on the left of the Cardo Maximus, a wide stairway leads up to the **Cathedral**. This is an area you can return to later, to explore the churches and their mosaic floors.

Just past the stairway you come to the monumental two-storeyed façade of the **Nymphaeum** on your left, elaborately decorated with carvings and with niches which would have held statues. High up on the left, a few traces of paint, green and orange, are visible in the niches. In front is a superb enormous stone basin, where on a hot day you can hallucinate that you are prostrate in the cascading water. The water supply to ancient Gerasa was always abundant, supplied by two springs, and the elaborate drainage system is still visible in parts, running under the middle of the street in true Roman fashion. Holes at intervals at the kerb sides conducted the water to the central drain.

Water hallucinations

Beyond the Nymphaeum you gain your first glimpse of the mighty columns of the **Temple of Artemis,** the most impressive of all Jerash's buildings in its sheer scale and power, as befits the patron goddess of the city. In the renovations of this century, the propylea (the entrance vestibule) was dismantled and rebuilt stone by stone, and in one part of the courtyard the columns had to be cleared of debris up to their capitals. Youths are often to be found loitering round these vast Corinthian columns, devising experiments to prove that the columns are moving in the wind. By wedging a coin in a tiny gap between two column drums, the fractional movement of the columns is magnified in the coin's movement and can be quite alarming as you look up anxiously to see them swaying in the breeze. The fact that they have withstood the earthquakes of past centuries suggests, however, that the wind is unlikely to blow them over like skittles now.

Temple of Artemis

Swaying columns

The temple itself forms the core of an elaborately planned series of stairways, gateways and courtyards, which led up in succession from the bridge over the river to the east. The central holy of holies was only ever entered by the priests, and the worshippers remained outside on the steps or in the courtyards.

One of the vaults under the colossal raised temple platform has been converted into a museum housing mosaics found on the site from churches which have today all but disappeared or are very dilapidated. Among the charming subjects are a rabbit eating a grape and a man carrying a lassoo.

Rabbit mosaic

After the rise of Christianity, when the temple ceased to function as such, the Byzantines built their hovels and stone workshops in the outer courtyards and used it as a quarry to build their churches. The Cathedral was built by the middle of the fourth century, and by the time of Justinian (531–565), as many as ten churches covered the city, all built from the stone of the ancient temple blocks, and though this was obviously damaging to the older buildings, it nevertheless gives a pleasantly harmonious effect to the juxtaposition of the various eras of buildings.

Church of the Viaduct

The most curious example of this mixed provenance is the so-called **Church of the Viaduct** on the Cardo Maximus, directly opposite the Temple of Artemis. The structure was originally part of the monumental approach to the temple, but merely by adding a roof and adapting the entrance, it was converted into a church. The paved street formed the nave, and the colonnades flanking the street formed the church's side walls. Though it no doubt offends purists, one has to admire the ingenuity of it.

From this point onwards, the Cardo Maximus becomes narrower and the columns revert from Corinthian to Ionic, until, after some 200m, you reach the **North Tetrapylon** at another road junction. Dedicated to Julia Donna, wife of Septimius Severus (193–211 AD), it is smaller and quite different in style from the one in the south.

Collapsing baths

Immediately opposite to the right, a path leads to the chaotic **West Baths**. Although quite badly collapsed as a structure now, it still has one of the earliest surviving examples of a dome on pendentives, i.e. a circular dome resting on a square room. Gerasa had two bathing establishments: this one, and a much larger one on the east bank, which now has to be sought out among the streets of modern Jerash. Bathing was in Roman times a social rather than a particularly hygienic pastime. Men gathered to have parties, all lads together, bathing in the same water and sitting together on their stone toilets. The women washed alone in their houses.

At the very end of the Cardo Maximus is the ruined North Gate, built in 115. From here the Romans constructed a road straight to Bosra in Syria. The first part of the street was originally lined with tombs and sarcophagi, a common Roman habit, and about $1^1/_2$km to the north reached a spring, still known today as **Birkatain** (Two Pools) which flowed out into two pools on the edge of which were two temples and a small theatre. Here, as late as the sixth century, a pagan water festival was held each year, involving licentious mixed bathing and riotous celebration. The pools and theatre can still be visited higher up the river valley.

Pagan water festivals

Forking left from the North Tetrapylon, a colonnaded way leads you to the **North Theatre**, which has only recently been excavated. Though small, it offers an attractive view of the valley to the north beyond the city.

Numerous churches

Retracing your steps to the Temple of Artemis you can now begin to explore the cluster of churches that lie behind and to the left of the great temple. The best

The northern Jordan river (Darke).

Bedu women leading their goats across Wadi Rum in search of grazing (Vine).

A Bedu family living at Petra near the entrance to the Deir.

Tobiad caves at Iraq Al Amir (Vine).

Wadi es-Sir from caves at Iraq Al Amir (Vine).

Some of the ruins at Jerash (Vine).

approach is probably to climb the steps just after the temple, which lead from the main street up into the Cathedral, the oldest of Gerasa's churches. More than 14 churches have been found in all, and there were almost certainly many more, now buried under the modern town or lost under the rubble of earthquakes. With the exception of the Cathedral, which dates back to about 350, all the churches were built between 400 and 600, and the fact that they were abandoned early (most by the eighth century) and that they were not adapted and rebuilt over the centuries, means that they show an unusual concentration of styles of early Christian architecture. The Umayyad caliph at Damascus in 720, Yazid II, ordered that: *'all images and likenesses in my dominions, of bronze and of wood and of stone and pigments should be destroyed'*. Many of the churches' mosaic floors were destroyed as a result, and the earthquakes of the eighth century finished them off.

The Cathedral itself is not well preserved, although its basilical plan, with three naves and an apse, is clearly recognisable. It was built on the site of a temple to Dionysus, whose blocks it has largely reused, and a section of the temple substructure is still identifiable as such. The stairway you climbed to reach it was originally the Roman approach to the temple, later converted and adapted by the Byzantines.

Ancient cathedral

Behind the Cathedral you come to a well-preserved paved courtyard, known as the Court of the Fountain after the square basin still to be seen here, where, according to an eye witness account dated 375, the annual celebration was held to commemorate Christ's miracle at Canaan of turning water into wine, an appropriate link between Dionysus and the later church.

Further west still, beyond the Court of the Fountain, two stairways lead to the **Church of St Theodore**, built from Roman blocks between 494 and 496. To the right of the entrance is the baptistry with the sub-ground-level font, and in a chapel on the left there are still some mosaics. A little of the original limestone-and-marble-patterned floor survives. The two rows of columns in the nave were felled by an earthquake but have now been re-erected. The remnants of the Roman heating system which are visible date from 455, when the hygienically minded bishop had baths erected alongside his church.

Church of St Theodore

Beyond St Theodore further to the west, you reach the **Church of St Cosmos and Damianus**, where the best preserved mosaic floor in Jerash is to be found. It was lifted and relaid on a firm bedding in the 1930s by the

Best mosaics

Department of Antiquities. The colours and design are attractive, with a variety of geometric patterns forming the background, and with highlighted white squares or diamond shapes containing pictures of animals, birds, plants and the heads of its two benefactors, a wealthy couple named Theodore and Georgia. The church is often kept locked, so you must content yourself with peering down on to the mosaic over the walls.

St John and St George

Immediately abutting this church but to the left or south, are two further churches, **St John and St George**, which together form a large ensemble with a shared atrium and portico. St John still preserves a section of its mosaic flooring which consisted of pictures of various cities of the Byzantine Empire, including Alexandria and Memphis. St George, though it was the later of the two still in use (eighth century), had its mosaics badly damaged by invading Arabs. The crumbling walls also reveal the poor workmanship of the construction, where the outer facings were in stone but the centre was filled with loose earth and debris.

Further west, behind the Temple of Artemis, are the two churches of **Bishop Genesius**, the latest yet found on the site at 614, and the **Synagogue Church**, so called because the Jewish population converted it to a synagogue in 530. Neither retains much of interest today and neither has been properly excavated. It is quite likely that further churches lie buried under rubble and debris, waiting to be unearthed.

On the east of the stream are two further churches. The first, the **Church of the Prophets, Apostles and Martyrs**, had fine mosaics but the new road was driven straight over it and it can now scarcely be recognised at all. The other, the **Church of Procopius**, is deep in the modern town, identifiable by its high columns rising above the houses.

The eastern town

If you want to stroll in this eastern area to get a feel for the extent of the ancient city, it is best done by returning down the Cardo Maximus to the South Tetrapylon, forking left and following a porticoed way which led down to the river and crossed it with a Roman bridge. Go to the right along the main road, then to the left, and you will reach a little mosque opposite the Roman bath, and then the heavily ruined but extensive **Eastern Baths**.

With the destruction of the great trade centre of Palmyra to the north, the commerce of the region dwindled. The real decline of the city set in with the Sassanid Persian invasion of 614, then the Arab conquest in 635. Successive earthquakes, especially that of 747, completed the destruction.

By the ninth century the city's population had shrunk to a fraction of its earlier size and was a mixture of Christians and Muslims.

In 1120 the Atabey of Damascus (1104–1128) converted the temple into a fortress, bricking up the main doorway and making a smaller entrance to the side. Baldwin II, the Frankish Crusader King of Jerusalem (1118–1131) burnt it to the ground when he captured the city. From that time on, the place was utterly abandoned till the Circassian settlers arrived in 1878. It was so desolate that a saying grew up in Arabic *'as ruinous as the ruins of Jerash'*. Perhaps now that Jerash has, thanks to the efforts of the archaeologists of this century, become the most complete example of a provincial Roman city in the world, a saying will in time evolve, *'as well-preserved as the ruins of Jerash'*.

Changing fortunes

Umm al-Jimal
Turning east through the modern town of Jerash, the road leads on via Mafraq to the extraordinary black basalt ghost town of **Umm al-Jimal**. The ruins lie just 50km east of Jerash, and can be visited in half a day, either from Amman or from Ajlun, returning to Amman for a late lunch.

Basalt ghost town

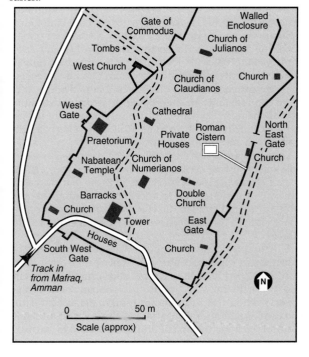

Umm al-Jimal site plan

The road winds through pleasant rolling hills, the valleys green with vegetables, the result of irrigation from nearby springs.

Mafraq means crossroads in Arabic and until 1920 it was indeed nothing but a crossroads. Then when the Iraqi pipeline from Kirkuk to Haifa was built, a largish town grew up around the junction.

Twelve kilometres east of Mafraq, you reach a road block, and leaving the Baghdad road to lose itself ahead in the endless desert, you fork off left on a track that gradually approaches the black sprawling ruins, some 3km off the main road. At first sight, the collapsed two- or three-storied buildings look like a burnt or bombed city. The **Eerie blackness** blackness of the stone, if lacking in beauty, certainly has an eerie effect. The town covers an area of 80 hectares or 200 acres, so a vehicle is indispensable to reach the different sections of town, which are all linked by tracks. Four-wheel drive is preferable, but by no means essential.

Woodless construction In the absence of any trees, no wood was used in the construction of the buildings; everything was made from the black basalt that was spat out in lava streams all over this area of the northern Jordan and southern Syrian desert by the volcanoes of the Jebel Druze. As a result, the buildings are unusually well preserved, often still retaining their ceilings and upper storeys, making Umm al-Jimal one of the best examples of a small Christian Byzantine city ever built on the edge of a Muslim Arab empire, complete with 15 churches, a cathedral, houses and administrative buildings. It is remarkable too, for its elaborate water system of cisterns and aqueducts, a trib- **Ingenious water systems** ute to the ingenuity of the people in a region devoid of natural springs. The extent of the city and its preservation also enables a picture to be built up of everyday life in a caravan and trading centre.

The open areas that lie between the various clusters of buildings, and that seem rather pointless today, were the *raison d'être* of the place, for it was in these that the camel caravans, on their way from Petra to Damascus and Palmyra, would unload, as it were in the womb of the city, giving it the name, Umm al-Jimal, Mother of the Camels.

The original caravan city was founded by the Nabateans in the first century BC, but apart from a dubiously identified Nabatean temple and a few large family tombs outside the walls, none of the remains date to that period. When the Romans under Trajan annexed the Nabatean kingdom in 106, Umm al-Jimal (known then as Thantia), was included. The impressive Roman barracks date from that period, with their large open courtyard. Though the floors of the three-storeyed tower collapsed in 1970, it is still the best preserved of all Umm al-Jimal's buildings. A superb basalt door still works on its stone hinges to afford you entrance. Inscriptions show that it was later converted into a monastery.

Stone door to the barracks

Christianity came early to the town and one of the churches, St Julianas, which was consecrated in 345, is the earliest yet found east of the Jordan. Of the 15 churches found in the town, some are in a square or rectangular plan with arcaded courtyards, while others are divided into three naves with a semicircular apse.

The track leads straight into the town through a breach in the walls and it is best just to get out and explore a section at a time, then drive on to the next major group of ruins. The buildings found in most profusion are private houses, mainly Byzantine, separated by narrow tortuous little lanes. In typical oriental style, they usually have an internal courtyard, from which basalt steps on basalt beams, now often very rickety but sometimes still useable with caution, lead up to the living quarters. Some had little stables for camels, horses, sheep or goats in the lower storey, with a hole in the basalt for tying horses; many others had a little semicircular washing basin by the door. Most houses had their own cistern. The vaulted roofs are often intact in the houses, and you can still marvel at the slabs of basalt, like huge tiles, laid across rafters and joists of basalt, sometimes looking a little precarious now as they hang above your head.

Private houses

The water supply of the whole town was dependent on the rains collected in winter in huge cisterns (some 24 in all), hollowed out of basalt and spread throughout the city. Some are still used by the local Bedouin. A kilometre-long aqueduct system links the largest of these to a wadi where seasonal rains were quite frequent.

Cisterns and aqueducts

In a small village not far from Umm al-Jimal to the east, some Bedouin families still live in a cluster of basalt Roman/Byzantine houses, unchanged for the last 1400 years, apart from the TV aerials.

Various American digs have taken place here, the last ones early in 1984, and these are due to recommence when funds come through.

A series of other basalt Byzantine cities are to be found in the black desert here, but none are as well preserved or as easily accessible as Umm al-Jimal. Of these, Jawa, further to the north-east and close to the Syrian border, is the best known as a result of extensive excavations which have been carried out there.

Jawa

Jawa continued to thrive under the Umayyad caliphs of Damascus, perhaps because of its closeness to the Arab desert palaces and the pilgrim route to Mecca, but in the mid-eighth century a severe earthquake destroyed the city. The timing coincided roughly with the fall of the Umayyads and the shift in the centre of power east to Baghdad, so the town lost its role and was not built up again. It lay deserted until the twentieth century, when a few Druze settlers from the northern Jebel Druze moved in between 1905 and 1909, and undertook some reconstruction, often not identifiable as any different from the old Byzantine buildings.

The Desert Umayyad Palaces

Enjoyable day trip

A circuit of the palaces of the Umayyad caliphs which lie strung out in the desert east of Amman is one of the highlights of a trip to Jordan, a most enjoyable and instructive sortie into a rarely seen side of early Islam. Now that they are all, with the exception of Qasr Tuba, linked on a new tarred road, a circuit can easily be accomplished on a day trip from Amman, with lunch and perhaps a swim at Azraq. Those wanting to look more closely, and to include the Qasr Tuba (for which four-wheel drive is necessary), could base themselves at the well-appointed resthouse at Azraq.

Architectural melange

The desert palaces have always excited controversy. There are over 20 of them scattered in Lebanon, Syria, Israel and Jordan, always in solitary locations, and showing a variety of confusing architectural patterns. Sometimes they resemble Roman/Byzantine castles, sometime Syrian Byzantine baths, sometimes Parthian/Sassanid halls or khans with four *iwans* or vaulted niches. The confusion was compounded by the fact that they quite frequently used existing buildings such as old caravanserais and earlier fortresses, and adapted them to their purposes. As a result, the palaces have been variously dated to 293 AD, the fourth and sixth centuries, and finally to the Umayyad period in the eighth century.

The Umayyads, under their leader Mu'awiya, were the first settled dynasty of caliphs in Islam. The Bedouin horsemen surging out of the Arabian Peninsular had conquered Egypt and all of the Levant at remarkable speed. Muhammad was dead and his followers had acquired a new empire which now needed to be administered.

First they needed a base, and in 660 they founded their new capital at Damascus, which was to be the centre of the empire for the next two centuries. As simple tribesmen now in charge of a huge machine, with all its

MAYSUN'S LEGACY

Mu'awiya, the supreme organiser, laid the foundations
of a stable, orderly Muslim society: he was the first to
introduce a registry system for recording the affairs of
state, and he began the first proper postal system, using
relays of horses. Yet from among his many wives he
chose as his favourite a Jacobite Christian, called
Maysun. Of Bedouin origins from the Kalb tribe of Syria,
she abhorred the rigid court life of Damascus and longed
for the freedom of the desert. She used to take her son
Yazid, later to be Mu'awiya's successor, to the desert
where they would roam with her tribesfolk, and where
the young prince acquired a taste for hard riding, hunting, drinking wine and composing poetry.

From this time on the tradition continued, and later
Umayyad caliphs, notably Abd al-Malik and Walid II,
built their country residences in the desert and called
them *al-Badiyahs*. Here, their pure Arabic language
escaped the corruptions of Aramic and other foreign elements, and they also avoided the infectious plagues
which befell the cities of Syria at regular intervals during
the seventh and eighth centuries. Here in the desert each
prince received what was held to be the perfect education: he learned to read and write Arabic, to use the bow
and arrow and to swim, as well as acquiring the ethical
ideals of courage, endurance of hardship, manliness,
generosity and hospitality, regard for women and the
keeping of promises. After all this, he would be termed
al-kaamil, 'the perfect one'. The results of this desert life
were not always so beneficial, and the caliph Hisham's
young son was killed when he fell from his horse on a
hunt. His father's wry comment was: 'I brought him up
for the caliphate and he pursues a fox!'

**A desert
education**

attendant ties and responsibilities, it was not unnatural
for them to long for the sporting life of the desert that
was in their bones, and in which they had been brought
up. Sometimes this longing for the old days was channelled into such exploits as raiding and looting the
southern coastal towns of Turkey, where they left a trail
of destruction through the seventh and eighth centuries.
On other occasions it took a more harmless form, the
building of fantasy palaces in the desert, where they
could escape the cares of government and administration, and enjoy instead hawking, camel racing, wine,
women, music and poetry, all the traditional Arab pleasures in their natural desert setting. They were never
really castles, as any defensive function they may some-

**Civil servants
longing for the
old nomadic
lifestyle**

times have had was always secondary to their primary function – the pursuit of pleasure.

Palace circuit

Jordan boasts the best and most readily accessible examples of these desert palaces, and no less than five may now easily be seen in the same day on a trip from Amman. Starting with Qasr el-Hallabat, which is reached via Zarqa, the circuit covered here continues to Qasr Azraq, Qasr Amra, Qasr Kharaneh, Qasr Tuba and finally Qasr Mushatta, just outside the perimeter fence of the new Queen Alia Airport.

Qasr el-Hallabat

Leaving Amman on the Zarqa road, the total distance to Qasr el-Hallabat is 55km, and takes about an hour. You take the turn-off to Azraq along a flat desert road that heads eventually towards the Iraqi border. Some 12km after the Azraq turning, Qasr el-Hallabat can be seen rising on a hillock to the left of the road. A track leads off to it at a blue police sign, and heads towards a group of sand-coloured huts some 500m off the tarred road. The track bears left after about 1km, and as you follow it you

Small baths *en route*

pass on your left the Hammam El-Sarakh, a small baths complex *en route* to the palace, which lies 2km further on. The whole hillock is now kept fenced off, but sounding

The ruins of Qasr el-Hallabat (Darke).

your horn as you arrive soon sends the guardian or his son scampering for the key. You can then drive up the remaining 500m or so to the very walls. The guardian will accompany you, and expects a tip for his duties, but there is no actual entrance fee at the time of writing.

The palace was originally a Roman fortress, built **Former Roman** probably under Marcus Aurelius to control the north-**fortress** eastern edge and to protect it against Parthian attacks from the east. This defensive function is clearly recognisable even now, not only from its raised position, but also from its high, thick outer walls built in a square and defended by towers at the corners. In 529 the emperor Justinian renovated the castle, and for a short period in the seventh century Christian monks used it as a monastery. The Umayyad princes took it over at the beginning of the eighth century and decorated it more in the style of a palace, with elaborate tiled marble flooring in geometric patterns and carved frescoes. Many of the stones used in the construction have Nabatean Greek and Latin inscriptions, and were probably brought from nearby Byzantine sites like Umm al-Jimal. Stairways lead up everywhere to the missing second storey, and in one of the smaller rooms there are extensive and finely **Animal mosaics** worked mosaics of animals like lions, bulls, ostriches, and bearded serpent and wildfowl, framed by foliage and a geometric edging. Nearly all the rooms in fact have mosaics, but they are covered with a protective layer of soft mortar.

The other striking feature in the building is the contrast between the sandy-coloured limestone blocks used for the western part and the black basalt ones which were used for other sections. This feature is especially noticeable from the outside eastern wall, where alternate walls of sand-**Black and** coloured stone and black basalt were used to give a striped **white stripes** effect. It has been suggested that the black basalt blocks were originally taken from Umm al-Jimal, which would explain the number of Greek inscriptions on the stones.

Immediately in front of the palace, the small building with three gateways is a Umayyad mosque. The Umayyads also constructed a complex water system on the edge of a wadi to supply the palace with dams, cisterns and water channels.

The nearby **Hammam el-Sarakh**, recently renovated **Hammam el-** and partly rebuilt by the Jordanian Department of **Sarakh** Antiquities, was a tiny independent hunting pavilion built around a set of small baths. It was erected in 725, and at the turn of this century early European visitors could still see traces of coloured frescoes on the bath

Deep well

walls, but these have since disappeared. A tiny mosque with marble paving remains, as well as a finely constructed well, 20m deep, to supply the water for heating. The three bath rooms were the caldarium or hot room, the tepidarium or luke-warm room, and the changing room. Surprisingly, there was no frigidarium or cold room. Beyond the baths, the audience hall stands only to ankle height, and the mosaics that once covered the floor are gone.

It is not certain which of the Umayyads lived in Sarakh or Qasr el-Hallabat, but from the dates of construction it could have been either Hisham or Walid II who may have used the little pavilion or the larger hilltop palace for hunting excursions or for gatherings with local Bedouin sheikhs.

Continuing south-east towards the oasis of Azraq, you pass a turn-off signposted 'Qasr Amra 17km via Wadi el-Harth'. This road is only a desert track and should be avoided, even with a four-wheel drive vehicle, as it is very tricky to tell, in the maze of desert tracks all of equal size, which is the correct one.

**Azraq
resthouse**

Some 50km further along the featureless main road, you reach a T-junction at the outskirts of Azraq. Here you turn left following the North Azraq signpost, and after about 1 or 2km come to a sign pointing left to the resthouse where you can take lunch. The castle itself lies a further 3km along the road. About 1km before it you will find the private As-Sayyad Hotel. The oasis is no great beauty spot, and though there are indeed palm trees and some lush vegetation, the sprawling half-finished modern constructions all around detract considerably from any charm the place may once have had.

Qasr Azraq

The lowering black basalt castle of **Qasr Azraq** lies directly on the left-hand side of the construction, so it cannot be missed. It was originally of Roman construction, built in the third century as one of three (the other two are heavily ruined) that guarded the northern edge of the Wadi Sirhan against the frequent surges of Bedouin from Saudi Arabia.

Walid II, one of the most pleasure-seeking of the Umayyad caliphs, came here in the eighth century attracted by the rich hunting to be found in the oasis. Lions and lynx, gazelles, antelopes and wild horses were all to be found here in abundance.

Climbing the stairs and entering the gatehouse, you will undoubtedly come across the guardian, a wizened old blue-eyed Circassian who starts whispering 'Awrence, Awrence' at you the moment you turn to enter the old courtyard. Knowing the Westerner's fascination for T.E. Lawrence, he is anxious to show off what has become the most important thing in the fort – the room above the gatehouse, reached by outside steps, where Lawrence stayed for a month after arriving from Aqaba and Wadi Rum. He waited there while all the tribal armies of the Arab Revolt collected before their final assault on Damascus in 1917. Among them was the current guardian's father. Viewing the bare, desolate black room today, you need all your powers of imagination to visualise Lawrence squatting here with his fellow soldiers.

Lawrence stayed here

The guardian will then lead you on a tour to point out the 'lesser' areas of the fort: a church with vaulted arches and columns that later became a mosque when the Umayyads added a *mihrab*; a prison in the far corner, with an adjacent stable for horses; the so-called House of the Roman Leader with its huge three-ton basalt door. Unfortunately the hinge is broken from the top, so the door no longer functions like the fine Umm al-Jimal one. Inside the house is an oven to the left of the door. The basalt ceiling slats are again reminiscent of the building techniques used at Umm al-Jimal. A fine deep well has steps leading down into it.

Impressive church/mosque

The castle was rebuilt in 1237 by Aybak, the able Mamluke governor of the Ayyubids, whom we came across earlier at Ajlun, and an inscription above the gateway proclaims this fact.

The oasis itself varies enormously according to season. In the winter months there are lakes and swamps, but from mid-May onwards the lakes become caked mud in the summer heat. The oasis waters are slightly salty, and in the summer months some 13,000 tons of salt are extracted from the surface. From mid-November to mid-March the oasis is like a miniature Camargue, a swampland favoured by thousands of migratory birds. Over 280 different species have been identified, mainly wild duck, herons, flamingoes and pelicans – see 'Flora and Fauna', *Section 1*.

Azraq oasis

Some 15km south of the fort, to the right off the road that leads eventually to Saudi Arabia, is the **Shaumari Wildlife Reserve**, a modest set-up where attempts are being made to reintroduce the oryx, a rare antelope with horns, sometimes said to be the original unicorn, now extinct in the Jordanian desert. The Jordanian Royal Society for the Conservation of Nature is carrying out the project with the help of the Worldwide Fund for Nature.

Wildlife reserve

Exiled goats

Scenes of pleasure

Gazelle and ostrich are also being introduced, though of the four ostriches shipped across from the United States, only one now remains. The goat, which single-handed brought about the devegetation of the once Fertile Crescent, is banned from the area.

In the mud of one of the oasis springs earlier this century, over 400 neolithic and paleolithic axes and spearheads were found, showing that even 200,000 years ago, hunters had started the process of whittling down the local wildlife.

The road from Azraq back towards Amman is badly rutted by the streams of petrol tankers that ply their way up and down it carrying oil from Iraq. In Europe the weight limit for such tankers is 50 tons, but here tankers of 60–80 tons lumber along, damaging the tarmac beneath them. Their long and boring routes lead to frequent accidents, and many a burnt out carcass can be seen littering the roadside from here to Amman.

Qasr Amra

A journey of about 25km from Azraq brings you to Qasr Amra, a tiny but charming palace, immediately to the right of the road. The guardian lurks in a nearby tent, and will scurry out to unlock to gate to the enclosure and the door to the *qasr* itself. The lavish frescoes decorating its baths are the best-preserved examples of Umayyad painting in the world, but their interest lies not only in their excellent state of preservation, but in their subject matter. Contrary to the strict Islamic view that the representation of human or animal forms in art was the prerogative of Allah alone, here at Qasr Amra the early Muslims had paintings of naked women bathing, scenes of frolicking and dancing, hunting scenes with men chasing dogs chasing gazelles into nets, men on foot spearing horses, bears playing lutes, and camels and horses working in the fields.

The basis for this ban lay in a quote from the Prophet Muhammad that on the day of judgement the most severely punished would be the 'portrayers', or 'image makers'. As a result of a subsequent strict interpretation of this passage, no human representation is to be found in any subsequent mosque, and almost all the decorative motifs throughout the Muslim world derive from plants or abstract geometric patterns.

The palace was built between 712 and 715 and this is therefore the earliest example yet known of Muslim picture art. The pleasure-loving Caliph Walid I was the builder, and he obviously chose as decoration scenes that

Best-preserved Umayyad painting in the world

Scenes of pleasure

THE PLEASURE-LOVING UMAYYADS

All the Umayyad caliphs were fond of entertainment. Even Mu'awiya set aside the evenings for listening to tales of past heroes and historical anecdotes. The favourite drink, especially with the women, was rose sherbet, which is still drunk in Damascus and many Arab towns. Drinking was to become a progressive weakness in later caliphs. Abd el-Malik, we are told, drank wine only once a month, though apparently when he did he drank so heavily that he would force himself to vomit afterwards to help him recover. Hisham drank once a week, after the Friday prayers, while Walid I drank every other day. Yazid drank daily, and trained a pet monkey to share in his revelling.

Walid II was definitely the most advanced however, and we have eye-witness accounts of his drinking parties, in which he would have the bathing pool filled with wine, then swim in it, gulping enough to lower the level visibly. Accompanied by dancing and singing handmaidens, he would frolic in the liquid until they all lost consciousness. Besides the orgies, however, these Umayyad soirées, be they in the desert palaces or the court itself, also produced much by way of music and above all poetry, notably love poetry, some of which has survived.

Ah for the throes of a heart sorely wounded!
Ah for the eyes that have smit me with madness!
Gently she moved in the calmness of beauty,
Moved as the bough to the light breeze of morning.
Dazzled my eyes as they gazed, till before me
All was a mist and confusion of figures.
Ne'er had I sought her, and ne'er had she sought me;
Fated the hour, and the love, and the meeting.
(Omar ibn Abi Rabi'a, died 720).

The women of these early Umayyad days seem to have enjoyed what would now be regarded as an unusual degree of freedom. In Medina, a proud and beautiful woman called Sukaynah was noted not only for her beauty and learning, but also for her poetry and song and sense of humour. She once sent word to the chief of police that a Syrian had broken into her apartment. The chief himself rushed over to find her maid holding out a flea – Syria was ever noted for its fleas. Accounts of the number of her husbands range from seven to nine, and she frequently made complete freedom of action a precondition to the marriage.

In Ta'if Sukaynah had a rival in the shape of Aishah, daughter of a Companion of the Prophet. She had the three qualities most prized in a woman among Arabs – noble descent, great beauty and a proud spirit. She notched up only three husbands, but when the second chided her for not veiling her face, she retorted: *Since God, may He remain blessed and exalted, hath put upon me the stamp of beauty, it is my wish that the public should view that beauty and thereby recognise His grace unto me. Under no conditions, therefore, will I veil myself.*

gave him the greatest pleasure. Experts claim that the work was probably executed by Christian and Sassanid subjects of the Caliph, but there is also an almost child-like primitiveness in the drawings, especially those of people, that makes them quite unlike any other form of painting. Al-Walid died at the age of 40, but during his pleasure-packed life he also had some of the finest Umayyad constructions built. He enlarged the beautiful great mosque at Mecca, and rebuilt that of Medina. In Syria he built many schools, mosques, and hospitals for the poor and the infirm. In Jerusalem he put a gilded brass dome, lifted from a church in Baalbek, Lebanon, on to the Dome of the Rock mosque which his father had built. In Damascus he converted the site of the Cathedral of John the Baptist into the Great Umayyad Mosque, still today the fourth-holiest mosque in Islam, after Mecca, Medina and Jerusalem.

The palace was discovered by the Arabist Alois Musil in 1898. He had heard stories of ancient palaces in the desert which were haunted by ghosts and decorated with wonderful paintings. Some restoration work was carried out in the 1970s by a Spanish team, for over the years the frescoes had acquired their inevitable share of graffiti, though relatively little considering their accessibility: perhaps their haunted reputation protected them to some extent. Some of the more recent vandalism is attributed to the army. The colours, shielded from light by the virtual **Rich colours** absence of windows have remained rich, with reds, greens, browns and blues the predominant colours.

On the right-hand wall, beyond the large painting of the woman rising from the bath, is a curious though dam- aged scene of six kings conquered by the Umayyads, with their names underneath in Greek and Kufic Arabic script. **Kings of the** These are 'Caesar', the Byzantine Emperor, 'Roderick', the **world** last Visigoth King of Spain before the Muslim Conquest, 'Chosroes', the Persian Sassanid Emperor, 'Negus', King of Abyssinia, and two other figure thought to be kings of China and India respectively. According to one scholar, this mural recalls one of the frescoes in a palace in Kermenshah, Iran, which was an illustration of a poem by Yazid III on the family of the kings of the world.

Tiny rooms Two tiny rooms at the end of the triple-vaulted audi- ence hall have patterned mosaic floors, and these are thought to have been the bedrooms of the princes. The overwhelming smell of urine betrays their current role. Between them is a throne niche which faced out into the audience hall. A door off left from the hall leads into the complex of tiny bath rooms, an apodyterium or changing room, then a tepidarium, and a caldarium, where the inmates would sit on benches in alcoves to perspire. Behind the caldarium is the room where the water was heated before being conducted in pipes to the caldarium, and beyond that in turn is an open walled space where wood and other stores were kept.

Just outside the palace, in front of the bathing complex, is a well, 22m deep, with a ruined cistern. The long wall which runs from a point to the west before joining the back wall of the audience hall was designed in this shape to break the west wind which used to carry drifting sand from the desert. The west wall of the audience hall has only a small window for the same reason.

Protection from drifting sand

The situation of the palace, which seems quite random, makes sense when you see it in the spring, for it lies in the Wadi Butm where pools of water collect after rain, attracting wildlife to drink. On a nearby hillock, some 250m to the north-east, are the scant remains of a little fort, showing that the palace also had a defensive role, probably to guard the caravan route that passed from Qasr Kharaneh to Azraq.

Qasr Kharaneh

Less than 20km further west the road passes just to the right of the impressive **Qasr Kharaneh**, the most strikingly defensive of all the palaces, extremely well preserved with two storeys and most rooms intact. A notice which greets you, exhorting 'Kindly no touching, writing, smoking or lettering' may ensure that it continues to be preserved.

Solid and square, the palace has fine towers on the corners, and interestingly decorated arrow-like slits in all directions. These were not in fact for shooting arrows, as they are too difficult to reach from the inside and too narrow: they were instead ventilation slits for the inner rooms. The inscription over the gateway to the south bears the date 711, although some believe that it was originally a pre-Islamic building, possibly a Sassanid fort, as some of its architectural features, such as the tree of life medallion on its upper storey, show Mesopotamian influence. Like Qasr Amra, its strategic importance is not immediately obvious to the layman, but in fact it lies at the intersection of the number of tracks at the head of a wadi, and was used as a caravanserai by the traders from Syria to all points south and east.

Former Sassanid fortress?

The long vaulted downstairs rooms on either side of the entrance were the camel stables. There were originally

99 rooms

99 rooms in the castle, the ground floor one plain and simple and used as storerooms, but the upper living quarters with fine carved arches, clusters of triple pictures and decorations in the pleasantly proportioned vaulted rooms. The most elaborately decorated room lies directly above the entrance gateway, and was probably the caliph's own room. The outer walls are at least 1m thick, built of local stone with earth and water mixed together to form a kind of bonding cement.

Two sets of steps lead up to the roof, now carefully restored, offering a fine view into the central open courtyard and a good feeling for the defensive command of the place. The army has also not been slow to see its advantages, and is often in partial occupation here. Military vehicles and personnel tend to be much in evidence on the road between Azraq and Amman, and a wide strip of land nearby is used as a runway.

A well just outside the entrance gateway supplied water for its original occupants, and is still in use.

Qasr Tuba

Large but undecorated

Immediately west of Qasr Kharaneh, a desert track leads south some 50km to **Qasr Tuba**, the most isolated of the desert palaces, but not particularly well preserved. A four-wheel drive vehicle is required, together with a compass or guide, and the journey is slow and sandy. Rather than incorporate it into a day's circuit with the other palaces, it would be better to make it the centre of a camping trip, spending some time in the desert. Real enthusiasts could even drive on down to Bayir, some 120km south of Kharaneh, where another heavily ruined Umayyad palace is to be found.

The palace at Tuba would have been one of the largest of all the desert palaces in area, but it was left unfinished in 744 when its builder, the caliph Walid II, was killed. Its name, Tuba, means brick, and indeed the main characteristic of the construction here is the brickwork, which is not found in the other desert palaces. No further decoration is to be found, for the beautiful stone-carved door jambs and lintels which once adorned the doors and gateways have been removed or broken up. Only a single example of a decorated lintel survives, and it is now in the Amman museum.

Remoteness has not spared two further palaces, Mushash and Muwaqqar from despoliation, for both are now reduced to mere foundations. Both lie just off the road between Kharaneh and Sahab.

Qasr Mushatta

Although many maps, including the one issued by the Jordanian Tourism Ministry, show a road from Muwaqqar to **Qasr Mushatta**, the last palace on the circuit, the road is in practice so bad, if you can find it at all, that it is better and faster to continue into Amman and then take the main road south that leads to the Queen Alia International Airport.

You then turn exactly as if you were going to the airport, but follow the road that leads to the right, circling the airport perimeter fence to the south. Although the palace itself lies on the northern perimeter of the airport, the only approach is by skirting the southern, then, eastern and northern perimeters as if driving round three sides of a square. As you approach a police check-point towards the end of the northern perimeter, you will see the palace lying some 100m to your right. The soldiers are instructed to allow visitors in, so the barrier will be raised and you can then drive right up to the now crumbling building.

Airport site

Although still impressive, Mushatta (meaning Winter Camp), would have been a great deal more so before 1903. Its entire façade was covered with elaborate and intricate carvings of vines, flowers, leaves and birds, but the Ottoman sultan at that time, Abdul Hamid, made a gift of the palace to the Kaiser, whereupon its sculptures were prised off and shipped to the Pergamum Museum in Berlin, where they can still be seen. A few fragments lying near the main palace entrance hint at what the whole façade might have looked like.

Stripped by the Kaiser

The palace, thought to have been built in the eighth century by Walid II, was, like Qasr Tuba, never completed. Parts of it were built of brick, though it was burnt brick, not the sun-dried brick of Tuba. The ground plan is quite complex with a variety of styles, from high vaulted brick domes almost like baths, to colonnaded open-air sections, reusing fine marble pillars from Roman sites.

Complex plan

Some 20km away, Walid was said to be building a new town that would bear his name. Many labourers died from lack of water in the project, finally causing a revolt in which the Caliph was killed. His successor Yazid III never made any attempt to complete this or any other of Walid's half-finished projects.

113

The Urn Tomb at Petra (Darke).

SOUTH FROM AMMAN

Southern Jordan Facts

The Dead Sea
The resthouse has a restaurant and snack bar but no overnight facilities. Camping is permitted. Swimming has to be done from the resthouse beach (there is a small entry fee), something you are likely to want to do anyway, to avail yourself of their showers immediately afterwards, before the salt cakes on. The resthouse also has an outdoor fresh-water pool. The newly opened **Dead Sea Spa Hotel** (*tel: 09-802028. fax: 09-665160*) further south offers four-star facilities plus a German-run treatment centre for skin diseases like psoriasis. Most treatment programmes last four weeks. Also on offer are fitness and anti-stress programmes, massage, mud-packs, a gym, jaccuzzi, tennis, squash, mini-golf, volleyball and a fresh water pool. The restaurants can provide special diets and vegetarian menus.

Zerqa Ma'in
The newly constructed ****** star Ashtar Hotel** (*tel: 545500. fax: 545550*) has a health clinic. The whole spa area has been laid out with private chalets, caravans, a supermarket, a tennis court and a children's playground. There is an entrance fee to cover the use of the pools. Day trips are now offered by JETT buses from Amman.

Kerak
Two hours' drive from Amman by both the King's Highway and the Desert Road. The government resthouse (*tel: 351148*) is on a precipitous edge immediately adjacent to the castle. It has 12 simple but adequate rooms with bathroom. Before this was built, it was possible to sleep in the cell-like rooms of the castle itself, where the government had set up a few beds.

Petra
Three hours' drive from Amman. One hour 40 minutes' drive from Aqaba. At peak season (March–May and September–mid-November, Christmas and New Year) it is vital to book as pressure on rooms is enormous. The hotels are:

**** Petra Forum Hotel (*tel:03-634200. fax: 634201*). The tarred road that drops down from Wadi Musa ends at this new hotel. 82 rooms. Small outdoor swimming pool. Souvenir/book shop. Car hire. Picnic boxes. Built in 1983, the uninspiring façade conceals a luxurious interior. The inside, with thick carpeting, marble floors and walls and waiters dressed in smart red uniforms, contrasts strongly with the experience of venturing into Petra with its cave dwellings and chronic water shortage. Tired, smelly and dusty on your return, you are transported into another world in two seconds. A 64-room extension is being built which will include further restaurants, bars, a health club and shops. The Forum also has a gravel camping ground, more suited to camper vehicles than tents, though tents can be hired from the hotel. Water facilities are provided.

*** **Petra Palace Hotel** (*tel: 602460*). A new 36-room hotel with airconditioning and TV, five minutes from the site entrance.

*** **Petra Panorama**. Under construction. 126 rooms.

Petra Resthouse (*tel: 03-83011*). Set just before the Forum, right at the entrance to the site, and opposite the Visitors' Centre. 32 rooms. Excellent value, with buffet-style lunch and dinner. The bar is converted from a huge hollow rock tomb and the owner must certainly be turning in his grave. Such vandalism of ancient monuments would be utterly taboo now, but that said, it is rather fun to sit in little alcoves where bodies would once have been neatly laid out instead of today's tables and chairs. Behind the reception desk is a bank where the exchange rate is considerably better than that offered by the Petra Forum. The Petra Resthouse also plans an extension for a further 36 rooms.

Tayiba Resort. This is a small farming village 7km from Petra which the owners of Kan Zaman Village near Amman are renovating. The 210 original houses and buildings of the village will be restored to provide 86 guest rooms, restaurant, an Oriental café, a bakery, a Turkish bath, a town square, a meeting hall, an Oriental fast-food restaurant, a bar with a garden, a swimming pool with a fitness centre, handicraft centre with 14 studios and a museum of village life. Scheduled for completion in January 1994, Tayiba will be unique as a place to stay.

Ain Mousa Hotel and Restaurant. A modest hotel with five rooms above the village next to Ain Musa, where the road from Aqaba and Amman begins the entry to Wadi Musa. At some 4km from the site entrance, transport is a must.

The Petra Visitors' Centre is where the tourist police are based. Tickets for horses, carriages and for guides are purchased here, and they also sell guidebooks, souvenirs, film, slides and postcards.

Inside the site, only simple refreshments, cold drinks and souvenirs are available. The smart Petra Forum Restaurant, contrary to its name and appearance, only offers sandwiches, cake and yogurt, though it does also offer wine, beer and araq. A picnic, prepared by the hotel or bought yourself, is often the best policy.

Wadi Rum

One hour's drive from Petra or from Aqaba. 4 hours' drive from Amman.

The self-catering resthouse offers basic accommodation. Camping is also possible for a small fee, and in the summer even preferable, as no tent is needed and your view of the stars is unobstructed. Bring your own food and drinking water. The simple cooking, fridge and bathroom facilities of the resthouse may be used.

At the small Bedouin settlement by the Desert Camel Corps post, there is a tiny shop where you can pick up the odd dubious tin of sardines, bread and the occasional water melon, but it is best not to rely on this. The Camel Corps soldiers on duty at the post, dressed in khaki robes, red tassles and red and white checked head-dresses offer traditional cardomum coffee to any passing visitor who cares to partake. Local Bedouin offer to hire their four-wheel drive Toyota trucks or camels for about JD10 for a few hours.

There is no public transport to Wadi Rum, so you will have to hire a car or taxi, or hitch a lift.

Aqaba

Four or five hours' drive from Amman on the desert road, and one hour 40 minutes from Petra. There are nine flights a week from Amman. JETT buses, fast and air-conditioned, also run five times a day to Amman, taking five hours one way. Tickets are bought at the JETT office on the waterfront near Al-Samakh Fish Restaurant. Service taxis also make the journey constantly, but cost the same as the JETT buses and are less comfortable.

Ferry to Egypt: Travel agents all along the waterfront sell tickets for the car ferries to Nuweiba and Suez in Egypt. The ferry terminal itself lies out of town some 10km to the south of the commercial port. Nuweiba is the more popular destination for non-commercial traffic, as it takes you to central Sinai in three hours. The Suez journey is 15 hours. There are two Nuweiba sailings daily, at 12 noon and at 4 pm (but these timings are not firm, so always check locally first) and you should arrive at the dock at least an hour before departure. Tickets can be bought on the day and there is rarely any problem with space for vehicles and certainly never with passengers. See also 'Travelling to Jordan' in *Section 1*. The Egyptian Consulate is about 15 minutes' walk inland from the beach hotels, (see Aqaba Town Plan) and is open 9–12 except Fridays. Visas are issued on the spot and cost JD7.

Local Transport: A minibus a day leaves Aqaba for Petra at about 10 am. Cars can also be hired from the big beach hotels. Rates fluctuate, so it is worth trying several agencies.

Accommodation: This is Jordan's winter resort, and the climate stays mild while Amman is cold in the winter months. The beach hotels are the best places to stay.

**** Aqaba Gulf Hotel (*tel: 316636. fax: 318246*). Aqaba's most luxurious hotel.154 air-conditioned rooms, with in-house video and minibar. Two restaurants, two bars. Large pool. Tennis court. Café, bookshop. Sea views. Travel agency. 24 hour room service.

**** Coral Beach Hotel (*tel: 313521*). 36 air-conditioned rooms. Private beach. Pool, tennis court, watersports.

**** Holiday Inn (*tel: 312426*). 162 rooms. Private beach. Pool, children's pool and tennis courts.

*** AquaMarina Hotel (*tel: 316251*). 71 rooms. Private beach, pool, sauna and massage. All watersports facilities, with snorkelling and diving. It also organises half-day or full-day (JD7.5) trips to Pharaoh's Island, 45 minutes' boat ride away just off the Egyptian Sinai coastline.

*** **Aqaba Hotel** (*tel: 312056. fax: 03-314089*). The oldest of the beach hotels and in some ways the nicest. It also has air conditioned bungalows with kitchenette (slightly more expensive) set among the palm trees of its garden.

*** **Aqaba Inn Hotel** (*tel: 316896 fax: 314339*). 46 rooms with TV and minibar. Swimming pool.

*** **Miramar Hotel** (*tel: 314340. fax: 314339*). Away from the beach. 97 rooms, health club and 25m pool

**** **The Alcazar Hotel** (*tel: 314131. fax: 314133*). 132 rooms. Two restaurants, bar and pub. Sauna, jaccuzzi and pool. It has a new diving centre for professional instruction at all levels and equipment hire.

Camping is permitted in the gardens of the Aqaba Hotel.

Watersports: Although all the beach hotels offer water-skiing, pedaloes, snorkelling and glass-bottomed boats, the diving clubs at the AquaMarina and Alcazar Hotels are centres for scuba diving. Aqaba is increasingly marketing itself as a winter watersports resort, and prices are generally higher from September to March to reflect this. To see the best coral and fish, diving is essential. In the area around the town and port, the fish and small patches of coral are generally disappointing. A trip in a glass-bottomed boat will soon reveal this. Take a snorkel and mask in the boat with you, as visibility through the glass is often murky. The best snorkelling is on the reef some 10km outside Aqaba on the way to Saudi Arabia, or around Pharaoh's Island if you make the day trip there.

Other activities: The town also has a horse-riding club.

Beaches: The best beaches belong to the hotels as they are cleaned and maintained. Bikinis can be worn on the beach, though Arab youths will always ogle. Toplessness is not advised. The beaches are rarely crowded except during the Muslim holidays.

Restaurants: The Ali Baba Restaurant, in the centre of town, a 15-minute walk from the beach hotels, has the best choice of fish. It has a pleasant atmosphere and you can sit inside or out. Credit cards are accepted. The local wines on offer are all from the West Bank: dry white Cremisan, red and rosé Latroun, red St Catherina. A meal for two with wine is around JD8.

Between the beach hotels and the town you will notice a pair of restaurants, set right down at the water's edge and shielded by burusti fencing: the Sinbad and the Al-Samakh. Both offer limited fish dishes, and are cheaper than but not as good as the Ali Baba.

The Indian restaurant in the centre of town does good food and you can sit out on its balcony for sea views.

Shops and Market: Aqaba's shops are good and varied and the market has plentiful fruit and vegetables of high quality if you are self-catering.

The Dead Sea

For most visitors to Jordan a visit to the Dead Sea for a ritual float is a must. It is an easy half-day excursion from
Amman, as the total distance is only 50km, and the drive
takes about 45 minutes. Heading south as if for the airport, you take the fork to the right signposted to Na'ur
about 15km south-west of Amman. Na'ur is one of the
towns where large numbers of Circassians were settled by
the Ottoman Sultan Abdul Hamid.

Once clear of Na'ur, the drive is a striking one, through
barren, lunar landscapes, as the road starts its descent into
this, the deepest and most enclosed area on the earth's
crust, 394m below sea level. Throughout its history it has
known many names. The Hebrews called it the Sea of the
Steppe, the Salt Sea or the Oriental Sea. The Greeks called
it the Asphalt Lake from pieces of black bitumen the water
was said to contain. The Nabateans sold the natural
asphalt at high prices, notably to the Egyptians, who used
it in the mummification of bodies. The Crusaders called it
the Dead Sea, and the medieval Muslim geographers
called it variously the Stinking Lake, the Lake of Sodom
and Gomorrah, and the Upsidedown Lake. In modern
Arabic it is the Sea of Lot, reference to the Prophet Lot,
who is referred to no less than 33 times in the Quran. The
sites associated with him and his people lie further south
on the Dead Sea shore, which are reached from Kerak, and
will be discussed in that section.

A multitude of names

Shortly after the road drops below the sea-level indica-
tor at the roadside, some vegetation begins to appear,
with palm trees on the valley bottom. Some 2km past the
sea-level marker, to the right of the road, you may be
interested to spot one of Jordan's largest and best preserved **dolmen fields**. The dolmens are prehistoric grave
markers in the form of a flat stone resting on three or four
supporting stones. Jordan is estimated to have had over
20,000 of these structures, but this group is one of the best
preserved and easily spottable.

Prehistoric graveyard

As you drop fully into the valley you will see straight
ahead the tarred road that leads to the King Abdullah
Bridge and to Jerusalem, an access route that has stayed
closed since 1967. Before reaching the road block, you follow the curve round to the left which then winds along to
the north eastern tip of the lake. From here it continues
south to the resthouse and the new Dead Sea Spa Hotel,
the two places from which most swimming takes place. It
is possible to swim from other points, but the shoreline is
usually foul-smelling and muddy, so most prefer the
sandy beaches of the resthouse and the hotel A small

Dead Sea

entrance fee is charged at both establishments, which entitles you to use the changing and shower facilities. Try to avoid Fridays and Saturdays, as the weekend crowds can be unpleasant.

Surface swimming

Serious swimming is impossible, as you cannot keep your limbs underwater to make the strokes, so to make any headway you have to make odd kicking and wriggling movements, propelling yourself along like some aquatic bug on the surface of the water. Bring a newspaper so that you can pose reading it for that well-known photograph. If you splash too vigorously, the water that gets in your eyes stings dreadfully. When you come out, the salt on your body feels so clammy that you will tend to rush for the shower. A dedicated few, however, seem to feel it is beneficial to sit and let the salt cake on.

Death to fish

The lake is a mere 16km wide, so the view across to the other side is usually clear. Its length fluctuates between 75 and 85km depending on the season. Depths of up to 400m have been recorded, although much of the southern half is very shallow, often no more than 10m. The salt content is ten times that of the Mediterranean, making the water feel oily and slimy on the skin. Fish carried down from the River Jordan die within a minute of arriving in the sea, and are found washed up on the shore stiff and rigid with minerals.

It was the Roman Emperor Vespasian who discovered that it was impossible for humans to drown in the water, when he had non-swimming Jewish prisoners tossed into the lake with their hands tied, only to find them bobbing on the surface hours later.

Best at sunset

In the summer months, the heat is fierce over the midday period, and visits would be best confined to early morning or sunset. The sea is often at its most attractive at these times anyway, with the colours on the water and the mountains changing dramatically as you watch. Evaporation is immense, estimated at 8.5 metric tons of water per day in summer, and some geologists have calculated that it will have dried up completely in 500 years' time. The crystallised salts coating the mud flats and rocks of the shore line, a phenomenon particularly noticeable in the more southern parts of the sea, give us some idea of what the whole Mediterranean must have looked like some five million years ago when it was a colossal evaporated basin with thick salt and mineral crusts.

The King's Highway

Route planning

The route south from Amman to Petra that runs along what has been known throughout history as the King's

Highway should be incorporated into all except the briefest of itineraries. It follows the ridge of mountains that skirt the east of the Dead Sea, dropping every now and again into spectacular valleys. It passes biblical sites, Crusader castles, Nabatean settlements and Roman cities. In this continuous variety of landscapes and relics of the past, it offers a total contrast to the tedious desert road that proceeds through monotonous wastelands of sand. This desert route from Amman to Petra is 262km and can be driven in under three hours. The King's Highway route is 274km and although it can be done in a day, that **Allow one day** only allows you time to stop off at the mosaics and **minimum** churches of Madaba and at one of the Crusader castles. To do the route justice, you should devote two days to it, stopping overnight at the pleasant hilltop resthouse of Kerak, just next door to the castle. It is the two-day itinerary that will be described here in detail, and from which you can select your preferences, as even two days will hardly allow you time to visit all the locations thoroughly. The desert route can be used on the return journey to save time. The first three sites – Madaba, Mt Nebo and Zerqa Ma'in – could also be visited in a day trip from Amman.

Madaba

Leaving Amman from the south as if going to the airport, you take the right-hand fork, signposted to Madaba after some 20km. The road climbs gently through the next 10km to the town, a centre of some 40,000 people with an important Christian community, mainly Greek Orthodox. Christianity gained a strong foothold east of the Jordan in the second and third centuries, but in Madaba it flourished above all in Byzantine times, when its churches and now-famous mosaics were built. The sheer profusion in churches and houses makes it the mosaic capital of Jordan. Today, besides the orthodox church and school, there is also a Melkite church and a Methodist mission.

At the edge of the town, a signpost points off right to **Mt Nebo** Dar as-Siyagha (House of the Monastery), the site of **Mt summit** **Nebo**, and it is probably best to visit this first before the churches of Madaba. The picturesque narrow tarred road runs along a ridge for a little under 10km till it reaches the church on the summit of Mt Nebo at 838m. It is a superb vantage point, with a view over the Dead Sea shimmering below to the west, and the Jordan Valley, and on a clear day to the palms of Jericho and even to Jerusalem, 50km away. This was the summit that God commanded Moses to climb in order to look over the promised land just before he died.

An example of the mosaics at Madaba.

And Moses went up from the plains of Moab unto the mountain of Nebo, to the top of Pisgah, that is over against Jericho. And the Lord shewed him all the land of Gilead, unto Dan... And the Lord said unto him, This is the land which I sware unto Abraham, unto Isaac and unto Jacob, saying, I will give it unto thy seed: I have caused thee to see it with thine eyes, but thou shalt not go over thither.

Moses' mystery grave

So Moses the servant of the Lord died there in the land of Moab... And he buried him in a valley in the land of Moab, over against Bethpeor: but no man knoweth of his sepulchre unto this day. And Moses was an hundred and twenty years old when he died: his eye was not dim, nor his natural force abated. (Deuteronomy 34: 1–6)

Inside the basilica the floors are covered in extensive mosaics, badly damaged in places, but still with some very attractive patches showing hunting scenes of men on horseback spearing bears and wild cats, with dogs leaping up to help. In front of the basilica a rusting metal statue erected by an American in 1984 is a representation of Moses lifting up the serpent in the wilderness. The Franciscans have built neat little huts containing the finds from the excavations and a small book shop.

About 1.5km before Nebo, a track off to the right (north) snakes down the hill to the so-called Spring of Moses, under tall eucalyptus trees. On the descent you may notice, to the right of the track, a prehistoric stone ring made up of two concentric circles, and a number of dolmens on the hillsides. Near the spring are the scant ruins of another monastery.

Some 3km before Nebo, you will have noticed a road forking to the left signposted to **Al-Mukhayyat**. This short detour is well worth making, to visit the two sixth century churches set in a picturesque valley: the St George Church and the St Lot Church. The bumpy road bounces off into the valley and you fork left at the next junction. Within 2km you arrive at the little village of Nebo huddled round a small acropolis hillock, with the St George Church at the top, and the St Lot Church at the foot. This place was one of the last stops for the Israelites on their journey to the Promised Land, and in Byzantine times it was a flourishing town. Both churches were lived in by local Bedouin families until relatively recently, as evidenced by the fire-blackened walls. A Bedouin woman with tatooed chin and black dress may emerge to complain that a Christian man came from Amman some years ago and bought the land from her cheaply. Not having appreciated the value of the churches and their mosaics at the time, she now feels hard done by.

Two early churches

From the outside the St Lot Church is totally plain, yet inside is an unusually well-preserved mosaic floor with highly original scenes of men harvesting and treading grapes. One man is playing a flute, while bulls, sheep and various mythological beasts are all intertwined in circles of trees and flora. On the hillock the St George Church is badly ruined, its mosaic floor mainly covered with earth. The bucolic scenes of men and animals depicted are similar to those in St Lot. Some 500m east of the acropolis hillock are the remains of a monastery spread out on a cliff with nearby caves.

Fine mosaics

Returning to **Madaba**, you can now visit the famous **St George Church** that lies in the centre of town, opposite the government resthouse. A total of 14 churches are known in Madaba today, but the major ones which are open for visits are the St George Church and the Church of the Apostles. The archaeological museum is also worth a tour, displaying mosaic floors from houses and churches in Madaba and some collections of Roman and Byzantine jewellery and pottery, all found locally. Choose your day carefully, as the churches are all closed on Sundays, while the resthouse (offering refreshment only) is closed on Fridays and the museum on Tuesdays. Nearby, there are shops, open most days, which make and sell the colourful Madaba carpets that have been woven in the town for centuries.

Avoid Tuesdays and Sundays

The town has a long history and is mentioned several times in the Bible in connection with the wars between the Ammonites and the Israelites. In Roman times it was a fine provincial town with temples and colonnaded streets, but today nothing remains of the Roman town except one cistern and the mosaics. The cause of its destruction was the arrival of some 2000 Arab Christians (Melkites) from Kerak in 1880, following inter-tribal clashes there. The ruined mound of Madaba had been uninhabited for centuries until that time, and the new arrivals built their houses and modern churches over the mosaic floors. Until the museum recently appropriated it, one mosaic floor was in use as a garage.

Famous Palestine map

The most famous mosaic, the map of Palestine, forms the floor of the St George Church. The church building itself dates from the end of the nineteenth century when the new Christian community arrived, though the mosaics belong to the early sixth-century basilica that stood on the same spot. As it is still a functioning church, there is no entry fee, though a donation is expected, and a Greek Orthodox priest often accompanies you to explain the map. It would originally have covered a north-south span from Lower Egypt to Sidon in Lebanon, but whole chunks are missing or badly damaged from centuries of neglect. The frequent wetting of the mosaics to sharpen the colours for the benefit of visitors also causes damage, making them bulge upwards and detach themselves from their limestone bed. In the late 1960s a German team of restorers lifted the entire mosaic and reset it in a new bed.

Jerusalem in mosaic

The central point of the map is the city of Jerusalem, fortunately one of the best-preserved sections. One can identify the Holy Sepulchre and the round dome of the Anastasius Church just below. Lower down on the right is Bethlehem with its basilica, and on the right is the Jordan River, complete with fish, emptying into the Dead Sea. The southern portion still shows an area of the Nile Delta.

In the south-east of the town, on the main road out towards Kerak, you will see the sign announcing the

Church of the Apostles just on the right of the road. The plain building with its corrugated-iron roof protects a large mosaic which you can walk around on a raised walkway after buying a ticket from the guardian. Though dusty and difficult to see properly, you can make out in the centre a striking woman's torso, a representation of the sea, bare-breasted and large-eyed, and surrounded by fish and mythological monsters. The Greek Thalassa (sea) is inscribed above her head.

The museum lies just 300m away back towards the centre of town and is signposted. Open from 8.00–5.00 daily, except Tuesdays, the main exhibits are further mosaic floors rescued from local private houses, together with Roman figurines, Byzantine ceramics, glass and jewellery, a few carpets, weapons and costumes.

The themes of all these mosaics are again of a Bacchus-like bucolic revelry, with men harvesting grapes, boys playing flutes, baskets of fruit, lush bushes and trees and all sorts of wild animals scattered amongst the vegetation. It is in these sorts of motifs that the inspiration for many of the murals in the Umayyad palaces like Qasr Amra may perhaps be found.

If your appetite for mosaics is still unquenched, a local guide can escort you to several private houses where owners will, for a consideration, allow you in to view their floors. Enquire at the resthouse of the museum.

Church of the Apostles

Bucolic mosaics

Zerqa Ma'in

On the road running through the centre of Madaba, beyond the St George Church, you will reach a crossroads signposted left to the museum, with a blue sign in Arabic to the right to **Zerqa Ma'in**. This excursion makes an interesting change from mosaics and now, with the completion of the new road and impressive hotel and spa amenities, it is an excellent stop for lunch in pleasanter surroundings than the rather squalid Madaba. The drive itself is also spectacular, as the road snakes down through the cliffs with gradients sometimes reaching 15 per cent and dramatic views across to the Dead Sea. At the moment, the road stops at the springs, though plans are in hand to extend it down to the Dead Sea at Ain Zara, some 4km away, identified with Callirhoe, where Herod the Great used to descend from his palace at nearby Mukawir to take the waters. This is the site of the new Dead Sea Spa Hotel.

Cut into a gorge-like valley, the hot springs of Zerqa Ma'in form an ensemble of natural basins, the water

Hot waterfall   temperatures varying from 55 to 60°C. The most spectacular spring cascades over the basalt rocks, forming a
wide natural waterfall where hot showers are popular
with men, if they can manage not to slip on the hot
slimy deposit left by the minerals. The women, usually
grossly overweight, seem to prefer to sit for hours in
rather stagnant enclosed spa areas that smell oppres-
sively strong. There are a total of some 60 springs, most-
ly hot but a few cold. They are said to benefit mainly
rheumatic disorders and skin diseases. This has long
been a popular place for weekend outings, sometimes
with whole families camping out beside the springs in
primitive tents. The construction of the hotel took rather
longer than envisaged and the springs were theoretically
closed to the public for some six years, but many families determined to seek cures managed to 'persuade' the
guards to let them through, and continued to camp
beside the springs.

Mukawir
Returning to Madaba, you can now continue your journey
south along the ridge of the King's Highway. The next
interesting diversion comes after some 14km at Libb,
where a road forks off to the right leading, after 20km, to
Mukawir, the spectacular site of Herod's Palace. Here it
Site of Salome's   was that Salome danced for the head of John the Baptist,
dance   and the eerie conical mound, looking rather like a nest
overlooking the Dead Sea, seems a strangely fitting site
for this spectacle.

The route is not signposted, so having turned right at
Libb (the only tarred road leaving the main road at a right
angle), you then bear right at the next junction in the village. Following this road for 18km you then reach a junction where you fork right again, arriving after a further
1km at a small village (also called Mukawir), where you
again bear right. Nearby is a ruined Byzantine church and
various architectural fragments. At this point, beyond the
village and slightly to the left, you will see the distinctive,
Distinctive   almost volcanic, shape of the hill, with its flattened top on
mound   which the palace stands. The final 3km is on a bumpy
rather rocky track, more suited to four-wheel drive, so
those with saloon cars can either take their chance and
drive very carefully or else make the interesting walk
down, examining at leisure the extraordinary cave tombs
cut into the moonscape cliffs and hills all along the way.

The track stops in an open space directly opposite the
mound, and from here you have no option but to walk.
The distance is, however, deceptive, for though the summit

The bute of Mukawir with caves visible at the foot of the cliff-face (Vine).

appears high and remote, you can be standing on top within 15 minutes. The approach is along the remains of a fine causeway that spans the saddle. Further cave tombs cut into the hills are to be seen on the way.

Causeway approach

On the summit little remains beyond foundations and walls, but the spectacular view alone makes the ascent worthwhile, quite apart from the fun of skipping from room to room imagining where John's beheading might have taken place. The graphic local name for the palace is Qasr el-Mishnaqa, Palace of the Gallows. Herod had two further palaces on hilltops round the Dead Sea, one near Bethlehem and the other near Jericho, and both are visible from here on a clear day, as are the towers of Jerusalem.

The first castle to be built on the mound was that of Alexander Jannius, King of the Jews in the first century BC. His widow Alexandra chose it as the safest place to hide her treasures and jewellery at the time of the Roman invasion, but Pompey destroyed it in 67 BC, leaving it to Herod the Great to rebuild again in 37–48 BC.

It was Herod Antipas (4 BC–39 AD), one of the sons of Herod the Great, who was tricked by the dancing of Salome into granting whatever she wished. John the Bapist was in prison for having spoken out against Herod's adultery with Herodias, his sister-in-law, and Herodias plotted to remove her denouncer. Knowing that Herod feared to put the Baptist to death because of the public outcry that might ensue, Herodias arranged for her

Dancing trickery

John the Baptist's head

beautiful daughter Salome to dance on Herod's birthday. Following her mother's instructions, when Herod promised her whatever she wished as reward she asked for the head of John the Baptist on a platter.

And the king was sorry: nevertheless for the oath's sake, and for them which sat with him at meat, he commanded it to be given her.
And he sent, and beheaded John in the prison.
And his head was brought in a charger, and given to the damsel: and she brought it to her mother.
(Matthew 14: 9–11)

Although little other than the foundations remain today, archaeologists have found hints of the luxury the palace once enjoyed. They have uncovered traces of lavish baths with mosaic flooring. The water was brought from numerous cisterns sunk into the hillsides and from an aqueduct to the east. Extensive storerooms for goods to withstand a siege lined the outer defensive walls, and three towers rose on the west, south and east.

Elaborate water system

That so little remains today is the result of the Jewish uprisings against the Romans, when many Jews fled from Jerusalem in 66 AD to Mukawir (or Machaerus as it was then known), this being the next safest stronghold. Like the more famous Massada on the other side of the Dead Sea, it remained a nest of resistance held by the rebel Jews until the Roman general reinforced by the Xth Legion, came in 72 AD and laid siege to it, building the ramp that today resembles a causeway from the eastern, most vulnerable side, from which to launch their attack. The Jews, realising that defeat was inevitable, and seeing one of the Romans' Jewish prisoners threatened with crucifixion, gave up in advance. They were allowed to live, but the palace itself was razed to the ground.

Massada-like ramp

From Mukawir you must return to the main road at Libb to continue south towards Kerak. There are plans for a road to link with the new highway under construction which will run along the eastern side of the Dead Sea, but at the time of writing this remains a difficult if exciting track, suitable for four-wheel drive only.

Some 20km south from Libb, the road passes through **Dhiban**, the biblical Dibon, where the so-called Mesha Stele was found, a basalt block detailing the battles of the Moabite king Mesha against the kings of Israel. This extraordinary record confirms and complements to a large degree the biblical account of these wars.

A French orientalist offered to pay the princely sum of £60 for it in 1868, and returned to his base at Jerusalem to

The desert Umayyad palace, Qasr Amra (Darke).

The black basalt castle of Qasr Azraq (Vine).

Attempts are being made at the Shaumari Wildlife Reserve to reintroduce the Arabian oryx (Vine).

Mosaic portrait of a young man in the church on the summit of Mt Nebo.

The spectacular hot springs waterfall at Zerqa Ma'in (Darke).

fetch the money. Meanwhile squabbles broke out among the local familes as to how the money would be split, and one of them, in a fit of pique, lit a fire on the stele and poured water over it, making the stone smash into pieces. The French scholar had fortunately made an imprint of the stone before he left, and copies, based on this imprint, are in the museums of Amman, Kerak and Madaba. The original was gathered up and sent to France for reassembly, and is now on display in the Louvre. The ruins today at Tell Dibon are a rather unimpressive and to the layman incomprehensible maze of Iron Age, Roman, Nabatean and Byzantine walls, though one area of well-built Moabite town wall still survives and is recognisable in the south-eastern section.

Family squabble

Enthusiasts with time to spare can make the 16km detour from Dhiban to **Umm ar-Rassas** where the extensive though heavily ruined remains of a Byzantine town are to be found, with numerous low walls and arches of houses and churches. About 1km to the north-west is a solitary well-preserved Byzantine tower some 15m high, thought to have been used by early Christian monks seeking solitude. The site is reached by turning east from Dhiban at the exit from the town near the police area along an asphalt road. The ruins can be seen after 16km directly to the left of the road. It is here that the remarkable Church of St Stephen has recently been excavated, with mosaics showing city plans from Egypt, Jordan and Palestine.

Umm ar-Rassas

Continuing south from Dhiban, you reach the edge of the dramatic **Wadi Mujib** after about 15km. The descent, some 400m into this Grand Canyon-like gorge, is one of the most dramatic visual experiences that Jordan has to offer. An excellent new road now hairpins down 9km to the valley floor, lush with vegetation and cultivation even at the height of summer. The width of the gorge at the top is 4km and the combined descent and ascent cover 20km of snaking bends, with a spectacular viewing point at the beginning of the descent. Whether it is the view that has distracted so many drivers or the steepness that has caused their brakes to fail, terrible accidents occur on this road with unfailing regularity, often involving lorries or buses.

Jordan's Grand Canyon

In the Old Testament the river which flows along it is known as the Arnon, disgorging eventually into the Dead Sea. On the ascent, to the left of the road, two Roman pillars mark the passage of the original Roman road.

From the edge of the Wadi Mujib the road runs along the high ridge passing several scattered villages to the right and the left on the hillsides. One of these, Al-Qasr, about 15km from Wadi Mujib, has many architectural fragments like decorated blocks built into the current villagers' houses, and nearby, to the right of the road, is a small ruined Nabatean temple.

Some 5km further south you come to the village of Rabba, the biblical Rabbath Moab, where the remains of a late Roman temple dedicated to Diocletian and Maximian are quite well-preserved, along with some Corinthian columns of a Roman porticoed way, to the right of the road. The remainder of the ancient town is now covered by the modern village.

Sodom and Gomorrah

A further 10km or so brings you now within sight of the imposing hilltop Crusader castle of Kerak, with the town spread out on the steep hillsides around it. Here you can break your journey at the resthouse immediately adjacent to the castle, either for a meal or for an overnight stop.

The sinners of Sodom

If you have the time and are interested in seeing the sites of biblical history, you can make a short excursion ($2^1/_2$ hours) down to the Dead Sea to view what is popularly believed to be the site of **Sodom and Gomorrah**, the evil 'Cities of the Plain'. Here the flat salty promontory called Al-Lisan (The Tongue) juts out in the shallow water of a basin of relatively recent geological formation. The earthquake which caused it is popularly associated with the catastrophic event that destroyed Sodom and Gomorrah and resulted in Lot's wife being turned to a pillar of salt: certainly the character of the Dead Sea in these southern areas, with its arid salty expanses, is quite different from the northern shore.

Abram dwelled in the land of Canaan, and Lot dwelled in the cities of the plain, and pitched his tent towards Sodom. But the men of Sodom were wicked and sinners before the Lord exceedingly.
(Genesis 13: 12–13)

And the Lord said, Because the cry of Sodom and Gomorrah is great, and because their sin is very grievous; I will go down and see whether they have done altogether according to the cry of it, which is come unto me; and if not, I will know.
(Genesis 18: 20–21)

The angels whom God sent to warn them were mocked by the men of Sodom, and even Lot, his wife and two daughters were so reluctant to leave that they had to be *'laid hold of'* and led away, being exhorted by the angels:

'Escape for thy life; look not behind thee, neither stay thee in the Plain; escape to the mountain, lest thou be consumed'.

Then the Lord rained upon Sodom and Gomorrah brimstone and fire from the Lord out of heaven; And he overthrew those cities and all the plain, and all the inhabitants of the cities, and that which grew upon the ground. But his wife looked back from behind, and she became a pillar of salt.
(Genesis 19: 24–26)

Lot's wife

THE SEARCH FOR SODOM AND GOMORRAH

In the early 1920s one Melvin Grove Kyle, a Doctor of Divinity at Jerusalem, set out with a party of fellow theologians and archaeologists to find evidence for the existence of the cities of the plain, and entitled his charming account of the journey, *Excavations at Sodom*. He and his party were the first people ever to be granted visas for entry into the new Kingdom of Transjordan, and at the Allenby Bridge, the new Jordanian passport officials examined their passports and visas from front and back and upside down to be certain that all was in order.

'The fascination of the horrible seems irresistible' is how he begins his narrative, and goes on to elaborate on how the land and the mountains of Moab have enjoyed an evil reputation for thousands of years, and other travellers, soldiers and pilgrims have told him of the 'fetid air', 'horrible smells', 'execrable water' and 'pestilential desolation' of the cities of the plain. Instead, he discovers a scenery of 'more romantic beauty and grandeur...than Luxor, with almost none of the annoyances of that Egyptian resort'. He finds a wadi with a broad 20ft flow of the most excellent water he has ever drunk, and eulogises the lovely colours – reds, yellows, and mauves – of the rocks and cliffs around the sea. The Bedouin women in their black tents would bake bread for them 'thin and black and dirty, but bread', with 'about the texture and much the flavour of a hot-water bottle'. They would also buy the occasional old tough hen from the Bedouin 'and after we had stewed it for a long time, we were able to imagine we had eaten a chicken dinner'.

The dedicated team scoured the hillsides and shores of the southern Dead Sea and were rewarded with discoveries of the potsherds of a Canaanite civilization of the twentieth century BC, i.e. early Bronze Age. Their most significant finds were at the site of Bab el-Dhra'a, 500 feet above the level of the Dead Sea, a vast Bronze Age settlement with a fortress over a thousand foot long, surrounded by massive rampart-like walls up to 13 feet thick in places. From nearby graves and within the fortress, they collected several thousand flint artefacts, mainly knives. Their date, they concluded, coincided with the date of the end of Sodom and Gomorrah, and there was no evidence of subsequent occupation of the site. These discoveries led them to deduce that Bab el-Dhra'a was probably the Great High Place of the inhabitants of Sodom and Gomorrah, where they came to make annual pilgrimages and performed pagan rites, 'the nature of which had better not be surmised'.

**Descent of
Sodom**

Nothing really tangible remains to be seen today except
the abundance of salt formations and the 'brimstone' in
the form of sulphur and sulphurous springs to be found
on the promontory of Al-Lisan, now a military zone and
out of bounds.

The descent from Kerak to Bab el-Dhra'a and Sodom
and Gomorrah is a striking one. The steep hillsides are
covered in cultivation of which the Kerak townspeople
are justly proud, with terraces of olives, figs and vineyards all down the Wadi Kerak. The road, which then
continues south through the Wadi Araba to Aqaba, is
much used by lorries carrying produce for export from
the Jordan Valley to the port at Aqaba. As you descend
further, the shapes of the now bare hills betray that they
were once under water, with strange watermarks baked
on by the heat at the varying levels over the ages. The
scenery is dramatic, and after the road block, the drop to
the bottom is very sudden. Of this descent, Melvin Kyle
said that it was so steep they had to dismount from their
horses, but even then things were not easy. '*We walked,
when we could, and climbed when we could not walk, and slid
when we could not climb*'. A pack mule which happened to
be carrying Kyle's bedroll, was lost over the edge, but the
bedroll was fortunately recovered below. So impressed is
Kyle with the landscape that he makes a prediction: '*When
Palestine becomes prosperous – and she is rapidly becoming so –
an automobile line from Jerusalem to the Dead Sea and a motorboat line on the sea will make this one of the finest winter health
resorts in the world.*' Politics have, alas, so far thwarted his
prediction.

The site of **Bab el-Dhra'a** is announced by a blue metal
sign set a few metres off to the right of the road just by a
couple of small concrete huts 2km after passing the village
of Al-Dhra'a and just 200–300m after a barriered turn-off
to the left. The landscape here is flat and rather featureless, and the site, despite excavations in the 1960s and
1970s, is impressive for its extent rather than the actual
remains, as to the untrained eye it is merely an immense
enclosure containing a series of hillocks and mounds.
Most of the significant pottery finds were in the graves
which lie to the south of the settlement, on the other side

20,000 graves

of the road. Their total has been estimated at over 20,000.

The destruction of Sodom and Gomorrah was utter
and no one survived to tell the tale. 600 years later, Moses
still talked of the land as '*brimstone and salt and burning*'
(Deuteronomy 29: 23). A further 600 years later, Isaiah still
said of the place: '*It shall never be inhabited, neither shall it be
dwelt in from generation to generation: neither shall the*

Arabian pitch tent there; neither shall the shepherds make their fold there.' (Isaiah 13: 20).

In fact 2500 years of silence followed the catastrophe, and there was no sign of any settlement in the area until the Byzantine era. The scene until then had been as desolate as these prophecies suggested. Melvin Kyle puts it graphically: *'Here was a dead land round about a dead sea, and harbouring the memory of a moral character that was dead and a stench in the nostrils of the whole world.'*

As to the actual site of the cities, nothing can be proved decisively. The Israelis also have a site called Sodom, just to the south of their side of the Dead Sea. Industrial potash plants grace the place today, and not far away, several pillars of salt are on display, one of which is popularly claimed to be Lot's wife.

The nostrils of the world

Kerak

The town of **Kerak** is totally dominated by its fortress, Jordan's finest Crusader castle, set on the hilltop summit at 950m. After Abbasid Arabs moved their capital away from Damascus further east to Baghdad in 750, Jordan was distanced from the prosperity of the new empire and lay semi-forgotten and decaying. The advent of the Crusaders brought the country into prominence again, for the region of Transjordan was the Latin kingdom of Jerusalem's major principality, extending from Wadi Zerqa Ma'in in the north to the Gulf of Aqaba in the south, and with Kerak as its capital. This fortress was the centre of all Crusader activity east of the Jordan, and other fortresses were built at Shawbak (called Monte Reale by the Crusaders) further south along the King's Highway, at Wadi Musa (Le Vaux Moyse) near Petra and at Jezirat Far'oun (Isle de Graye), a small island in the Gulf of Aqaba.

Jordan's finest crusader castle

The Crusader armies concentrated in these fortresses would attack the Muslim caravans that plied between Damascus, Mecca and Egypt, often in violation of truces. Qal'at ar-Rabad, at Ajlun (see 'North from Amman'), was built by one of Saladin's generals to harrass the Crusaders and to protect these caravans.

From afar, the appearance of Kerak Castle is deceptive, for it seems to consist of nothing but defensive walls. Certainly the remainder of the town has little to offer the visitor besides a picturesque setting on the steep slopes and the government resthouse, which is extremely well situated on the cliff edge adjacent to the castle entrance. The town still has a significant minority of Christians, and has both a modest Melkite and a Latin church.

Deceptive interior

As you go through the iron gate (open from dawn till dusk) into the castle precinct, the whole place seems at first glance to be ruined. As you walk further in, however, all the vaults and buildings below the current ground level come into view, with steps leading down in many directions to colossal vaulted tunnels and rooms, whose functions have been variously interpreted as banqueting halls, sleeping quarters and stables. A torch is helpful for exploring the darker recesses.

In Crusader times, the castle could be entered by three underground passages which led from the hillside under the walls directly into the enclosure. Two of the entrance tunnels can still be seen, one on the eastern hillside, the other to the north-west. The original Crusader gateway is blocked today.

Fine museum

The castle enclosure is large and extensive, and you should allow a minimum of $1^1/_2$ hours to see it all properly. At the lower level is a fine museum, built into one of the vaults, some 100m long and 15m wide. A deep well shows just how far the whole structure goes down into the hillside. The museum contains an assortment of objects found in the region, from Bronze-Age pottery to Byzantine glass, attractively decorated Mamluke ceramics and Ottoman coins. Of the ruins to be seen today, however, only those of the Crusader period remain, with the exception of the rear end of an early basalt lion, now set into the corner of a house near the castle gate.

The name Kerak is a corruption of the Frankish Crusader name Le Crac which is in turn the same as that given to the famous Crac des Chevaliers in Syria, one of the best preserved of all the Crusader castles. Its full title was Crac des Moabites or Le Pierre du Desert, and throughout the Crusader period it remained the chief city of the province of Oultre Jourdain.

The original fortifications here were built in 1136 by one Payem, Lord of Kerak and Shawbak (Kerak's sister castle to the south). Its most notorious lord however, was the French Reginald of Chatillon, an adventurous and unscrupulous leader. In violation of local treaties, he would pounce on innocent caravans that passed peacefully beneath his walls, frequently during periods of supposed truce, and pillage the pilgrims on their way to Mecca. Saladin vowed to kill this Frankish boor with his own hand, and when he captured him, he kept his word; all the other captured Templars and Hospitallers were also publicly executed.

Pillaging the pilgrims

On a colourful occasion earlier in 1183, when Saladin was laying siege to the castle, it happened to be the time of the wedding of the 11-year-old Princess Isabella to the 17-year-old Humfried von Toron, heir to Kerak. Honoured and noble guests were present, and while stone blocks were being hurled against the walls outside, the celebrations continued inside with singing and dancing. The bride's mother herself collected a selection of wedding dishes which she had sent out to Saladin. At this point, ever chivalrous, he enquired which tower the young couple were staying in, and ordered that it be avoided by the siege machinery. The arrival of support troops from Jerusalem a month later meant that Saladin had to withdraw without taking the castle.

Saladin's chivalry

Saladin's brilliantly conducted victory at the Battle of Hittin in 1187 was the beginning of the end for the Crusader kingdoms and following their huge losses there, Jerusalem and a whole succession of Crusader strongholds fell to the Arab Muslims. At Kerak, Reginald's widow, Etienette, resisted capture for more than a year, but was finally forced to surrender by famine. By 1189 the Frankish knights were virtually swept out of the Levant, and only the three strongholds of Antioch, Tripoli and Tyre remained in their possession.

Kerak was taken over by Malik al-Aadil, Saladin's younger brother, and from this base he proceeded to acquire sovereignty for himself over Egypt and much of Syria. In 1263 the castle was taken by the energetic Mamluke Sultan Baybars, who saw himself as a second Saladin in defending the Muslim towns from the Crusader invaders. He demolished the venerated Church of Nazareth that had stood within the castle walls.

Ibrahim Pasha, the elder son of Muhammad Ali of Egypt, occupied the castle in 1840 and had many of the fortifications torn down. In Ottoman times a period of fighting and anarchy between local tribes resulted in the departure of the majority of Kerak's Christian population north to Madaba.

Entering the citadel, you can easily distinguish the different building techniques from the stone used. The Franks used large blocks of hard volcanic rock, black or dark red, found locally, while the Muslims built from softer greyish or yellowish limestone, more carefully dressed and in wider blocks, which were brought from a more distant quarry. From this you can see that though the Frankish plan was preserved, the Arabs reinforced the defences at numerous points and totally rebuilt them at others.

Varying building techniques

At the far southern end of the enclosure is the tall four-storey dungeon building, with a crenellated parapet,

Troglodyte accommodation

Disposal of prisoners

Picnic possibility

built, as you can see from its stone, by Muslim Ayyubids and Mamlukes. In front is a large ditch which also served as a cistern to furnish water to the garrison.

The underground rooms on the upper courtyard level of the enclosure, in front of the dungeon tower and reached by numerous stairways down into the hillside, are thought to have been the living quarters of the lord and his family. They were located underground to help avoid the summer heat. Nearby, half-underground, are the remains of the little Byzantine Church of Nazareth, round which the Crusaders built the fortress, which was destroyed by Baybars in the thirteenth century.

Having been built solely for military purposes, the castle has very few decorative architectural features. The sheer drops from some of the battlement walls, especially to the east and south, are impressive, and unwanted prisoners used to meet their end by being tossed over the walls, their heads carefully encased in wooden boxes to prevent them being inadvertently knocked unconscious before landing at the bottom.

Some 10km south of Kerak the road passes through the village of **Mu'tah**. Though marked as an archaeological site on the Jordan Tourist Ministry map, there is actually nothing to be seen here. The site is purely historical, for it was here that the earliest battle between Muslims and Byzantines took place in 629. The small but dedicated Muslim army had been sent out from Medina by the Prophet, but was defeated by the larger and better-equipped Byzantine forces. The Muslim dead were buried at Mazar, a village 3km further south, where a large new mosque now stands over the tomb of Ja'far ben Abi Talib, a cousin of Muhammad, who was among the martyrs of the day. Muslim tradition says that, having had his hands cut off in the battle, he clutched the standard of the Prophet to his chest with the stumps of his arms. Muhammad confirmed that he had seen him in a dream, flying among the angels of paradise with two bloody wings. As a result, he is sometimes referred to as Ja'far Flying in Paradise.

The little site of **Dhat Ra's**, signposted off to the left of the road some 5km south of Mazar, is worth a short detour, and is quite a good spot for a picnic. The fork off the main road runs east for some 4km, until you see the ruins of a tower over on the top of a hill just to the left of the road. Here you can perch in the shade of a breach in the wall to contemplate the scene.

The village itself was once the site of the Byzantine town of Kyriacoupolis but today, apart from a few scattered blocks and columns to be glimpsed between the houses, the major relic is a large Roman mausoleum of the second or third century, still remarkably well preserved and now in a fenced enclosure in the middle of the village. It is kept locked, and the guardian has to be found nearby. All but the dedicated archaeologist will, however, be content to look from the outside. Some experts believe it is more likely to have been a Nabatean temple, for it has the characteristic flight of steps leading up to the roof.

Returning to the King's Highway and continuing south, you begin almost immediately the impressive descent into the **Wadi el-Hassa**. The river flowing along the valley bed, marked the boundary between Moab to the north and Edom to the south in ancient biblical times. As you climb out again you may notice the maze of little tracks all over the hillsides made by the Bedouin as they descend to collect water from the wadi. In the season (midsummer) the region is rife with prickly pears for sale by the roadside. They make a refreshing snack, although they require considerable dexterity with a knife to eat.

Land of prickly pears

From this point south the terrain changes, and sandstone becomes the dominant rock. The limestone of the Moab district made for gentle plateaus with rolling hills, but in Edom, the hills take on a jagged appearance with sharper contours and valleys. Immediately to the west of the road, after crossing the Wadi el-Hassa, there is a high isolated hill on the summit of which stands the Nabatean temple called **Khirbet Tannur**, (literally, Cabbage Ruins, from its shape).

The site is rarely visited today for two reasons: first the journey is difficult, involving a bad road followed by a final 20-minute climb to the top; secondly, the temple, though originally beautifully adorned in statues and carvings of local Nabatean deities, has now had the greater part of these removed to the safety of the museum on Amman's citadel. You may therefore not feel inclined to make the effort, but if you do, you will be rewarded by sensational views and a sense of achievement in struggling to see the only Nabatean temple ever to have been fully excavated. The track to it branches off the main road some 6km after crossing the river, as the road climbs out of the valley. It is suitable for four-wheel drive vehicles only, and deteriorates into a path for the final approach to the summit.

Difficult ascent

Dating to the first century BC, the temple consists of an outer paved courtyard leading to an imposing façade with a central doorway. This façade originally had as decoration in its niches all the statues that are now in the

Sacrificial temple

museum. Inside the doorway is the shrine and main high altar, its façade also originally decorated with statues of the deities. Steps lead up from the side of the altar to the top, where the sacrifices would have been made. Today the whole structure is largely reduced to foundations, but some 200 years ago, when the white limestone blocks stood out against the bare hillside, no traveller along the King's Highway could have missed it. The temple was rediscovered in the early 1930s by a Jordanian police officer, and the excavations began in 1936 under Nelson Glueck, who considered the temple to be the most important of all Nabatean sanctuaries. The bones of numerous animals were found by the archaeologists, showing that burnt offerings were the main form of sacrifice made here.

Some 20km further south, the road begins the steep winding descent into a valley with the picturesquely situated town of **Tafila**, set among the olive groves, clinging to the hillsides. The Crusaders fortified it, though today only a simple square building, some 200m west of the road junction, remains as any indication of their attentions.

Edomite settlement

Seventeen kilometres further on, a sign points off right to **Buseira**, a small village 3km to the west of the King's Highway, where an extensive early Edomite settlement of the seventh and eighth centuries BC has been excavated since 1971 by the Edomite specialist Mrs Crystal M. Bennett of the British School of Archaeology. Driving straight through the village, you come to the modern secondary school slightly to your right, with an iron gate and a high concrete wall. The ruins are actually within and beyond the grounds of the school, but when the school is closed you can still reach the ruins by following the road past the gates, then bearing left after the last houses to do a large loop round and enter the excavated area from the north-west. Identified as the biblical Bozra, the town was a major seat of the Edomite kings. The foundations of palaces and temples have been found on and around the little acropolis mound, while on the lower terraces all about were the houses of the Edomite inhabitants. For a non-specialist the site today is not especially impressive, although the hilltop setting with the valleys falling away beyond is fine.

Fine setting

The road now continues south and after passing the Wadi Dana, you can look out for a stretch of Roman road, its paving blocks still visible, beside the modern road.

Shawbak

Some 40km south of Buseira, the King's Highway reaches the intersection with the main approach to Petra from the desert highway. Excessive volumes of traffic and over-laden lorries mean that, despite frequent resurfacing, travelling on the link road to the desert highway can often feel like driving along a bumpy rutted staircase.

Forking right towards Petra, within a kilometre or two you will reach the small tarred turn-off (currently sign-posted for the benefit of those coming from the opposite direction only) that leads up and over the bare wind-blown hills for some 3–4km to make the approach from the rear to the impressive Crusader castle of Shawbak, all alone on its conical hilltop. The castle is not visible from the main road, and the turn-off seems at first unlikely, leading off as it does at an angle of only some 25° from the main highway.

Hilltop castle

The castle now lies deserted and dignified and its high walls make a good spot for a lofty picnic. Some 20 years ago it was inhabited by a number of peasant families who had built their dwellings and huts within the walls, but they have now been persuaded to leave.

The road leads right round to the imposing gateway through which you climb up into the castle. Though badly ruined, a fair amount still remains to be seen, much of it dating to the fourteenth century when the Mamlukes restored it. The original structure, called Monte Reale, was built by Baldwin I in 1115 as part of a chain of fortresses to protect the route from Damascus to Egypt. It was captured in 1189 by Saladin after a year and a half of siege. The site dominated the two main east-west routes to the Wadi Araba, and while the surrounding landscape today looks bleak and desolate, the contemporary medieval descriptions reveal the valleys at that time to have been rich in corn, vineyards and olives. The fruit, especially apricots, of the region, was so abundant that much was exported to Egypt. In the fourteenth century some 6000 people lived in and around the castle, mainly Christians, presumably the descendants of the original Frankish knights.

Isolated site

After Saladin's conquest, the castle remained in Ayyubid hands for nearly 70 years, and the inscriptions built into the main entrance gateway date from this period.

After 1260 the Mamlukes chose Shawbak as their head-quarters for controlling southern Jordan, and rebuilt and restyled much of the castle. In the nineteenth century the Ottomans under Ibrahim Pasha made further changes when they used the place as a barracks. These differences of period and reconstruction are evidenced in the many different types, both in colour and size, of building blocks that can still be distinguished.

Inside the walls, above the entrance gateway are the remains of two churches, and crosses can still be seen carved into the walls. They were subsequently used as mosques, and the roof, and until recently the mihrab or prayer niche in one of them, was fairly well preserved. Higher up on the hill you will find the entrance shaft leading down 356 slippery stone-cut steps into the depths of the hillside to a well. This shaft is thought to have been the work of the original Crusaders, and it is still possible, though not very pleasant, to climb right down to the water level. A powerful torch and shoes with good grips are necessary: the descent is trickier than the ascent, because of the sloping worn steps, and it takes about 20 minutes to reach the two chambers in the centre of the hillside. One has a muddy puddle, the other has rock benches round the edge. There is just about enough room to swing a cat. This remarkably labour-intensive construction is thought to be unique in Crusader architecture, and the safe water supply it guaranteed enabled Monte Reale to stave off Saladin's onslaughts considerably longer than its sister castle Kerak to the north.

356 slippery steps

Siege water

Petra

From Shawbak the road south brings you after some 25km to the Wadi Musa, the beginning of which is heralded by the charming little three-domed white building which houses Ain Musa, the spring which gushed forth when Moses struck the rock. Women and children come from all around to fill their huge plastic containers, and the water is wonderfully cool and clear. Just beyond is the modest Ain Mousa Hotel and Restaurant. From here a winding descent of 5km brings you through the sprawling village of Wadi Musa and on to the government resthouse and the Forum Hotel, both set on the very edge of the archaeological zone of Petra.

Moses' spring

Even as you begin this drop into the valley, you will notice the change in the geology of the landscape. Gradually the rocks and hillsides all around, and especially to the west, take on strange and distinctive formations, often showing hints of reds, mauves, yellows, blue and black. The rock city of Petra sits in the middle of this huge geological freak of nature, over 200sq km in area. Earthquakes, watercourses, wind and rain have created out of the soft natural sandstone a landscape of fantasy where dramatic puffy rock formations suddenly give way to abrupt gorges, narrow defiles and deep fissures.

Geological freak

In some ways even more remarkable than the natural phenomenon is the man-made contribution, for the

Nabatean architects of Petra were no more than a humble tribe of nomad camel drivers from the deserts of northern Arabia. It has been speculated that it may have been one of the first permanent settlements used by nomads, around the fourth century BC. From their capital at Petra they established an elaborate network of caravan routes which brought spices, incense, myrrh, gold, silver and precious stones from India and Arabia , to be traded on to the west. From the wealth they acquired, they adorned their city with palaces, temples, arches and monumental ways. Many that were free-standing have largely disappeared, but many were carved into the rock – the Treasury, the monumental tombs, the High Place of Sacrifice – and these still remain today in a condition of perfection so staggering that you feel you must have entered a time warp.

Caravan network

Eroded sandstone at Petra (Vine).

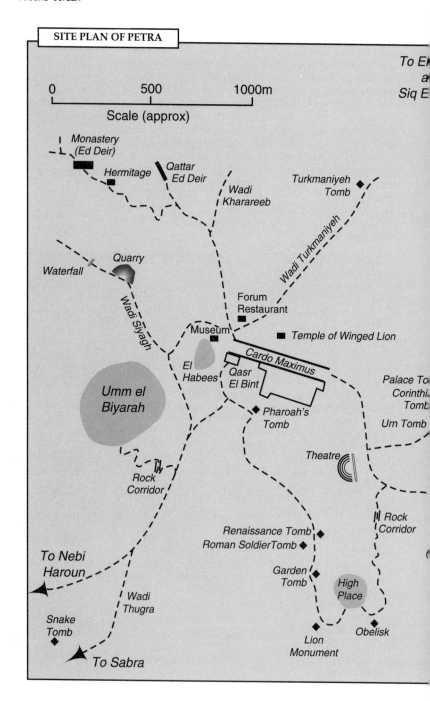

SITE PLAN OF PETRA

To El
a
Siq E

0   500   1000m

Scale (approx)

Monastery
(Ed Deir)

Hermitage

Qattar
Ed Deir

Wadi
Kharareeb

Turkmaniyeh
Tomb

Wadi Turkmaniyeh

Waterfall

Quarry

Wadi Siyagh

Forum
Restaurant

Museum

Temple of Winged Lion

Cardo Maximus

El
Habees

Qasr
El Bint

Umm el
Biyarah

Palace To
Corinthi
Tomb

Urn Tomb

Pharoah's
Tomb

Theatre

Rock
Corridor

Rock
Corridor

Renaissance Tomb
Roman SoldierTomb

To Nebi
Haroun

Garden
Tomb

High
Place

Wadi
Thugra

Snake
Tomb

Obelisk

To Sabra

Lion
Monument

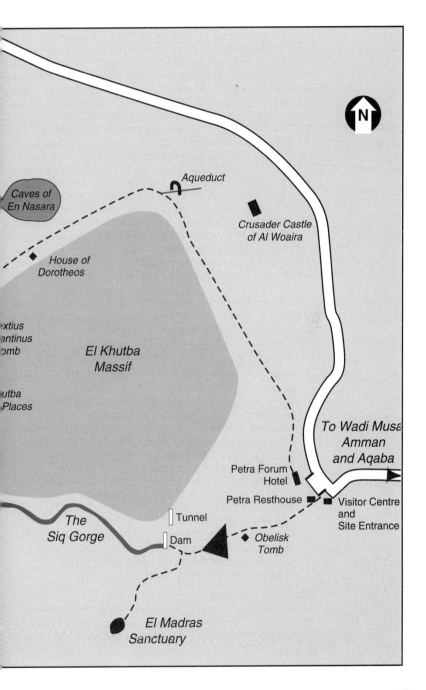

Caves of En Nasara

Aqueduct

Crusader Castle of Al Woaira

House of Dorotheos

xtius entinus omb

utba Places

El Khutba Massif

To Wadi Musa Amman and Aqaba

Petra Forum Hotel

Petra Resthouse

Visitor Centre and Site Entrance

The Siq Gorge

Tunnel

Dam

Obelisk Tomb

El Madras Sanctuary

Comfortable footwear

Itineraries

The great majority of visitors to Petra come for one day only. Some even make it a day trip from Amman, which is not to be recommended unless it is totally unavoidable. If you are here for one day only, it is essential to make the most of that day. Depending on your age and fitness, you can select the appropriate circuit from those that follow. Any tour of Petra involves walking and some climbing, so it is vital to have comfortable footwear. The rock underfoot is generally firm and easy to walk on, although the approach walk through the Siq (the name given to the narrow 2km gorge that leads to the heart of the city) is on sharper, loose stones. A hat is not a bad idea if you are sensitive to the sun, and a bottle of water is definitely a good idea. A compass will be useful for following some of the directions given later. Simple food and refreshments are available inside the site, although you can always take your own light picnic if you prefer. With the heat and exertion it is advisable to eat lightly, the better to savour an evening meal later as your reward.

One day itineraries

One Day – Energetic: This tour represents about the maximum it is possible to do in a day, especially if you choose to walk rather than ride the full length of the Siq. It makes an excellent introduction to Petra, involving two longish climbs, one in the morning, the other in the afternoon.

1. Walk through the Siq to the Treasury (or ride if you prefer).
2. Ascend to the High Place of Sacrifice (rock path begins just before the theatre and is signposted).
3. Descend from the High Place via the Wadi Farasa and Pharaoh's Pillar to Qasr el-Bint (Palace of the Maiden).
4. Light lunch at the tent near Qasr el-Bint or at the Forum restaurant.
5. Climb to Ed-Deir, the Monastery. (The afternoon is best as the climb is largely in the shade, while the sun strikes the façade of the monastery for the best lighting and photographs.)
6. Return from Qasr el-Bint along the Cardo Maximus, the main street of Petra, looking at other monumental tomb façades en route, finally returning to the Treasury.
7. Walk or ride back through the Siq.

One Day – Average:
1. Ride through the Siq to the Treasury. Leave the horses.
2. Ascend to the High Place and return by the same route.
3. Continue past the Theatre down the Cardo Maximus to Qasr el-Bint.

4. Lunch near Qasr el-Bint.
5. Climb to Ed-Deir.
6. Return to Qasr el-Bint and go up the Cardo Maximus to the Treasury.
7. Meet your horses for the return through the Siq.

Two Days: Two full days is really the minimum time necessary for a proper visit to Petra. It means that you can visit the various places without excessive fatigue and haste, and also sit somewhere quietly out of the way in a favourite spot from 11.00 to 3.00. This is the hottest part of the day, and also coincides with the period when the day tours from Amman are disgorged into the site for their lightning visits.

Two day itinerary

Day 1: The same as the One Day circuit, choosing the energetic or the average version, according to your taste.

Day 2:
1. Ride through the Siq either to the Treasury or all the way to Qasr el-Bint.
2. Climb the rock (known as El-Habees) behind Qasr el-Bint, to reach the ruined Crusader fort on the summit. With the help of a guide, it is possible to return a different way to arrive at the museum, which is cut into the rock-face above Qasr el-Bint, and the refreshments area.
3. Walk along Wadi es-Siyagh to reach the spring and waterfall.
4. Lunch in the Qasr el-Bint area.
5. Strenuous but exciting afternoon climb up Umm al-Biyarah mountain (Mother of the Cisterns), the highest point in Petra, and the site of the earliest settlement here. Take a Bedouin boy as a guide (from the refreshments tent area) as the path is tricky and not always clear.

Additional Excursions
If you have more time at your disposal, you may care to select from the following excursions:

Extras

Siq al-Baared and Beidha. By car this can be a short 1^1/$_2$–2-hour return trip from the resthouse, or alternatively a five hour return trip on foot from Qasr el-Bint. Al-Baared is likened to a mini Petra, in its own gorge 10km from the resthouse. Beidha, next to Al-Baared, is the site of an extensive neolithic city dated to 7000 BC. With your own transport, this is quite a good trip to do as an introduction if you arrive at Petra in the late afternoon, when it is not worth entering the site proper but there are still a couple of hours of daylight left.

Woairah. From the road that leads to Siq al-Baared and Beidha, a five-minute walk and scramble brings you to this heavily ruined Medieval Crusader castle, called by the Crusaders Le Vaux Moyse.

Es-Sabrah. A fairly strenuous 11-hour round trip takes you to a separate mini-city, a good two hours' walk or ride from the theatre at Petra. Take your own provisions and water and a local guide. Official guide fees are JD15 from the Visitors' Centre.

Jebel Haroun. It is a strenuous $2^1/_2$-hour ascent from Qasr el-Bint to the little white sanctuary on the summit of Jebel Haroun, where tradition holds that the Prophet Aaron is buried. The route is often unclear and a local guide is useful.

El-Madras. This site is a 45-minute walk from the rest-house, heading as if for the Siq, but turning left before the dam and the Siq entrance, up a series of rock-cut steps, arriving eventually at a cult sanctuary area with tombs and inscriptions. This is another good excursion to do if you arrive at Petra in the late afternoon, with only a couple of hours of daylight left.

Background Information

The site is open officially from 7.00 am to 6.00 pm, but in practice from dawn to dusk. The best months to visit are March–May and September–November. From December to February it can be very cold, especially at night. Sometimes it even snows, leaving a white covering up to 10cm thick. The altitude of the central Petra basin is about 1000m. From June to August it is extremely hot, although you have the advantage of longer evenings, which means that you can rest from 12.00 noon to 2.00 pm during the heat of the day. During the peak spring and autumn seasons the number of visitors can reach 1000 per day, which is another reason why the independent traveller may prefer an off-peak visit.

Extremes of hot and cold

The entrance fee, which is paid at the gate, is JD1 per person and tickets are valid for one day only. The Visitors' Centre sells tickets for horses at JD2 per horse for the return trip (plus a tip for the owner at the end), and arranges official guides at fixed prices if you require them. It also sells a selection of guidebooks, film and souvenirs. The Bedouin boys with their horses will assail you as soon as you step past the gate. The ride down takes some 35 minutes and you are led by the reins all the way, the boys walking in front. Even a total novice can manage it, though there may be some anxious moments when you first mount. Having arrived where you want to be dropped, you simply arrange a time and place with the boys for the return ride at the end of the day. Do not give in to pressure to make this earlier than you would like. Horse-drawn carriages are now also available (with sunshades) for a slightly higher price.

The walk down through the Siq takes about 40 minutes, so the difference in time between this and riding is minimal. The walk is highly recommended, especially on your first visit. It gives you a chance to absorb your surroundings and fully appreciate this unique and dramatic approach to what must be ranked as one of the most spectacular sites in the world.

Best to walk on first visit

Petra's earliest inhabitants were the Edomites, a Semitic agricultural people mentioned several times in the Bible as the sons of Esau. They are mainly remembered for refusing the Israelites passage through their land and along the King's Highway during their Exodus from Egypt to the Promised Land.

And Moses sent messengers from Kadesh unto the king of Edom, Thus saith thy brother Israel, Thou knowest all the travail that hath befallen us:
How our fathers went down into Egypt, and we have dwelt in Egypt a long time; and the Egyptians vexed us, and our fathers:
And when we cried unto the Lord, he heard our voice, and sent an angel, and hath brought us forth out of Egypt: and, behold, we are in Kadesh, a city in the uttermost of thy border:
Let us pass, I pray thee, through thy country: we will not pass through the fields, or through the vineyards, neither will we drink of the water of the wells: we will go by the king's high way, we will not turn to the right hand, nor to the left, until we have passed thy borders.
And Edom said unto him, Thou shalt not pass by me, lest I come out against thee with the sword.

No passage for the Israelites

And the children of Israel said unto him, We will go by the high way: and if I and my cattle drink of thy water, then I will pay for it: I will only, without doing any thing else, go through on my feet.
And he said, Thou shalt not go through. And Edom came out against him with much people, and with a strong hand.
Thus Edom refused to give Israel passage through his border: wherefore Israel turned away from him.
(Numbers 20: 14-21)

This initial confrontation set the tone for the enmity that was to continue between the Hebrews and the Edomites.

**Idols of the
Nabateans**

The Nabateans, a nomadic tribe from northern Arabia began to move northwards into the biblical land of Edom in the early sixth century and gradually displaced the indigenous Edomite population, emerging as an independent and powerful force by the fourth century BC with their base at Petra. Its attractions were evident: a naturally defensive position, safe water supplies, fertile farming and grazing land, all combined with a strategic location near the junction of the silk and spice trade and caravan routes to the north and east. They brought from the Arabian Peninsula their worship of idols, their main gods being the male Dushara and the female Al-Uzza, the latter a fertility goddess identified with caravans and the morning star. Dushara, literally 'He of Sharra', was named after the Sharra mountains of the Petra region. These mountains are called 'Seir' in the Old Testament and Jehovah is also called 'He of Seir', suggesting that they were one and the same god. The Greeks later assimilated Dushara with Dionysus. Both Dushara and Al-Uzza are generally represented throughout Petra as blocks of stone or obelisks.

In character the Nabateans were known to have been unwarlike and hard-working. The classical historian Strabo, writing in the first century BC, gave us an interesting description of them:

A peaceful folk

The Nabateans are temperate and industrious...Having few slaves, they are served for the most part by relations or by each other, or they serve themselves, and the custom extends even to the kings. They form 'messes' of thirteen men each and two singing girls to each mess. The king in his great house holds many 'messes'. No one drinks more than eleven cups in one and then another golden beaker. Thus the king is a democratic one, so that in addition to serving himself he sometimes even serves others...Their cities are unwalled on account of peace. Most of it abounds in fruit except the olive: they use oil made of sesame. Their sheep are white haired, their oxen large; the country does not produce horses, camels render service instead of them...They think dead bodies no better than manure; as Heraclitus says, corpses are more to be thrown away than dung heaps. Wherefore they bury even their kings beside their privies. They honour the sun, setting up an altar in the house, making libation on it daily and using frankincense.

When they were threatened with attack, their preferred tactic, rather than fighting, was to buy the enemies off with valuable gifts. This they did successfully with the Greeks and the Romans, and during the turbulent history of the region, they managed to remain in practice largely

independent, though sometimes paying tribute to nomi-
nal rulers. When the last Nabatean king died in 106 AD,
Petra was incorporated into the new Roman province of
Arabia, and became its capital.

The Romans moved in and redesigned the city on
Roman lines, building the main colonnaded street, the
temples and the baths. After the second century BC the
Roman caravan city of Palmyra took much of Petra's
wealth as the trade routes changed and moved further
north. As in the remainder of the region, Christianity
made an early impact on the population, and by the
fourth century Petra had its own bishop and one of the
Nabatean tombs was converted into a church. The population dwindled over the next few centuries and nothing
is heard of Petra until the twelfth century when the
Crusaders settled there briefly, building two castles, one
inside and the other just outside the main valley. From
then until the nineteenth century, it sank into oblivion,
thought of by learned Europeans as a fabled city of leg-
endary wealth, like Atlantis.

In 1812 the interest in Petra was rekindled by the
curiosity of a young Anglo Swiss explorer, James
Burckhardt (1784–1817). Born in Basle, Switzerland, he
went to England in 1806 and had himself sponsored for a
period of ten years by the African Association, to make an
overland journey of discovery in the interior of Africa. He
devoted the next three years to the study of Arabic and
Muslim society and customs, for it was clear that he could
only make such a journey, travelling with caravans
through the Near East and Egypt, if he was disguised as a
Muslim pilgrim.

Setting off in 1809, aged 25, he was travelling from
Damascus to Cairo when he heard tales from his guides of
a remarkable ruined city hidden in rock mountains. When
he tried to enquire further about it, he found the locals
very defensive, and it was clear that they did not want
foreigners to find the place for fear that they would seek
its treasure and interfere with its activities. Such secrecy
was of course only fuel to the fire and Burckhardt, feign-
ing total disinterest in the city itself, announced his desire
to make a sacrifice to Aaron, knowing that Aaron's tomb
lay within it.

The guides saw little harm in this and duly led
Burckhardt, sacrificial goat in tow, down through the Siq,
where the first European eyes for six centuries fell on the
Treasury façade. Unable to conceal his excitement at this
discovery, he aroused the guides' suspicions, and one of
them even threatened him with a rifle. To save himself

BURCKHARDT'S PROVERBS

In between his travels, Burckhardt returned to Cairo and Alexandria for spells of recuperation, and it was in Cairo that he began collecting popular proverbial sayings. Unfortunately, in the editing process that occured after his death, many of the earthier sayings were omitted as too *'grossly indecent'* to be laid before the public *'although it must be acknowledged that they excelled in wit'*.

The following is a selection to chew over, perhaps at rest points during your tour of Petra:

If a serpent love thee, wear him as a necklace.
If the turbans complain of a slight wind, what must be the state of the inner drawers?
If the winding sheet be ragged, and the corpse washer one-eyed, and the bier
   broken, and the burial ground a saltish soil, then truly the deceased must
   belong to the inhabitants of hell.
If there be grease on thy hand, rub it off at thy nearest neighbour's.
Climb like a cucumber, fall like an aubergine.
Not everything round is a nut, not everything long is a banana.
An unmarried man is Satan's brother.
He who makes light of other men will be killed by a turnip.
He would burn down a city to light a cigarette.
He can swallow a camel but chokes on a mosquito.
Just like a goat, they bleat from afar and butt when they are near.
Better to ride a dung beetle than to tread on soft carpets.
Who does not think his fleas are gazelles?
The well is deep but the rope is short.
He who takes a donkey up a minaret must also bring it down again.
Bring your hearts together but keep your tents apart.
How many friends I had when my vines produced honey, how few now that
   they are withered.
After puberty, a husband or a grave.
As soon as they are told to save water everyone begins to drink.
Guests and fish stink after three days.
A woman's house is her tomb.
Everyone is perfectly satisfied with their own intelligence.
The whole world is nothing but the scraping of a donkey.
Three things prolong life: a big house, a swift horse and an obedient wife.
Good luck comes to him who has it, not to him who seeks it.
The unlucky mouse sees the cheese but not the cat.
The beauty of a man is in his intelligence: the intelligence of a woman is in her beauty.
However many times she has been passed over, marry the woman of noble birth.
Be good to your own wife and you can have your neighbour's.
The dung beetle, seeing its child on the wall, thinks it sees a pearl on a thread.
It is better to herd cattle than to rule men.
Spit upwards and it lands on our moustache, spit downwards and it lands on our beard.
For every bean full of weevils God supplies a blind grocer.
When I saw the mirage I threw away my water; now I have no water and no mirage.
What camel ever saw its own hump?
Use your own brains, for no one else will lend you his.
People who live on promontories know how to swim.
He flies from the drain and discovers the gutter.
Who has seen tomorrow?

Burckhardt proceeded without delay to the foot of Jebel Haroun, where he sacrificed the goat.

The party returned from the valley after dark, so he saw no more of the ruins. He continued his arduous journeys and died eight years later, his body utterly exhausted and worn out. He kept diaries throughout, but never lived to see them published.

Diaries and proverbs

Though Burckhardt's record of his findings at Petra was published in his book *Journeys through Syria and Nubia* the difficulty in reaching the remote location, together with the hostility of the local Bedouin, meant that very few foreigners visited the site until well into the twentieth century. The oft-quoted line describing Petra as '*a rose-red city half as old as Time*' was in fact written by an Englishman who had never left England's shore, in a poem created for an Oxford University competition in 1845!

The Site

As you set off from the entrance gate, the valley is at this stage, and for the first 15–20 minutes, quite wide and open. This section is the approach to the narrow gorge and is known as the Bab es-Siq, Gateway of the Siq. The first monuments you pass in this section are the curious **Djinn** (Arabic for 'spirit' or 'ghost') **Blocks**, a cluster of three free-standing rock cubes just to the right of the track. All three are thought to have been grave chambers; the third is the most elaborate as well as the largest. Its deeply grooved exterior also bears the crow-step pattern, a common Nabatean decoration and hallmark of Petra. Behind these Djinn Blocks are three wadis running north-south, in which the intrepid with plenty of time to spare will find further rock tombs and funeral monuments.

Three Djinn blocks

Continuing along the main path you come to the **Obelisk Tomb**, carved out of the cliff, on the left. It is in fact two superimposed tombs, the upper one with its four obelisks which catch the eye, the lower one a triclinium (grave chamber with rock benches round three sides), where relatives of the deceased would sit and feast at funeral banquets. Some 107 chambers of this sort with benches have been found throughout Petra, and it is thought that some of them were probably used purely for domestic purposes, like eating or even sleeping, rather than having definite funerary associations. Both components of the Obelisk Tomb date from the first century AD, the period of the last Nabatean kings. The tomb shows a strange mixture of influences – Egyptian in the pyramid-like obelisks and classical in the pillars, pediments and statue niche.

Obelisk Tomb

On the other side of the path, directly opposite the Obelisk Tomb is an inscription carved into the rock some 5m above the ground. It is written in both Nabatean Aramaic and in Greek, and announces the burial place of one of Petra's citizens. The Nabateans, being an Arabian tribe, spoke an Arabic dialect and by the late fourth century BC had adopted a form of vertically elongated Aramaic script, having become the lingua franca of the whole region when it was under Persian rule. It was from this Nabatean script that the elongated Kufic script and subsequently the conventional Arabic script evolved.

Origins of Arabic Script

The valley now turns to the right, but for those with time to make an extra detour of 45 minutes or so, a blue sign to the left of the path points to **Al-Madras**, a cult sanctuary area with a variety of monuments, almost like a separate suburb of Petra proper. Just 2m to the right of the Al-Madras sign is a tallish tree and from here the path begins, running behind the low stone wall obliquely to the south-west towards a group of rock cliffs. After crossing scrubland for five minutes, you arrive at the edge of an open rocky area, and from here on you must look out for the cairns that mark the way. Head in a westerly direction following the cairns for about another five minutes until you come to an open flat area of heavily weathered rock with a hollowed-out overhang above you to the left. Walking over to the far (west) edge of this flat area, you will join the original rock-cut stairway, badly worn but quite broad. Climb this as it heads to the south-west for a further ten minutes, until you emerge to see in the distance a large tree slightly to the right (at about 2 o'clock on an imaginary clockface) from which a group of four connected staircases leads up to Al-Madras. Scrambling up one of these, you enter a grassy enclosed area with rock-cut tombs, cisterns, niches, more staircases, various chambers and water channels. Slightly above is a twin-pooled area with an altar for sacrifices, or high place as these are called in Petra. Some 100m further to the north, reached by walking under a rock overhang, is another high place with two linked pools and many carved niches. Staircases lead off to further areas with caves and rockchambers, many bearing Nabatean inscriptions. One of these cites Dushara as the god of Al-Madras. All around are fabulous views of the distinctive Petra landscape, especially lovely at sunset. If you are just making the excursion to Al Madras, allow two hours for the round trip from the resthouse.

Detour to Al-Madras

Splendid sacrificial sites

Just after the right-hand bend in the valley you reach the entrance to the **Siq** gorge itself, by walking up a

Siq entrance

small ramp over a dam, then dropping back down again to the level of the gorge. This dam was built to seal off the Siq entrance, after a group of 23 tourists was drowned in a flash flood in 1963. While constructing it, the builders came across the traces of an original Nabatean dam and water channels, and were able to build on the old foundations to some extent. Clearly the Nabateans too had wanted to use the Siq as the entrance to the city all the year round and so had to protect it from the winter floods. At the same time, they had devised an elaborate water system for their needs, whereby water was channelled along canals cut into the rock wall of the Siq, and ,this channel can still be seen, especially on the left-hand side of the gorge, running at about head height. On the right-hand side are some sections of ceramic water pipe.

Almost immediately after entering, look up and you will notice the remains of a triumphal arch some 16m above the ground, which was intact until about 100 years ago. In Nabatean times the entire length of the Siq was paved with limestone blocks, though today only fragmented sections remain, raised up a little above today's more eroded canyon floor. **Collapsed arch**

If you are lucky, you can walk down the Siq in total silence, with perhaps just the occasional clatter of horses' hooves. Wheeled traffic is forbidden except for the trucks of the local inhabitants, transporting supplies or their families from the old city to their new settlement near Al-Baared. Noise is magnified by the high-sided ravine, but there are so many twists and turns along the way that horses clattering along just one or two bends away cannot be heard until they have virtually caught up with you.

At its narrowest point the gorge is a bare 2m wide, which makes the 100m high cliffs seem even more dramatic. The colours of the rock are mainly reds and browns, and among the shapes which the wind and water of eons have formed you can still spot the occasional niche containing carved blocks or pyramids of stone, primitive symbols of the Nabatean god. Fragments of rockstairways can be seen at many points leading off tantalisingly to neglected sanctuaries hidden in the cliffs. **Narrowest point**

The walk through the Siq takes little more than half an hour, yet it somehow seems longer because of all the twists and turns and because only rarely can you see ahead more than 20m. All the more remarkable then, is the moment when you first see, appearing in an unreal vision of sudden light, the magnificent façade of the **Treasury, Al-Khazneh**, awaiting you at the end of the **Breathtaking façade** blackened gorge. On your first visit, time your arrival here for between 10.00 and 11.00 am in summer months, or between 9.00 and 10.00 am in winter, to ensure that the sun will be striking the façade, bringing to life the natural rosy redness of the rock. If this is not possible, try late afternoon on your way back, when the setting sun can even enhance the natural redness. The Bedouin call the Treasury Al-Jerrah, the Urn, after the 4m high urn that sits on top of the circular middle section of the upper storey. Local superstition holds that in this urn is hidden Pharaoh's treasure. The urn itself is consequently the most damaged section of the façade, pockmarked with the rifle shot of relentless attempts to dislodge it or break it open to release the treasure. In fact, like the remainder of the monument, it is solid rock.

Pure perfection

In its sheltered position, the Treasury's architectural outlines have remained sharp and the decorative friezes and statues clear. The German scholar who saw it in 1911 described it as *'the most perfect two-storeyed façade which has been preserved in the East from antiquity until now'*.

Its original purpose, and even the exact date of its construction, have long remained a mystery. Some scholars dated it to the first century BC, others to the first or second centuries AD. Research in recent years has dated it to Aretas IV (died 40 AD). Some thought it was a temple to Isis/Tyche, the goddess represented in the centre of the upper storey, while others concluded from its plain interior, that it was the monumental tomb of a Nabatean king.

A puzzle for the experts

The absence of inscriptions has made the debate especially tricky, for stylistic characteristics are all that the experts have had to go on. The unique mixture of Hellenistic, Middle Eastern and Egyptian influences make this a fascinating study. Most scholars feel that foreign workmen and architects were brought in for the construction, as so many elements are alien to Nabatean design. The temple columns and capitals are Corinthian in inspiration, while the two giant obelisks which connect the top of the structure to the natural rockface are Egyptian. In the various niches and scattered among the other architectural features are many carved animals and humans; winged sphinxes, a lion, a panther, a snake, a man leading a horse, and dancing Amazons. The central statue of Isis/Tyche stands draped holding a cornucopia in her left hand, and shows a marked Alexandrian influence – Petra had extensive trading and cultural links with Alexandria. Others have seen her as Al-Uzza, the local goddess of caravan and caravaneers.

The main doorway into the interior, as well as the two smaller side entrances, originally had functioning wooden doors, for the door jambs can still be seen in the stone floor. The central chamber, in stark contrast to the façade, is disappointingly plain, a 12m hollow cube roughly carved from the rock, leading to other simple chambers.

In recent years a Bedouin with a camel has taken to lurking almost permanently by the Treasury touting for photographs and inviting you to mount.

Touting camels

Opposite the Treasury, to the right as you exit from the Siq, is another tomb, known as Tomb 64, and those with a love of rock-climbing and heights can scale the rocks to the left of it to arrive above its façade, for an excellent view across at the Treasury, making an interesting variation on the usual angle for photographs.

The path now continues round to the right and then to the left again, the cliffs on either side bearing many rock tombs of various designs and sizes. To the left of the path, just before the steps leading up to the High Place, a rock fall, the result of an earlier earthquake, has partially smashed the façade of what is generally considered one of the earliest Nabatean monuments.

As the Siq opens out considerably now, just past the sign and steps up to the **High Place**, you will see to your left a whole series of chambers (44 in all), cut into the cliff on four levels, and often therefore called the Four Streets of Façades. Again, the stylistic types are varied, and many are thought to have been dwellings rather than tombs. Some 100m further on, also on the left, is the Theatre, which you can visit on your return. For now, however, it is best to take the signposted steps up to the High Place, to the left just before the Streets of Façades.

This route to the High Place, which returns via the Wadi Farasa to Qasr el-Bint, takes about two and a half hours, so if you have arrived at the start around 10.00 am you can time your arrival at Qasr el-Bint and the refreshments area nicely to coincide with lunch. A morning ascent is also best as the route is largely in the shade until noon.

The steep climb up rocksteps and corridors takes about 35 minutes and is impressive for its sense of ascending into a different world, hushed and remote from the heart of Petra. It has the feel of a ceremonial way and it would indeed probably have been up these steps and along these corridors that the priest would have led the processions on their way to make their ritual sacrifice at this, the most important of Petra's many high places. As you reach the top of the narrow defile, it opens out, and to your

Ceremonial ascent

Obelisk deities   right (west) you will see two free-standing obelisks on a platform above you. Heading towards these, the way is generally clear, but if in doubt keep a look-out for the blue squares that are painted on rocks along the route.

The 7m high obelisks are unusual in that they were formed by cutting away all the rock, thereby creating a huge sandstone platform all around them. Like the obelisks in the temples of Egypt, they serve to mark the entrance to the sanctuary on the summit above, and it is presumed that they represented the two main Nabateans gods, Dushara and Al-Uzza.

Immediately above and to the north of the obelisks is the fort, thought to have been built with the rock that was chiselled out to form the obelisks. Heavily ruined, it has never been excavated or studied and there is consequently much dispute about its date. It has been seen as Nabatean, Roman, Byzantine or even Crusader.

From the fort, the approach to the High Place itself is to the north, towards the main valley of Petra, up the wide, heavily weathered rock steps and then a short clamber over the flat rock to reach the huge open summit.

Spectacular views   From here, it is the view which will captivate you first, with the dramatic volcanic mountains of Petra laid out all around you. To the left, at approximately 10 o'clock on an imaginary clockface, is the dramatic table mountain of Umm al-Biyarah, the highest of the local mountains and the site of the earliest inhabitants of Petra, the Edomites. This colossal rock has been identified by some scholars with the Sela of the Bible. The climb to the summit is one of the most arduous but exciting in all Petra. The love of high open places is thought to have been passed on by the Edomites to the Nabateans, along with their worship of male and female fertility gods.

Also to your left, but at about 11 o'clock, you will see the tiny white shrine on the top of Jebel Haroun. This is reputed to be the tomb of the Prophet Aaron, revered by Muslims and a place of pilgrimage for the devoted. At an angle of about 11.30 you can also see, if you know what to look for, the colossal façade of the Deir, or Monastery, the place you will be climbing to in the afternoon. Only the upper section of the façade is visible, seen as from the side, for the building faces west.

Cult sacrifices   The cult installations of the High Place are carved into the natural sandstone, and the major sacrifice area is the large rectangular altar with steps and the adjacent raised circular altar with channels where the blood of the animals would flow down to be collected in basins. The central court is a sunken rectangle with a bench cut round on three sides where the participants or observers of the sacrifice would probably have sat. Nothing is known for certain about the ceremonies that took place here, although the likelihood is that it was animals rather than people who were the offerings.

The path for the descent via the **Wadi Farasa** is not as clear as the ascent from the Theatre, but it is difficult to get lost, and the chances are that other visitors will be making the descent ahead of you, so you can always follow them.

Descending again past the fort, you will notice the makeshift refreshments area usually manned by a local Bedouin family, with simple chairs and tables laid out, selling tea and cold drinks and the odd postcard. Continuing some 50m past it (to the south), you follow the straight line of the rock, until you notice on your right some rough steps leading down into a gulley between the rocks. The path leads on across a red stony track for about 100m until you reach a fork where you continue straight on to see an area with a flat grey façade bearing some Nabatean Aramaic inscriptions near the bottom. Steep steps lead down from here, before going up, then down, then up again. They lead to a flat area with a strangely shaped overhanging rock carved with a fine 1.5m tall medaillon, hidden behind a group of small boulders. It consists of a human bust thought to be the female fertility goddess Al-Uzza, and a Dushara block beneath.

Steps up...
...and
down

The path now leads on through a narrow stone corridor which passes out into an open terraced area with a huge headless lion carved into the rock on your left. Beside it are the remains of a water cascade, and water would originally have been channelled out of its mouth and into a large basin below. The Nabateans often used the lion to represent deities, and it has been suggested that it could be the male god Dushara. It is this lion which gives its name to the Wadi below, Farasa meaning 'beast of prey' in Arabic.

Headless lion

From the lion, steep steps wind down through an impressive rock corridor overhang and past weird rock formations. You can see down into the wadi floor quite clearly. The total time for the descent to the valley bottom from the High Place is about 45 minutes.

From the foot of the staircase, you will see the first main monument of the Wadi Farasa on your right, known as the Garden Tomb, a fine classical façade with two free-standing columns in the centre. Immediately to the right of it, just by a huge wall, a worn staircase can be clambered up to see the huge cistern which collected the water from all directions. The water system at Petra was highly

Garden Tomb

Roman Soldier tomb

Elegant arch

Shelterless walk

Pharaoh's Pillar

sophisticated, and water was conducted to several main cisterns from large distances all around.

From the Garden Tomb, steps lead down into a large wadi which opens out to reveal the next tomb, that of the Roman soldier on the left. The three niches above the door contain badly weathered statues, the central one of which is a headless male figure dressed in a Roman soldier's short tunic. Opposite is a fine carved triclinium or three benched feast room which has the most remarkable interior of any monument in Petra, with carved pillars in multicoloured sandstone with red marbled swirls.

More steps now lead on down to the wadi and you will see on your right, the elegant façade of the arched Renaissance Tomb, the only tomb with this style of façade in Petra. Fifty metres further on, you have to turn and look up the cliff into a raised terrace area to your right to see the Broken Pediment Tomb, its façade facing out towards the north, the direction in which you are walking. A worn staircase leads up to it and the rock colours are again in fine bright reds. From the excess of droppings all around and the pungent smell, it is clearly still in frequent use as a goat pen.

From here it is a further 30 minutes' walk along sandy paths and with no shelter from the sun, northwards to reach Qasr el-Bint and the main street of Petra. Following the line of cliff tombs from the Broken Pediment Tomb round to the right, you then continue straight on along a path that leads across the summit of a rubble-strewn hill. Heading straight across the ridge of this hill, you have a fine view of Corinthian tomb façades in the distance to the right. Continuing along the ridge, you bend round to the left (south) of a small protrusion which has tombs converted into houses underneath. As the path leads on, you can see a small area of excavations below, where traces of the southern city wall still run. The ground is often littered with fragments of Nabatean pottery, mainly from the first and second century AD, and from the amount of debris, this is thought to have been the city rubbish dump in Roman times.

The path leads on round the north side of a further hillock to reach the solitary **Pharaoh's Pillar**, known by the locals as Dhibb Far'oun or Pharaoh's Penis, a tall column of ten rather stumpy drums. Next to it are the fallen segments of a similar drum, and the two are thought to have marked the entrance to a Nabatean palace or temple, possibly similar in role to the two obelisks as fertility symbols marking the approach to the High Place.

From Pharaoh's Pillar you can walk along the upper path to the north-west to where a blue sign announces **Al-Habees Crusader Castle**, at the foot of the rocky outcrop. You can walk down to the refreshments area at the base of Al-Habees (The Prison), or, if you still have the energy, make the short but steep ascent to the castle on the summit, returning on the other side of the hill via the museum, then on down to the refreshments area. The climb to the lowest level of the castle takes no more than ten minutes and is up a path heavily strewn with goat droppings. The castle is surprisingly well constructed. Wooden planks lead across to the higher level, and from the highest point, the small square keep, you have a fine view over the city below. The role of this castle was thought to have been an observation post, subsidiary to the main castle of Al-Woairah which lies on a rocky outcrop outside the main valley of Petra, and is more defensive in nature. The Crusaders only occupied Petra for a relatively short period, and abandoned it at the end of the twelfth century.

Ascent to Al-Habees castle

To make the descent via the Al-Habees High Place and the museum, you head towards the northernmost point of the rock summit, from where you will see the beginning of a rock staircase, very small and rather sandy. Descending carefully, as the sand can make it slippery, you come after a few minutes to a fine area with open shelves of rock from where you have good views down into the Wadi es-Siyagh to your left. In this area you will notice the large sunken court of the high place and many tombs cut into the rock all around. A fine rock corridor leads along the northern edge of the Al-Habees outcrop, and suddenly you come out on to the side of a final flight of steps down to the **museum**. It is open from 8.00 am to 4.00 pm and consists of a long straight hall carved out of the hillside with windows cut at intervals. Above the entrance is a Pharaoh's head carved like that of a Greek god, and inside is a selection of Edomite exhibits, with fragments of Roman carving and sculptures of Roman gods. Below and to the side, many houses are carved into the hillside, and the guardian of the site and the museum lives here.

Rock-cut museum

Down in the wadi, set low and surrounded by oleander bushes, the rather smart modern building is the grandly named Forum Restaurant (which in fact serves only cold snacks and drinks), where you can have a well-earned rest. Alternatively, you can choose any of the refreshment tents that are grouped around Qasr el-Bint. One of these, called the Nabatean Shop, is run by the sons of the local

Refreshments round Qasr el-Bint

sheikh, the mukhtar or headman of the Bdul tribe, formerly resident in Petra, but now rehoused by the government in their new breeze-block settlement on the Beidha road. The sheikh is a hard-working and diligent man, and has single handedly constructed a rough road to his cultivated piece of land in an off-shoot valley. Here, like a true descendant of the Nabateans, he has devised complex water channels for irrigation and is proudly growing tomatoes, cucumbers, melons, aubergines, grapes, olives and sunflowers in profusion.

Whilst resting and gaining strength for the afternoon ascent to Ed-Deir, you can gaze at the imposing Qasr el-Bint, the only free standing building remaining at Petra. You can also see the large unfinished tomb cut into the façade of Al-Habees next to it, which illustrates well the technique of carving from the top down. Just adjacent to it **Dovecote tomb** is the Dovecote or Columbarium Tomb, carved with numerous tiny square hollows in which it is thought the Nabateans placed urns containing the ashes of their dead. Some scholars have seen it rather as a later Byzantine construction for keeping doves and pigeons.

Qasr el-Bint (Palace of the Maiden), the most important Nabatean temple at Petra, was built in the first century BC. The maiden referred to is thought by one early scholar to be the daughter of the Pharaoh, who lived in the temple but deplored the lack of water. She announced that she **To marry for** would marry the man who laid on a water supply to the **water** palace. One suitor finally succeeded with the help of 'God, men and camels', and married the princess. Excavations have indeed revealed a stone water channel and drain at the foot of the temple.

The imposing building, made from blocks of local sandstone, still rises in places to about 25m high and its monumental approach stairway is still well preserved. At the heart of the temple is the holy of holies, where the sacred object would have stood on the raised central platform. There is no longer any trace of this object, but excavations here in 1959 discovered a possible clue to what it was in the form of a fragment from an enormous clenched human hand in marble. From the scale of this hand, the statue to which it belonged would have stood over 7m tall.

The external decoration of the temple is still well preserved in places, with Doric friezes, roundels and rosettes. In a few places at the back and on the western wall, there **Traces of colour** are still traces of the coloured plaster which once covered the walls. The human busts which had adorned some of the niches were destroyed, along with many of Petra's human representations, in a fit of iconoclasm. The temple

Morning light captures the pink glow of carved sandstone on the Treasury at Petra (Vine).

The Palace Tomb at Petra (Darke).

The spectacular Wadi Rum (Vine).

The Dome of the Rock, Jerusalem (Darke).

Church of the Resurrection, Jerusalem (Darke).

*Church of St Anne, Jerusalem
(Darke).*

fell into disuse in the late Roman period, but it was reused in Byzantine and medieval times when it seemed to have been adapted to serve as living quarters or stables.

For many people the ascent to **Ed-Deir** rivals the climb to the High Place as the most exciting and memorable excursion at Petra. It is longer, 50–60 minutes depending on age and fitness, but exceptionally scenic throughout, with magnificent vistas over the rocks and gorges of the whole Wadi Musa area. The round trip from the refreshment area will take about 2½ hours, and the afternoon is the best time, both to benefit from the shade on the way up, and to get the effect of the sun shining directly on the façade of the monument when you get there.

Afternoon ascent best

From Qasr el-Bint you head north down over the new bridge across the wadi, past the Forum Restaurant on your right, and follow the track into the valley. Half the building housing the Forum Restaurant serves as the Department of Antiquities Administration and Conservation Centre. It was built in the early 1980s by the Petra Forum Hotel. There was a heated dispute over who should run the restaurant. The local Bedouin were against the foreign management coming in and controlling the tourist trade and taking all the profit for themselves – it was closed for some years, but is now open again.

After five minutes' walk along the path beyond the Forum Restaurant, you reach a short ravine where some blue and white signs mark the **Lion Triclinium**, a fine carved tomb, whose classical façade you can see over the signs. A brief detour from the path takes you to see this tomb up closer, with twin lions flanking each side, and two Medusa heads in its frieze below the pediment.

Twin lions

Returning to the path, you now reach the first flight of steps, and shortly afterwards you slide past a huge rock from an earlier landslip which nearly blocks the path. After another 15 minutes, the ravine divides and you take the left fork. If you wish, a 15-minute detour into the ravine to the right will bring you to another tomb, known as the Wadi Kharareeb Biclinium.

Rock landslip

The main track climbs up, zigzagging sometimes in stairways, sometimes just on rocky paths, and the clear air and the superb views are unforgettable. After 40 minutes of climbing you reach a wide rock platform where the stairs make a sharp turn to the west (left). Leaving the main path at this point and clambering over the rock to the north (right), a further detour brings you after about ten minutes to a dramatic 50m rock ledge with an overhang cut into the west wall of a steep ravine. This is a rock sanctuary, known as **Qattar ed-Deir** or El-Hammam (the

Watery rock sanctuary

Bath or Pool), from the water which drips down the rock and collects in moss-covered basins carved out of the corridor floor. Niches are cut into the rock wall, and from the ledge there is a vertical drop into the ravine.

Returning to the main path and continuing the climb for a further few minutes, you reach the sign pointing to the **Christian Hermitage**. Here, immediately to the right of the path, is a series of caves with crosses carved inside them, thought to have been etched out by early Christian hermits.

Early hermits

Just five minutes beyond this, after a scramble over a rock wall, you find yourself quite suddenly on the edge of a huge open sandy terrace with the colossal rock façade of **Ed-Deir** dwarfing you to the right. At 45m high by 50m wide, it is easily the largest monument in all Petra. The urn on the top alone is 10m high. Its name, meaning The Monastery, originates from the number of small crosses carved into the interior rear wall, which suggest that the place was used by the early Christians of Petra in the fourth century, attracted by its isolated position. It is generally thought to have been a Nabatean temple originally, but some experts also consider it likely that it could have been the unfinished tomb of one of the Nabatean kings – unfinished because the niches appear never to have held any statues or decoration. It is dated to the first century AD, a little later than the Treasury, to which it obviously bears a strong resemblance, though its stone colour is much yellower, and its lines much bolder and more imposing. Inside the single rockchamber is a recessed arch which would have held the sacred object of worship.

Largest monument in Petra

Temple or tomb

The route you have ascended from Qasr el-Bint was the original processional way up to Ed-Deir, and the size of the open courtyard in front of the monument suggests that ceremonies took place here on a huge scale.

Those with a love of climbing will not be able to resist the temptation to climb up to the urn on the top of the monument itself. The route is not particularly difficult and was evidently used by the priests. It begins on the rocky outcrop that juts forward from the left (northern) side of the façade, and on approaching, you will notice a series of rather worn steps cut into the rock. Following these, you soon come to a large altar area where sacrifices were presumably made, and from the altar, the steps continue in little flights to the upper edge of the façade, from where a simple scramble round the back brings you out on to the dome of the urn. A friend from below could photograph you there, to give an idea of the scale of the building.

Clamber up to the urn

Built under an overhanging rock opposite Ed-Deir is a refreshment stall offering cold drinks. The family running it lives just behind in a house carved from a free-standing rock cone. A TV aerial protrudes incongruously from the rock roof, and the Bedouin mother hangs out the washing on the line while the children and goats play beside her. In the rocky outcrop directly facing the façade of Ed-Deir you will see a huge gaping chamber, inside which is a small carved temple façade as well as much modern grafitti.

The comforts of home

Walking still further west away from the Ed-Deir façade you will come out onto a wide ledge with an excellent view down over the Wadi Araba. The little white sanctuary of Aaron stands out on a distant hilltop, and beyond the ledge a little path leads to the north-west towards another cluster of caverns. One of these, a three-benched triclinium is sometimes kitted out with cushions and used by the Forum Restaurant to serve lunches to tour groups.

Dramatic viewing spot

If you have more time or do not want to make the strenuous climb up to Ed-Deir, a pleasant walk can be spun out to about an hour into the **Wadi es-Siyagh**, perhaps whilst waiting for companions to return from Ed-Deir.

Heading past the museum and the post office installed in a tomb, you follow the line of the mountain of Al-Habees round to the left (westwards) to enter the wadi. The cliffs on both sides are riddled with caves and chambers. A newly built staircase on the right leads up to a room, now kept locked, which still has traces of Nabatean wall paintings on plaster. It is not possible, unfortunately, to be shown these paintings, but they are mainly in panels of red, brown or yellow ochre with blue or black edging, some depicting doorways, some with pediments and an eagle on top.

After a few minutes you come to a junction where the Wadi es-Siyagh leads to the right and the Wadi Kharroub to the left. Keeping to the Wadi es-Siyagh, you will soon reach the large Nabatean quarry to your right. As you stroll on further, the wadi floor becomes sandy and the vegetation grows lusher until you reach the spring, Ain es-Siyagh, the most abundant water source in Petra. In summer it is a fairly small trickle, but in winter it can swell sufficiently to create a waterfall a little further on.

Petra's water source

From Qasr el-Bint, the most challenging and strenuous half-day climb is to **Umm al-Biyarah**, the high rock massif that dominates the whole valley of Petra. In summer the ascent is best made in the afternoon, when the approach is mainly in the shade, and a local guide is advisable as the path is tricky in places and not always clear. One of the boys at the refreshments tent will be pleased to assist for a fairly nominal fee. Three hours should be allowed for the return trip from the starting point of Qasr el-Bint, spending about 45 minutes on the summit.

Heading off in the direction of Pharaoh's Pillar, you climb over the ridge and walk down into the Wadi el-Thugra, from where you have a good view of the fine and varied façades carved into the base of Umm al-Biyarah. Some are thought to have been tombs, others simply dwellings. Just to the left of these a blue sign announces Umm al-Biyarah. A crevice in the rock behind this point **Processional** was where the original processional way up the mountain **ramp and** would have begun, but a landslide has now blocked it **stairway** totally with debris, forcing you to continue further south to make a five-minute detour before turning uphill just past a solitary tree. A short ascent up loose rubble from here brings you suddenly to the cliff face where the Nabateans cut a spectacular high-sided rock stairway and walled corridor ramp, the most impressive of any in Petra, with a truly processional feel to it as it zigzags magnificently upwards.

Further on however, it is blocked by a huge fallen rock, and the path narrows considerably and leads along loose rubble or a series of worn steps, often obstructed by debris and frequently close to vertiginous drops. It is in fact more like a climb than a walk, with several sections of **Scrambling** scrambling on all fours up narrow gulleys where the orig- **over rockslips** inal stairway has been blocked by falling rocks. You reach the summit from the south side after about 40 minutes' climb from the monumental rock corridor, and once on top, the summit is surprisingly extensive. Totally exposed and shadeless, it slopes off slightly uphill to the north, and it takes a good 15 minutes to walk from one edge to the other. The majority of the Edomite settlement is in fact towards the centre of the summit. The British archaeologist Mrs Crystal Bennett conducted excavations on this summit for three years in the mid-1960s. The team of **Helicopter** excavators camped here and their food and water sup- **deliveries** plies were delivered by helicopter.

Petra's earliest The low walls of the Edomite dwellings are remarkable **dwellings** largely for their age, dating to the seventh century BC, predating the first Nabateans by some three centuries. The walls are built from flat slabs of limestone, broken off in their natural horizontal formation, and the settlement is calculated to have housed no more than 100 people.

It was long believed that Umm al-Biyarah was the biblical Sela, referred to in Chronicles and Kings II in

connection with King Anaziah of Judaea. This king took
10,000 Edomites prisoner and marched them to the summit of the rock at Sela and had them thrown to their
deaths. The excavations by Mrs Crystal-Bennett however, revealed that the Umm al-Biyarah Edomite settlement
began 100 years later than the Sela episode in the Bible.

Continuing to the far eastern edge that faces out over
the Petra valley towards Qasr el-Bint, you come to a
superb man-made sitting terrace area cut from the rock
on the very rim. It is like a small rectangle and is thought
to be part of a Nabatean temple. Perched beside the vertiginous drop here, it seems like the ideal spot from
which to cast unwanted prisoners. Nearby, scattered on
the hillside, are various blocks of Nabatean carvings,
among which are two especially fine sculptures, one of
which shows an angel-like figure with splayed wings,
while others have fine floral designs. Along the north-
eastern edge are nine rock cisterns coated with plaster to
make them water-tight. They are thought to have been
Edomite rather than Nabatean, and it is from them that
the mountain takes its name, Mother of the Cisterns.

Dizzy edge

**Mother of the
Cisterns**

It is now worth walking back across the summit to the
far western point, from where the view over the Wadi
Araba and the Jebel Aaron makes one of the most spectacular volcanic landscapes you are ever likely to see.
From this vantage point, you can almost visualise the
moment when these jagged black rocks seethed and
erupted from the earth's crust. Far to the south, the guide
will also point out the valley of Sabra, a whole day's
excursion.

From the Qasr el-Bint you can walk back along the
main street through the heart of ancient Petra. Most of the
buildings are now reduced to low walls and foundations,
the result of the major earthquakes in 363, 551 and 747.

The first 200m is the open temenos area or holy precinct
for the Qasr el-Bint temple, with low walls and rows of
benches where dignitaries would possibly have sat to
watch the religious ceremonies. Marking the entrance to
the sacred precinct at the end of the temenos is the
Monumental Gateway which with Qasr el-Bint is the
tallest and best-preserved of the structures left in the city
centre. Built in the mid-second century AD it is styled like
a traditional Roman gateway, with one main doorway
flanked by two smaller ones, though the linking arch is
now missing. Just to the right of the gateway a vestibule
leads to the baths, a series of three rooms, each capped
with a dome. Looking down through the light-hole in the
roof into the oddly deep and narrow interior, you can

**Monumental
gateway**

make out eight half-columns built into the walls. In some rooms nearby, which have also been excavated recently, traces of coloured plasterwork can still be seen, mainly reds and yellows.

Immediately after the Monumental Gateway you reach the **Cardo Maximus**, the paved colonnaded main street of Petra. Its total length is 240m, and in excavations in the 1950s it was cleared of the 40cm layer of dirt and rubble with which the Christian Byzantine inhabitants had covered it. The lack of wheel ruts in the paving stones suggests it may have been a pedestrian zone, or perhaps camels continued to be used in preference to horses.

Petra High Street

To the left after passing through the gateway, a staircase begins the climb to higher ground, where the remains can be found of what is generally called the **Temple of the Winged Lions**, dating to the first century AD. A bridge used to cross the Wadi Musa river bed from these steps, and then lead on up to the hillock, but now it is easier to follow the path up to it. The temple is worth a visit for the lovely decoration carved on the blocks of the column capitals showing winged lions crouched on floral beds. Excavations on it began in 1973. Its raised position makes it a good vantage point and behind it, further to the north, you can see the track that leads into the Wadi Turkmaniya, where the Turkmaniya Tomb with its famous inscription can be found.

Raised temple

To the right after passing through the Monumental Gateway, a large staircase leads up to the unexcavated building generally known as the **Corinthian Temple**. From the size and number of the column drums and blocks, it has been speculated that this might have been the Petra equivalent of a city hall, the centre of its commercial and administrative affairs. Today the collapsed drums look like colossal round biscuits that have fallen in a row out of the packet. As you continue along the street, all the area to the right is thought to have been markets and shops dating from Roman and Byzantine times. The local Bdul today continue the tradition with souvenir and refreshment stalls.

Petra city hall

As you reach the end of the Cardo Maximus, the late afternoon sun will be striking the façades of the four Royal Tombs cut into the mountain known as **El-Khutba**. They were thought to have been used for the burial of the Nabatean royal family in the first century BC.

Double-decker Urn Tomb

The first tomb you come to is the **Urn Tomb** which stands out from the others because of the two-storeyed arched vaults which jut out in front. The local Bdul refer to these vaults as As-Sijn, The Prison, and to the whole

The Deir at Petra (Vine).

tomb as Al-Mahkama, The Court. If indeed the building was ever used for these two purposes, it was certainly also used as a church in the fifth century, and the Bishop of Petra had the monumental staircase built to approach it. The main tomb façade is simple, with the unusual feature of a window carved out of the rock. Among the decorations are some heavily eroded human busts, thought to be either Nabatean deities or possibly the inhabitants of the tomb.

Monumental staircase approach

The next tomb along to the left is the **Corinthian Tomb**, strongly influenced in its façade by the Treasury. Its lower storey is curiously assymmetrical, with each of the three doors in a different style.

Largest façade in Petra

Next door on the left is the **Palace Tomb**, reminiscent of a Roman palace design, and boasting the largest façade in all Petra, with three storeys. Much of the uppermost storey has collapsed, as it was stone-built rather than cut into the rock, and the whole is quite badly weathered from its exposed position. Restoration work is currently being attempted.

A few minutes' walk further beyond the Palace Tomb you will notice to the left the edge of the Byzantine ramparts and the harmonious façade of the **Tomb of Sextius Florentinus**, Roman governor of the province of Arabia in the second century AD. Two rock ramps lead up to a terrace. Among the decoration over the door is a faint relief of a Medusa and the hydra, and an eagle.

With the help of a guide, it is possible from here to walk back to the Petra Forum Hotel, avoiding the Siq altogether. It is about 3km and takes about $1^1/_4$ hours, but if you attempt it without a guide, take a compass and allow about two hours for wrong turnings. Skirting around the west face of El-Khutba, there are numerous caves, rooms, cisterns and niches cut into the rock to the

House of Dorotheos

right, the largest of which the **House of Dorotheos**, 400m beyond the Sextius Florentinus Tomb. On the opposite side of the wadi, the cliffs of **Mughar an-Nasara**, Caves of the Christians, riddle the rock face. You continue to follow the course of the wadi as it skirts the edge of the mountain block of El-Khutba, and after you have left El-Khutba about 500m behind and the wadi course becomes small and narrow, you must head right (south) and climb across the rock until you reach the ridge which allows you to see in the next wadi to the south.

From this ridge you must comb the landscape in front of you until you see, tucked into a small wadi a little to the right (south-east) about 500m away, a single arched

Roman aqueduct

Roman aqueduct spanning a narrow gulley. Its stone blocks, which still stand almost intact, are the same colour as the surrounding rock, making it quite tricky to spot. This is the key landmark, and you must now head over the ridge and down the other side to enter the wadi that runs virtually due south, about 200m to the right of the aqueduct. This is the wadi that will eventually disgorge you into the area just north of the Petra Forum Hotel, but it is still easy to lose your way, as there are many confusing offshoots and deceptive goat tracks. Stick to the left side of the wadi as you enter, and after following the small path for about ten minutes, you will come to a rock staircase, the upper end of which has been blocked by a colossal rock over five cubic metres in size.

To continue on the path, you have to slither through a small gap that remains between the rock and the cliff face. Carved into the fallen rock is a group of three niches. At this point you are on the right-hand side of the wadi, but about ten minutes later, as the wadi opens out slightly, you cross to the left-hand side, where you will notice a water channel carved into the cliff side. Following this channel for a few more minutes brings you out into an area of white boulders and above them in the distance you will see the Petra Forum Hotel.

Slip between the rocks

On the top of El-Khutba mountain is the largest complex of **high places** in Petra, and of the four possible ascents, the most comfortable begins to the right of the Urn Tomb. Just after the beginning of the staircase approach to the tomb, you turn off south-east onto an ancient staircase which, in a tiring 30-minute climb, leads through small wadis and gaps in the rock, to reach the summit. To your left and above you as you emerge is an unusual rock altar approached by steps and within a 100m radius you will come across two more well-preserved high places. With the help of a guide you can find the wide staircase that leads down to the Sextius Florentinus Tomb, to make the descent by a different route if you wish.

Tiring ascent

Beyond the Royal Tombs, retracing your steps towards the Siq, you come to the **Theatre** on your right. Despite heavy weathering it is still impressive for its size and for the work it must have entailed to cut 40 rows of seats out of the rock. Dating, like the Treasury, to the time of Aretas IV (died 40 AD), it was later reworked by the Romans after they took Petra in 106 AD, but all the masonry collapsed in the violent earthquake of 363. It would have held some 8000 spectators.

Rock seats

Directly opposite the Theatre you can clamber up to an unnamed series of tombs, some of which have splendid natural colourings in all shades of yellows, reds, mauves and even blue. From the terrace in front of the highest cluster, you can get an unusual view down into the central basin of Petra to the west.

In the area of the Theatre and throughout the approach down the main road to Qasr el-Bint, there are several caves selling soft drinks and souvenirs.

If you arrive at Petra in the late afternoon or early evening with only an hour or two of daylight left, there are two possible excursions to choose from: the walk to El-Madras, described earlier, or the drive to Siq el-Baared and Beidha, visiting Al-Woairah, the ruined Crusader castle *en route*.

Petra suburb

The drive to **Siq el-Baared** makes a good introduction to Petra, as it is like a miniature suburb, sometimes referred to as 'Little Petra'. The new tarred road starts just by the Petra Forum Hotel and runs for 10km away from the Wadi Musa to the north. After 2km, as the road begins to climb, you can see on your left the crumbling remains of **Al-Woairah**, well camouflaged against the rock, looking distinctly less impressive from here than it does once you have walked up to it. Stopping when you are directly opposite the ruins and at the same height as them, you can walk straight over towards them, following the course of a small gulley which leads round in about five minutes

Splendid castle entrance

to the surprisingly splendid castle entrance across a vertical moat-like chasm. Steps lead up into the castle precinct through a hollowed rock. Inside, little remains beyond a few walls and odd rooms, but the site itself is impressive, sheer-sided and totally inaccessible except from the man-made entrance. Al-Woairah is the major Crusader castle of Petra, considerably bigger and more important than the subsidiary castle on the summit of Al-Habees. Built in the twelfth century, its Crusader name was Le Vaux Moise, the Valley of Moses, or in Arabic Wadi Musa.

From caves to breeze-block huts

Continuing on the way to Beidha, the road passes through the new breeze-block housing settlement of the Bdul, the local inhabitants of Petra. They used to live in caves and tents within the valley of Petra itself, but the government moved them up to this settlement and laid on water and sanitary facilities. This is where the mukhtar now lives in his two houses, one for each of his wives. By his Egyptian wife he has eight children and by his Jordanian one five. Like many other settled tribes, they feel that whilst their material comforts may have improved, their quality of life has suffered.

Where the tarmac stops, a sign points left to the ruins of Beidha, while straight ahead is an iron gate entrance to **Siq el-Baared**, presaged by the fine carved rock temple to the left, and often surrounded by Bedouin tents and grazing flocks. A guardian will appear with the keys, and you can then enter the miniature gorge. It is impressive for its

Set of three gorges

compactness, with three narrow openings leading to three gorges. Everywhere there are traces of Nabatean water channels and there are even rock hooks for tying up animals while they drank. To judge from their height, they were designed for camels, not for horses. On almost every cliff face there are steps, some heavily worn, some less so, leading up to mysterious high places. The most impressive and the most accessible of these is in the second of the three areas, to the right immediately as you enter.

Pushing through the branches of a tree that grows right up against the rock face, you will come to the flight of steps that leads up to an altar area, and higher still, a second altar area which makes a good point from which to savour the view.

Flowering pink oleander bushes lend attractive colour to the gorges, and families still live in some of the caves, in what appear to be quite well-appointed dwellings. At the end of the third gorge, a final staircase leads up onto an open terrace and out into the top of the adjacent valley. Steps lead down and beyond, giving a good idea of how all these extraordinary valleys are linked through endless series of steps and networks of paths.

The Stone-Age site of **Beidha**, dated by excavations to 7000 BC, lies 1km from the Siq al-Baared entrance, along a rough dirt track. As with many neolithic sites, it is unimpressive to the layman, appearing like a series of house foundations, now fenced in. Many of the houses still have the large stone hollowed out in the centre that was used as a communal eating bowl by the family. The old Bedouin guardian here, skinny as a rake and with one gold tooth, looks after the two sites and spent four years helping Mrs Diana Kirkbride with the excavations some 20 years ago. She earned his undying loyalty by living in a tent nearby and paying him regular amounts of money.

Loyal guardian

Sabra and Jebel Haroun

This is a whole day's excursion and needs to be done with a guide, taking your own water and provisions. Like Siq al-Baared, though much larger, it is a self-contained Nabatean suburb, even having its own rock theatre. It takes some two hours to reach from the Qasr el-Bint area, either on foot or on horseback. The scenery *en route* is fabulous, as you go through a succession of wadis and past several mountains, including **Jebel Haroun** with its white sanctuary on the summit at 1396m.

Fabulous scenery

To climb this takes a further two hours starting from Qasr el-Bint, but the path is unclear in places and a guide is recommended. All but the last 20 minutes can be done on horseback. The tomb itself was restored by the Mamluke Sultan Qal'aoun in the thirteenth century, and Greek Orthodox monks lived in it until that time. It is now kept locked and is still venerated as a holy shrine by Muslims and Christians alike.

The death of Aaron

And the Lord spake unto Moses and Aaron in mount Hor, by
the coast of the land of Edom, saying,
Aaron shall be gathered unto his people: for he shall not enter

*into the land which I have given unto the children of Israel,
because ye rebelled against my word at the water of Meribah.
Take Aaron and Eleazar his son, and bring them up unto mount
Hor:*

**The death of
Aaron**

*And strip Aaron of his garments, and put them upon Eleazar
his son: and Aaron shall be gathered unto his people, and shall
die there.
And Moses did as the Lord commanded: and they went up into
mount Hor in the sight of all the congregation.
And Moses stripped Aaron of his garments, and put them upon
Eleazar his son; and Aaron died there in the top of the mount:
and Moses and Eleazar came down from the mount.
And when all the congregation saw that Aaron was dead, they
mourned for Aaron thirty days, even all the house of Israel.*
(Numbers 20: 23-29)

The Pilgrim Trail

From Petra, the final stage of the King's Highway continues south for some 20km to join up with the Amman-
Aqaba desert highway. Whereas the road along the King's
Highway follows the ridge along which castles and towns
were built by the Crusaders, the faster desert road, finished in 1961, follows the old Darb el-Hajj or Pilgrim Trail,
the ancient road for pilgrims heading to Mecca.

**Pilgrim route to
Mecca**

After the Crusades, the history of Jordan is a virtual
blank. The Egyptian Mamlukes took some interest in the
country for a while, building a fort at Aqaba and repairing
Kerak and Shawbak. Then, under the Ottoman Empire,
where it formed part of the *vileyet* or province of Syria, the
Turks built a chain of fortified watering places for the
benefit of the pilgrims. Since that time, in the sixteenth
century, the pilgrim route to Mecca followed this chain of
fortresses or *qal'as*, spaced out at rough intervals of 35km,
a day's caravan journey. The qal'as were guarded by a
handful of Turkish soldiers and usually had a resident
Bedouin family to see to food and water requirements.
Two reservoirs were maintained at each fort, one for animals, the other for people, and during droughts, Bedouin
and villagers were enlisted to fill the reservoirs in advance
of the great caravan. The building of the Hejaz railway
put an end to this traditional foot pilgrimage once it was
built as far as Medina in 1908.

In the nineteenth century a number of Europeans followed this route, including Doughty and Burckhardt. In
1876 Doughty joined a hajj caravan of 6000 pilgrims and
10,000 beasts, and described his experiences in his book

Jolly caravans

Arabia Deserta. These caravans were jolly affairs, and
wherever they stopped for a couple of days' rest, a market

fair was held to coincide with it. At some major junctions, where the caravan would stop for several days whilst waiting for pilgrims from other routes to join it, these fairs would last for days amid much revelry. At Zerqa, the pilgrims would amuse themselves hunting the then plentiful wild boar.

Wadi Rum

Today, the major distraction *en route* to Aqaba is the fabled **Wadi Rum**.

We were riding for Rumm, the northern water of the Beni Atiyeh: a place which stirred my thoughts, as even the unsentimental Howeitat had told me it was lovely...Day was still young as we rode between two great pikes of sandstone to the foot of a long, soft slope poured down from the domed hills in front of us. It was tamarisk-covered: the beginning of the Valley of Rumm, they said. We looked up on the left to a long wall of rock, sheering in like a thousand-foot wave towards the middle of the valley...The hills on the right grew taller and sharper...They drew together until only two miles divided them: and then, towering gradually till their parallel ramparts must have been a thousand feet above us, ran forward in an avenue for miles...The crags were capped in nests of domes, less hotly red than the body of the hill; rather grey and shallow. They gave the finishing semblance of Byzantine architecture to this irresistible place: this processional way greater than imagination. The Arab armies would have been lost in the length and breadth of it, and within the walls a squadron of aeroplanes could have wheeled in formation. Our little caravan grew self-conscious, and fell dead quiet, afraid and ashamed to flaunt its smallness in the presence of the stupendous hills...Landscapes, in childhood's dream, were so vast and silent.
(T.E. Lawrence *Seven Pillars of Wisdom*: Ch LXII).

Greater than imagination

To get anywhere near the level of expectation which Lawrence's account arouses, it is necessary to spend a sunset, a night and at least one full day in Wadi Rum. Many visitors come up on a day trip from Aqaba, encounter greedy Bedouin charging outrageous amounts for camel rides or the hire of four-wheel drive vehicles, and return greatly disappointed.

Now that the Wadi Rum resthouse, simple though it may be, is open, you should try to spend a night here, timing it, if possible, for full moon. The resthouse provides basic accommodation only, in the form of space, mattresses and bedding. It has bathrooms, cooking facilities and a fridge, but you should bring your own food and water, as local supplies are very limited. Rubbish is

Basic resthouse

collected daily and taken off in a truck by a local to the Wadi Zibalah, Valley of Rubbish, of whose location you are better remaining ignorant.

From Petra the drive to Rum takes about an hour and a half, passing *en route* the spectacular vantage point of **Ras el-Naqab**, from where you can look down for the first time into the weird moonscape of Rum. Stopping for tea or coffee at the Ras el-Naqab resthouse at 1200m will give you the opportunity to take in this panorama properly. At sunset or early in the morning the lighting is at its most effective, when the reds, purples, greys and browns take on a surreal sharpness and clarity which adds to their moonscape effect. The many lorry drivers stop here, not to admire the view, but to drink the camel's milk which the Bedouin sell at the roadside, and which is reputed to give extra sexual prowess.

The benefits of camel's milk

From Aqaba the drive to Rum is less than an hour: 40km to Rum the turn-off, then a further 30km along the narrow tarred road to reach the police headquarters, set at the entrance to the vast corridor of Wadi Rum, and the motley collection of huts and black tents which form the village of Rum itself. The resthouse is the first modern building you come to on your right, a low white structure with a somewhat unfinished air. The Desert Police Post lies some 300m further on, and you pass through a checkpoint, where the tarmac ends. Affectionately known as the Camel Corps, the patrol here was first established in 1931 when King Abdullah, Hussein's grandfather, used them to control dissident tribes and to patrol Jordan's desert borders. Their first commander was Glubb Pasha, a British officer, John Bagot Glubb. Today their role is merely to check on tribal movements, to rescue sheep from starvation by transporting them to waterholes, and generally to monitor any grievances. The force numbers some 1000 men, but the specially trained camels have dwindled from 150 to a mere 40.

Desert Police Post

From here transport can only be on foot, by camel or by four-wheel drive. On foot there is obviously a limit to what you can do. By walking further into the large corridor you will come, some 500m after the check-point and slightly to your right, to the foundations of a Nabatean temple dating to the first century, almost completely buried in the sand. An Italian team excavated the prehistoric Bedouin sites here for six years, finishing in 1986.

From here, looking up at the right-hand wall of the Rum corridor, you will notice a slight indentation where a few trees are growing. This is **Ain Shelaleh**, about 800m from the temple ruins. Starting at the rock boulders on the valley floor it takes some 20 minutes to scramble over the tumbled blocks up into the crevice itself, where the spring comes out from the rock wall. Beautifully cool and clean to drink, even in the height of summer, this is the most plentiful spring in the Wadi Rum. The rocky clamber is also used as a commando desert ranger training area, as evidenced by the rifle ranges and mock soldier targets.

Walk and scramble to a cool spring

The standard camel ride lasts for one or two hours and consists of a trek out of the Rum corridor and into a rock crevasse in a nearby mountain. Primitive Thamudic inscriptions and drawings can be seen here carved into the rock face, and you can clamber back a long way into this curious slit in the mountain.

CAMEL RIDING

The extraordinary motion of camel riding should be experienced at least once, for it is not only backwards and forwards, but also side to side, as if the saddle is about to slip off. The saddle has two wooden pegs to hang on to, one in front, one behind. The getting up and sitting down motions take some getting used to as well, for, from the sitting position in which you mount, the camels are trained to straighten their back legs immediately they feel your weight, catapulting you forwards without warning, only to be catapulted backwards again once their front legs are straightened. Given that all this happens in a space of seconds, it does not give you much chance to get your body weight back in the right place. All Middle Eastern camels are dromedaries (from *dromos*, Greek for runner). The heavier, hairier, two-humped Bactrian variety is only found in colder climes like eastern Turkey and Central Asia. A group of tourists eyeing some camels at the roadside were heard to comment: *'Of course, those aren't riding camels. There's no where to sit!'*

There is a surprising amount of butterfly and bird life in the valley. As you sit still or lie back in the sand gazing up at the towering rocks and the sky, the only sound is the birds soaring above and the gentle gusts of wind in your hair. In summer months the sunset tends to be more golden yellow than red, but at all times of year the open valleys and weird rock shapes take on a surreal glow as the sun descends. By moonlight too, the mountains possess an eerie glow. At dawn Bedouin girls set off into the valley with their flocks of sheep.

The magic of sunset

With the aid of a guide and four-wheel drive vehicle you can get to a further valley, 10km from the police post, in which there is an extraordinary rockface covered in profuse Thamudic drawings of camels, other animals and people. The tribe of Thamud is now extinct, but it came originally from the town of Al-Hijr in Saudi Arabia, north

Early drawings

175

of Medina. Mentioned in Ashourite texts as early as the eighth century BC, they were reputed to be a wicked pagan people, and their town was later destroyed. The Nabateans subsequently conquered them.

The splendid rock bridge

One of the most exhilarating and memorable excursions into Wadi Rum is the climb to the natural rock bridge, which is pictured on the back cover of Tony Howard's *Treks and Climbs in the Mountains of Rum and Petra*. Sponsored by the Ministry of Tourism, Tony Howard and his party of climbers spent several months in Wadi Rum, spread over a period of three years, exploring the full gamut of climbs on offer.

If you are a total novice, do not be misled by the book's 'easy' rating of the climb, for it has its tricky moments, and is especially not to be recommended at midday in August, barefoot: the rock can get extremely hot underfoot. Wear suitable clothing, as descending rock chimneys in a skirt or dress, for example, is not compatible with observing the relationship of your feet to footholds. The bridge lies 25km away from the police post, on the very edge of the Wadi Rum, and the drive to it should only be attempted with a guide and four-wheel drive. It takes about 45 minutes. The ascent itself takes a further hour, and the descent slightly less.

Aqaba

A few days spent at Aqaba, Jordan's window to the sea, is an ideal way to relax on the beach at the end of a tour round the country. The natural setting is impressive, with the narrow bay, the country's only port, ringed by mountains and fringed by palm trees. The port area lies round to the east of the town, and Jordan receives most of her imports from this route. During the Iran/Iraq war and after the Gulf War imports destined for Iraq came in this way to avoid the Persian Gulf, thus vastly increasing the shipping as well as the lorry traffic. Trucks still ply their way ceaselessly up and down the desert highway before forking off to the Iraqi border. On their return they bring back Iraqi oil. Just a few kilometres away, intriguingly close yet distant, is Eilat, Israel's rival resort on the Red Sea, far more heavily developed with large concrete hotel monsters along the beach.

Low-rise resort

Aqaba has remained low-rise, and of the several beach hotels, none offers more than 150 rooms. The town has several mosques, all of them modern, but the calls to prayer cannot be heard at all from the beach hotels. Development is, however, gradually gathering pace: the major new project is the 500–600-chalet Sultan Qaboos Holiday Village at the southern beach area. These chalets

```
┌──────────────────────────────────────┐
│  DANGEROUS MARINE LIFE  │
└──────────────────────────────────────┘
```

Stonefish: These ugly fish half bury themselves in the sea bed round Aqaba and indeed all around the shore of the Red Sea. They are highly poisonous and well camouflaged, looking rather like greyish-brown stones. If you are unfortunate enough to step on one, the spines inject a poison into your foot, resulting in severe and immediate pain. It can be fatal unless the antidote is given, and a doctor should be sought immediately. The Princess Haya Hospital in Aqaba keeps the anti-stonefish serum. Interim treatment is to bathe the foot in extremely hot water, as hot as you can bear. The safest way to avoid this unlikely but very unpleasant experience is to wear plastic shoes or sandals with hard soles in the water. This also protects from sea urchins and sharp coral. Ordinary gym-shoes are not sufficient.

Lionfish: These dramatic fish are much easier to spot and can therefore be avoided more easily. They swim about rather slowly, are quite large and black and white, with a mane of black and white poisonous spines sticking out about 15cm all around their heads.

Jellyfish: These, especially the purplish Portuguese man of war variety, sometimes come in shoals swimming close to shore. It is best to stay out of the water to avoid the very painful sting. There are smaller fairly harmless types of jellyfish which are totally transparent and brush against you when swimming, and you may notice a slight but sudden burning, stinging sensation as if you have swum into fragmented glass. Although disconcerting at the time, they do not leave any after-effects or mark the skin.

Although the Red Sea does obviously have far more nasties than the Mediterranean, the chances of encountering one and coming to grief are slim, far slimmer than having a road accident, so if you are that worried you probably should not be in Aqaba at all.

will not be for package tours, but for sale to both Jordanians and non-Jordanians as holiday homes. Skin-diving and snorkelling are the favourite sports, to see the coral reefs of the Red Sea, though the best coral, at the Yamaniyeh reef, is in fact outside Aqaba, some 10km down the road to the east of the gulf on the road to Saudi Arabia. Water-skiing and pedaloes are among the gentler aquatic pursuits available, as well as rides in glass-bottomed boats.

About 12km south of Aqaba, a little beyond the ferry terminal, where the coral reefs are far more spectacular than in Aqaba itself, is the Royal Diving Centre, open seven days a week, where equipment is hired out and lessons are given not only in diving but also in swimming and, snorkelling and marine photography. The centre has a cafeteria offering light snacks and refreshments. The Alcazar Hotel also has a new diving centre.

Diving lessons

An interesting day or half-day excursion can be made by boat from the AquaMarina Hotel to **Pharaoh's Island**, a tiny volcanic rock island 250m off the Sinai shoreline of Egypt. Here, a Crusader castle, known as Isle de Graye, was built under Baldwin I in the twelfth century or, as the Egyptians claim, an Islamic citadel built in 1170 by Saladin to defend the Arabian Peninsula from infidel incursions. Totally restored by the Egyptian Antiquities Organisation in 1986, the castle now boasts a carrier-pigeon tower, a tiny mosque, living quarters, an elaborate baths and cisterns. It also has a well-maintained little restaurant prettily set round a man-made sea lagoon where you can swim or paddle. A coral reef surrounds the island giving it its other name, Coral Island, and the snorkelling here is far better than anything in Aqaba. Come equipped with protective shoes. Despite the fact that it is now in Egyptian hands, the formalities for the visit are minimal. It is also visited from the Sinai main land via a little motorboat that shuttles to and fro, though the majority of visitors are from Eilat, which runs a boat service like Aqaba.

Coral Island

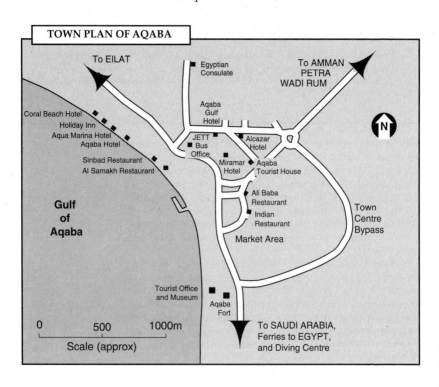

TOWN PLAN OF AQABA

To EILAT

Egyptian
Consulate

To AMMAN
PETRA
WADI RUM

Aqaba
Gulf
Hotel

Coral Beach Hotel
Holiday Inn
Aqua Marina Hotel
Aqaba Hotel

JETT
Bus
Office

Alcazar
Hotel

N

Sinbad Restaurant
Al Samakh Restaurant

Miramar
Hotel

Aqaba
Tourist House

Ali Baba
Restaurant

**Gulf
of
Aqaba**

Indian
Restaurant

Town
Centre
Bypass

Market Area

Tourist Office
and Museum

Aqaba
Fort

To SAUDI ARABIA,
Ferries to EGYPT,
and Diving Centre

0   500   1000m

Scale (approx)

Opposite the new Aqaba Gulf Hotel in the town centre you can see the recently discovered seventh-century Islamic walled city of Ayla, currently being excavated. The other main monument to see in Aqaba town is the fourteenth-century fort, near the waterfront round by the port. A section of it houses the Visitors' Centre, and another section boasts a small museum with some old photographs of Winston Churchill, Faisal and King Abdullah, some of the key players in the Arab Revolt.

THE ARAB REVOLT

The Arabs, disillusioned by years of backward Ottoman rule, had by 1914 roused themselves to unite against their oppressors. Under the leadership of the Hashemite Sherif Hussein of the Hejaz the tribes joined together in a dream of Arab unity, to oust the Ottomans. Encouraged by the Allies, and in particular T.E. Lawrence, Hussein was given to understand that Britain would back him if the Arabs rebelled against the Ottomans and fought for the Allies. When the revolt began in June 1916, however, Britain and France had already met one month earlier and secretly agreed to divide between them the lands they had promised Sherif Hussein and his sons Faisal and Abdullah. After the war, Iraq, Palestine and Jordan were duly put under British mandate, while Syria and Lebanon went to the French. The majority of the Arabs felt betrayed. Even Churchill referred to Britain's conduct as *'a confusion of principles'* and Lawrence called it *'a despicable fraud'*. The British had broken their wartime promises, a betrayal which was compounded by the 1917 Balfour Declaration, which supported *'the establishment in Palestine of a national home for the Jewish people'*. It was in partial recognition of this earlier betrayal that Churchill, as Colonial Secretary, in 1921 agreed to allow the separate mandate of Transjordan to be established under the administration of Abdullah, Sherif Hussein's son. At that time, the population of the Emirate of Transjordan was about 400,000.

Balfour Declaration

King Hussein, in his autobiography, Uneasy Lies the Head, sees the failure of the Arab Revolt as the death knell of Arab unity. Since then, he feels, the various Arab countries have pulled apart, finding it imposible to forget their domestic ambitions: *'As people we are one, seeking the same goal. As nations we lose each other down the different paths we choose by which to fulfil our national objectives.'*

His grandfather, King Abdullah, described the problem well at the time the Arab League was formed. It was, he said, *'a sack into which seven heads [the original seven Arab countries] had been forced tied by ribbons of foreign domination and Arab ignorance. Such a creature could breathe, but if it attempted to move, it would choke itself to death'*.

The Desert Road

This 336km route can be driven comfortably in five hours, or indeed less if you keep up a steady 120kph. It is dual carriageway in so far as the two directions are separated, but road lines or markings, when present, are somewhat erratic. Although it is the quickest route to the capital, it is a tiring drive because of the large numbers of heavy lorries which frequent it: fragments of burst lorry tyres line the entire route. Accidents remain commonplace, perhaps for lack of distraction. From Ras el-Naqab northwards, 75 per cent of the journey, the scenery is excruciatingly dull with little or nothing to see or to break the flat desert horizons except perhaps the occasional phosphate factory. Near the Wadi Rum turn-off, one very wide section of road doubles as an aeroplane runway, a military precaution.

Flat horizons

The town of **Ma'an**, 30km north of Ras el-Naqab, is the chief town of the Bedouin Howeitat tribe, the major one of Jordan's eight nomadic or semi-nomadic camel rearers. The paramount sheikh of the Howeitat lives at the village of Al-Qurain, south of Ma'an, with his three wives in separate but equal establishments, in accordance with Quranic prescription. Until the beginning of this century, the Bedouin were still in the habit of raiding the oasis towns to supplement their livelihood. Now many are semi-nomadic, the women and children living in a permanent settlement made up partly of breeze-block huts, and partly of tents, while the younger men take the camels off to roam for days or even weeks at a time in search of pastureland in the desert wadis.

The next resthouse to break your journey for a meal or refreshments is at Qatrana. It is confusingly called the Petra Resthouse and is on the left of the road. The nearby junction is in fact the turn-off to Kerak rather than to Petra. There are also petrol stations at these resthouses. From this point northwards, the journey to Amman takes another 1½ hours.

Section 3: THE HOLY LAND

Travel Facts

Jerusalem

The Southern Circuit

The Northern Circuit

The pools at Bethsaida (Darke).

INTRODUCTION

This section in no way claims to offer comprehensive coverage of all biblical sites, but it has been added in recognition of the fact that the majority of people visiting Jordan will wish to include a trip to Jerusalem and probably to a few other famous sites such as Massada, Qumran, Jericho, Bethlehem and the Sea of Galilee. Most of these sites lie within what used to be known as Transjordan, and was indeed Jordanian territory until it was lost to Israel in the 1967 war. Known since then as the Occupied West Bank, this area in November 1988 unilaterally declared itself 'The Independent State of Palestine'. To avoid the political implications of this and all other titles, this section has been called The Holy Land. For the tourist, these changes in nomenclature will make little tangible difference, and the procedures for crossing from Amman to Jerusalem remain, at the time of writing, unaffected.

TRAVEL FACTS

Crossing from Jordan
There is only one land border crossing which is open at present, and that is the King Hussein (formerly Allenby) Bridge across the Jordan river. No cars, private or hired, may be taken across the bridge in either direction, and the only way to cross is therefore as a foot passenger on one of the buses that shuttles to and fro between the border posts. A pass, which must be applied for at least 48 hours in advance from the Jordanian Ministry of Interior enables you to cross over and back, and means that your passport will not get an Israeli stamp: this is important as such a stamp would automatically invalidate your return to Jordan or indeed to any other Arab country. Full details on how to obtain this pass are given in *Section 1*.

From Amman the drive to the bridge takes about 40 minutes. The best method by far, rather than go by taxi, is to take one of the comfortable air-conditioned JETT buses which set off from Abdali Station (see Amman street plan). There are several departures a day, starting from 6.00 am (except Saturdays when the bridge is closed), and seats should be booked in advance. The advantage of these buses is that they ferry you through the customs and border procedures in the smoothest possible way. It is best to make an early departure because, although the bridge does not close officially till 1.00 pm, it will close earlier if the maximum allotted number of people have already made the crossing that day. The whole business is now far easier than it used to be, since new facilities were built in 1982 which keep tourists and all foreigners entirely separate from the terminal where Palestinians are processed. On the Israeli side too, a new terminal has been built in which foreigners are kept separate, and the procedures, though still lengthy and tiresome, are considerably less so than they are in the non-foreigner terminal, where the crossing generally takes most of the day and includes humiliating body searches and extensive baggage checks.

Once clear of the customs procedures, you are free to go out and catch a service taxi to Jerusalem, the rate for which is fixed in shekels and displayed on a board near where you leave the terminal building: it generally equates to about £5.00 or $7.50. Remember to keep some shekels for the obligatory exit tax on your return: this is usually the equivalent of about £9.00 or $13.50, but it is best to establish the exact amount so that you are not caught unawares as you return to Jordan.

The drive up from the Jordan Valley, past Jericho to Jerusalem takes about 40 minutes, climbing through gaunt hills, once the Wilderness of Judea. On the summits of these mountains, where the Devil brought Christ to tempt him, there now crouch eerie Israeli settlements, their appearance like futuristic military garrisons. As the road swoops over the final ridge, you have your first view down on to the old walled city of Jerusalem, the golden Dome of the Rock rising unmistakably in its centre. The taxi swings right down into the valley to skirt the eastern walls, passing the Garden of Gethsemane to your right, then climbing the hill again to deposit you at either the Damascus Gate, the New Gate or the Jaffa Gate, according to your choice: there is no difference in price.

A day before you plan to return to Jordan, you should go to reserve a place in one of the service taxis called sherut in Israel at the main office which is diagonally opposite the Damascus Gate, outside the walls. Without a reservation, you may have difficulty getting a seat at peak season and therefore be forced to take a private taxi which is very expensive, as only certain taxis are allowed past the check-point. The earlier your departure, the quicker you will be processed at the border.

At the Israeli departure terminal, a substantial exit tax has to be paid in shekels (equivalent to about £9 or $13.50 but check in advance) by queuing at the 'Post' kiosk in the foreigners' building: on payment you are given a little white receipt. You must now queue at Passport Control and show the receipt before waiting for the small JETT bus to arrive. An unseemly scramble ensues, and the bus then makes the three-minute journey back across the bridge to the Jordanian embarkation point. This costs a further JD1.5 or $5 paid to the bus driver if you have not purchased a return ticket from Amman in advance. Passports are then checked and collected by the Jordanian officials before the bus is free to set off to Amman.

Flights
Direct flights to Tel Aviv (the nearest airport to Jerusalem) are run by British Airways and El-Al, from about £250 return.

Car Hire
This is expensive throughout Israel, costing in the region of $150 for three days unlimited mileage. In high season and holiday times, hiring cars can be a problem, as there is a shortage, and Israelis themselves frequently hire them as well. Petrol is slightly cheaper than in Europe, but anyway, distances are so small that this is hardly a factor.

Food
For lunch in the Old City, and indeed throughout Israel, the staple is *falaafel*,

sold from stalls everywhere. It consists of pitta bread stuffed with fried chick-pea balls, *tahina* (sesame paste) and salad. Hygiene can be suspect, so choose your stall carefully. Freshly squeezed fruit juices are also good in summer. Most restaurants in East Jerusalem are uninspiring, and if you want first-rate food you tend to be better off eating in the hotels, especially the American Colony.

Money
The Israeli shekel rates are always sliding, as the country is perpetually in the grip of rampant inflation. As a result, many prices are given in foreign currency, generally US dollars.

The money changers around the Damascus Gate area offer about the best rates and are very quick, with the minimum of paperwork. Many are closed on Fridays as they are Muslims. Shekels are needed for entry fees, buses, taxis, cafes and restaurants, but most hotels prefer foreign currency or travellers cheques, and tend to display rates in US dollars. Banks are open *8.30 am–12.30 pm and 4.00 am–6.00 pm on Sunday, Tuesday and Thursday, and 8.30 am–12.30 pm on Monday and Wednesday. On Friday they are open fron 8.30 am–12.00 noon. They are closed on Saturday.* Credit cards are widely accepted in hotels, good restaurants and larger shops.

Visas
UK passport holders do not require visas. Make sure your passport does not get an Israeli stamp: customs officers are used to this request, and simply stamp a separate loose card which is tucked into your passport.

Vaccination and Health
Tap water is safe to drink throughout the area. There has been a recent polio outbreak, so make sure your polio immunisation, and typhoid, are up to date.

Climate
At an altitude of 762m, Jerusalem is cold in winter, especially from November to March (7°C in January). There is quite a lot of winter rainfall. Spring and autumn are the best times, but the summer months are never unbearably hot, with Jerusalem temperatures rarely exceeding 32°C.

Christmas and Easter are popular times to visit. The Eastern Church follows the old Julian calendar which is 13 days behind the Western Gregorian one, and Eastern and Western religious holidays are therefore on different days. The Western Christmas is on 25 December, Orthodox Christmas is on 6 January, and Armenian Christmas is on 19 January.

Bethlehem is the most festive place for Christmas Eve, with midnight mass celebrated in the Church of the Nativity. Tickets, obtained free well in advance from the Franciscan Pilgrims Office at the Jaffa Gate, Jerusalem, must be presented. Carol singing at Shepherds' Fields, Beit Sahur, is also a memorable experience, singing 'O little Town of Bethlehem' as the first stars appear over the town.

At Easter, Jerusalem is alive with colourful processions, which are held throughout Holy Week by all the different sects. Programmes giving the various celebrations and services can be obtained from the Tourist Office, major hotels, travel agencies and the churches themselves.

Clothing
For any visits to churches, mosques and synagogues, arms and legs must be covered, so avoid shorts and sleeveless tops.

Where to go for Information
In Jerusalem **The Tourist Offices** are at *24 King George Street* and at *Jaffa Gate*, and free handouts of city maps and the weekly booklet *This week in Jerusalem* are issued. This is useful for its listings of events, hotels, embassies etc. The **Israeli Government Tourist Office** in London is at *18 Great Marlborough St London W1V 1AF (071-434 3651)*.

The Intifada
The Palestinian uprising, now referred to internationally by its Arabic name, Intifada, flared up in Gaza in December 1987, in response to the killing of Palestinian civilians by the Israelis. What began as a spontaneous lashing out against the Israeli Defence Force has now become a way of life throughout the Occupied Territories. Hundreds of Palestinian and scores of Israeli lives have been lost and the economic cost to both sides is immeasurable. Neither side is about to stop however, and the visitor should therefore keep himself informed of the latest developments and take advice from the tourist offices.

Intifada leaders did not expect the struggle to last so long: they hoped their actions would attract world attention and force political change. Now they recognise that the world's interest in their problem, already dwindling, has been overshadowed by events in eastern Europe. *'The reality that we see'*, say the leaders, *'is the continuation of the Intifada, even though our people realise it is a slow death. But to halt it now, after all the casualties and suffering, would mean a quick death to the Palestinian people.'*

Gaza remains the most violent area, and travellers crossing from Egypt at the Rafah border post are advised to make a detour round the edge of the Gaza Strip. Other towns best avoided are Hebron, Nablus, Ramallah and Jenin. Generally speaking hire cars can be driven throughout the Occupied Territories, though it is always advisable to check your itinerary with the Tourist Office first, as the situation can change daily.

In East Jerusalem shops and restaurants inside the walled city can close inexplicably, and occasional strike days are called when everything stays shut. Mosques and churches remain open, however, and the streets of Old Jerusalem are safe for foreigners to stroll round. Beyond the walls opening hours are as normal, except on strike days when the whole of East Jerusalem closes. West Jerusalem of course stays open.

Touring the Holy Land
Tourism has obviously fallen off since 1988, but a surprising number of international tour groups still visit. Israeli firms like Egged and Galilee still offer coach tours that cover the Holy Land. These may be the best bet for those who

have made their own way here but who would prefer the protective cloak of a tour agency.

Alternatively, by hiring a car for just three days you can see a surprising amount of the Holy Land beyond Jerusalem, as distances are really very small. A suggested itinerary would be one day to the south, returning to Jerusalem for the night, followed by two days to the north. The beauty of this itinerary is that it requires only one night spent out of Jerusalem, and the only stretch of road you drive twice is the short section between Jericho and Jerusalem.

JERUSALEM

There is obviously a wealth of accommodation in Jerusalem. The following is a selection of hotels covering a range of categories:

***** **7 Arches Hotel** (*tel: 282-551*). Superbly sited on the Mount of Olives overlooking the Old city from the east. 200 rooms. Pool.

***** **King David** (*tel: 221-111*). The grand and famous hotel, ten minutes' walk to the west of the Jaffa Gate. 258 rooms. Pool. Very popular with tours.

**** **American Colony Hotel** (*tel: 282-421*). On Nablus Road, 1km from the Damascus Gate. An ex-pasha's residence dating from 1850, with quality service and excellent food. 106 rooms, furnished in the old style but with modern plumbing. Pool. Lovely central courtyard where meals can be taken in summer months.

*** **Jordan House** (*tel: 283-430*). Prettily set in pine trees to the north from Herod's Gate. 25 rooms in a local stone built house furnished with Middle Eastern antiques.

*** **YMCA East**, or **Aelia Capitolina** (*tel: 282-375*). A hotel despite its name. Up the Nablus road. 57 rooms, with grand Middle Eastern decor. Pool in the basement.

** **New Orient House** (*tel: 282-437*). Off Salah ed-Din St to the north of Herod's Gate. A Turkish residence with grand public rooms and 22 adequate hotel rooms.

* **Knights' Palace** (*tel: 282-537*). Once part of the Latin Patriarchate. Excellently located within the walls, close to the New Gate. 36 simple rooms with tiny bathrooms. Breakfast buffet, but no other meals.

* **Az-Zahra** (*tel: 282-447*). Just north of the Old City in a fine old Arab house. 24 simple rooms, with a pretty terrace where breakfast and drinks can be taken. No other meals.

On the Mount of Olives itself is a cluster of places with good views, a taxi ride from the Old City. They are the *** **Commodore** (*tel: 284-845*, 45 rooms), the ** **Astoria** (*tel: 284-965*, 23 rooms) and the ** **Mount of Olives Hotel** (*tel: 02 284-877*, 63 rooms).

Historical Background

Three times holy

Within the Holy Land, Jerusalem has always been the most holy city, but holy to no less than three of the world's major religions, in order of time, Judaism, Christianity and Islam. It is the focus of faith for a third of the world's population. No other city has been so fought over and evoked such passions in so many hearts. For the last 4000 years it has been conquered, destroyed and rebuilt more times than can be readily recalled.

The mixture of communities here has always been diverse, and each has striven to maintain its separate identity and culture rather than integrate with its neighbours. In the mid-nineteenth century the population was half Jewish, a quarter Christian and a quarter Muslim. Today, some two-thirds of the population of East Jerusalem is Muslim Arab, and one-third Christian (from some 30 different denominations). These proportions have fluctuated greatly over the centuries and will no doubt continue to do so, as will the constant tug of war between the various factions.

Israeli claims

The Jews claim Jerusalem as their own eternal city, based on the writs of the Talmud and the Old Testament, as well as their history dating back some 1000 years before Christ, when the Kings David and Solomon ruled ancient Israel from here. The Wailing Wall, all that remains of Herod's once-magnificent temple, is Judaism's most sacred site. When the Israeli army stormed St Stephen's Gate on 7 June 1967, a Jewish State was in command of all Jerusalem for the first time in 1800 years.

Muslim claims

The Muslims have regarded Jerusalem as a holy city since the seventh century when Muhammad made his ascent to heaven from the Dome of the Rock, Islam's oldest religious structure. For a time, it replaced Mecca and Medina as the holiest city of Islam and Muslims turned to face it to pray rather than to Mecca. The city has been under Muslim rule for most of the last 1200 years. The resident Arabs insist that East Jerusalem belongs to them, while the PLO claims the whole city for the Palestinian people, and the newly declared state of Palestine has claimed Jerusalem as its capital.

Christian claims

For Christians, Jerusalem is the holy city where Christ preached and was crucified, and in the West many people unquestioningly regard the Christian claim as the most valid. In practice, the city was only under Christian rule for three relatively short periods in its history: first, the Byzantine era for three centuries from 324; second, under the Crusaders for less than a century from 1099; and third, 30 years of British rule after the First World War, when after five centuries of Turkish Ottoman rule, it surrendered to the Allied troops under General Allenby.

Britain administered Jerusalem as part of the territory of Palestine under its mandate, and allowed both Jewish and Arab immigrants to surge into the city. It was a troubled period of Arab and Jewish guerilla warfare, and in 1947 a UN plan proposed the partition of Palestine into separate Arab and Jewish states, with Jerusalem as an international zone under UN control. Full-scale war erupted the moment the British mandate ended in 1948, and the Israelis seized the west of Jerusalem, while the Arab Legion held on to the Old City. A UN ceasefire left the city divided into Jewish west and Arab east, with a wide no man's land running under its eastern walls.

Jews, Christians and Muslims therefore all lay special claim to the city and each claim has its validity. The Jewish claim to have 'reunified' the city in 1967 when they overran the eastern walled section in the Six Day War is **Disputed status** clearly wishful thinking, and neither the UN nor the United States has acknowledged this annexation or Jerusalem's 'capital' status. After 1967, the Israelis proceeded to confiscate some 5000 acres of Arab land for 'public purposes', which turned out to be the building of settlements on an extraordinary scale. As a result the Jewish population of East Jerusalem grew spectacularly. Today, you do not have to look very hard to see the tension that pervades the place: the Arabs fear expulsion, the Christians fear their diminishing status as a minority, the non-religious Jews fear being overrun by the ultra-orthodox whose birth-rate is three times the average, Israelis fear to pass through East Jerusalem and especially to enter the walled city. Unviable solutions to the problem abound, but most impartial observers would accept that Jerusalem is a unique city with special needs, requiring a special status. One novel idea is for the city to serve as capital to two states, Israel and Palestine, with equal numbers of Israelis and Palestinians, about 450,000 each. To achieve this the borders of the municipality would have to be extended to include Bethlehem and Ramallah, and the Israeli settlements of Ma'ale, Adumim and Mevasseret.

Itinerary
Though today it covers less than 1 per cent of the new Israeli city's total area, for most tourists and visitors Jerusalem means the Old City, the square kilometre enclosed today within the Ottoman walls of Suleyman the Magnificent. The Roman Emperor Hadrian rebuilt the city on the ruins of Jewish Jerusalem, and his two main roads

SITE PLAN OF JERUSALEM AND THE OLD CITY

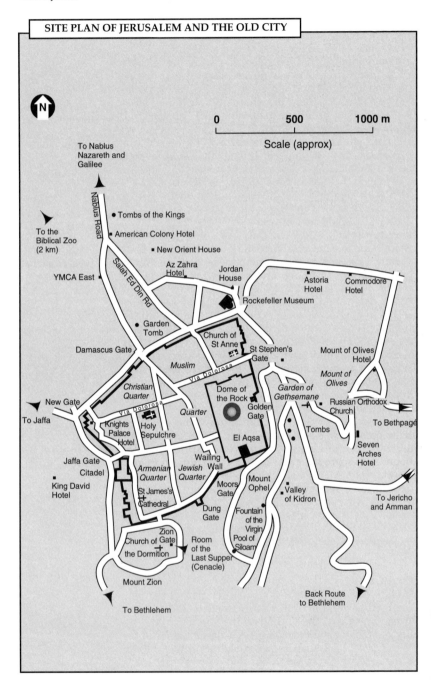

cut the city into the same four segments which still today define the boundaries between the Muslim, Jewish, Christian and Armenian quarters.

It is also interesting to stroll around the area immediately to the north of the Damascus Gate to get a feel for the city outside the walls, and the **Rockefeller Museum** (*open 10.00 am–5.00 pm*) near Herod's Gate is certainly worth a visit (allow about two hours). With the notable exception of the **Biblical Zoo** (containing many of the animals described in the Bible and *open daily from 9.00 am–4.00 pm*), the western city holds little for most visitors beyond various modern Israeli museums depicting the Zionist struggle, and the Knesset.

The following is a suggested two day programme in Jerusalem, and the text follows the order of this programme:

Two-day itinerary

Day 1: Inside the walls
Morning. Walk of the ramparts from Damascus Gate, descending at St Stephen's (Lion's) Gate. Visit Haram esh-Sherif (the Temple Mount), which accounts for nearly 20 per cent of the area within the walls, with the Dome of the Rock and Al Aqsa mosque. Visit the Wailing Wall.

Afternoon. See the Via Dolorosa, the Holy Sepulchre Church, the Pool of Bethsaida and St Anne's Church. Take an evening stroll around the Armenian and Jewish quarters. Attend the *son et lumière* performance at King David's Tower.

Day 2: Outside the walls
Morning. Visit the City of David (just south of today's walls, though within the walls at Christ's time), the Tomb of David and the Last Supper Room (Cenacle). Walk down to Gethsemane via the Pool of Siloam.

Afternoon. Visit the Rockefeller Museum. Climb to the Mount of Olives for sunset.

Inside the Walls
Of Jerusalem's 11 gates (of which four are closed), the **Damascus Gate** is the largest and most impressive. It leads into the heart of the Muslim quarter, the area most alive with bustling shops, street vendors and money changers. Outside the gate is a large open area which, early in the morning, has acquired a role in recent years as a so-called 'slave market', for it is here that, partly as a result of it being the bus terminal for East Jerusalem, Arab workers pour in daily from outlying villages or from East

Damascus Gate

The Damascus Gate, Jerusalem (Darke).

Jerusalem, hoping to be picked up for a day's work, almost mobbing each Israeli car or truck in a desperate attempt to be chosen. Ironically, most of this work is on Israeli construction sites, where they then help to build settlements on land that was originally Arab.

The Damascus Gate itself, like the walls, was built in the sixteenth century by Suleyman the Magnificent, when Jerusalem and the whole of Palestine fell under Ottoman Turkish rule. Before you enter, a small kiosk tucked below the bridge just to the left of the walls sells tickets for the **Rampart circuit** circuit of the ramparts. This makes an interesting walk, and affords excellent views down into the Muslim quarter and over the Garden of Gethsemane and the Mount of Olives. The tickets are valid for two days, so at a later point you could walk in the other direction, west from the Damascus Gate looking down into the Christian quarter, descending at the Jaffa Gate. The walk is closed at 5.00 pm, after which you can only leave from the iron turnstile at the Damascus Gate. For now, however, it will suit the purposes of the itinerary to walk eastwards along the walls past Herod's Gate, sometimes up and down quite narrow steps, sometimes along wide rampart walk-

Gethsemane and the Mount of Olives (Darke).

The Jordan River site where Jesus is said to have been baptised by John the Baptist (Darke).

The evocative fortress of Massada (Darke).

ways, descending finally at St Stephen's (Lion's) Gate. The walk stops here anyway, since the rampart passage does not lead on into the Haram esh-Sherif itself. At the point where you descend, the Church of St Anne and the Pool of Bethsaida (described later, in the afternoon walk), are immediately on your right.

You can now enter the **Haram Esh-Sherif** (The Temple Mount). The Arabic name literally means 'the noble sanctuary', and this is the sacred area which contains the most famous Muslim shrines: the Dome of the Rock and Al Aqsa Mosque. The rules about which of the nine entrances non-Muslims must use to enter the walled enclosure change frequently, but in general the three gates which are permitted are the Bab an-Nadhir (also called the Prison Gate or Majlis Gate), the Bab es-Silsileh and the Bab el-Maghariba or Moor's Gate by the Wailing Wall. All three are along the western edge of the sacred enclosure, and the safest time to be assured entry is between 8.30 and 11.00 am. The whole area is closed to foreigners on Fridays, on Muslim religious holidays, and on all days at prayer times. If your attire is considered too scanty, you will be issued with a hooded robe for which you are expected to give *baksheesh* (a tip) on your departure. You can leave from any of the nine gates.

Limited entry

Once inside, you can stroll around freely in the 30 acres of gardens and on the various levels of the artificial terraces. You cannot, however, enter the mosques themselves before buying special tickets on sale at the ticket office at the bottom of the steps by the Dome of the Rock. One ticket gives entry to three places: the Dome of the Rock, Al Aqsa mosque and the Museum. Fear of terrorist attacks means that no bags are permitted inside the buildings, which tends to mean that you must take it in turns to go inside, always leaving one person to guard your possessions outside.

The **Dome of the Rock** is without doubt Jerusalem's most famous building, prominent and unmistakable in postcards. It is one of the more curious quirks of the Western mind that many people think of it as a Christian shrine, and it therefore comes as something of a shock to realise that it is Islam's oldest surviving religious structure, its third most holy sanctuary after Mecca and Medina. The Roman Emperor Hadrian had built a pagan temple on the mount, but this was destroyed, like all other pagan shrines in the city, by Queen Helena, mother of Constantine (the first Roman emperor to adopt Christianity as the state religion), when she visited Jerusalem in the fourth century. Curiously, new Christians thereafter regarded the area as

The Golden Dome

**The Bible in
the Quran**

The same God

MUHAMMAD AS THE 'SEAL' OF THE PROPHETS

The Quran is full of stories from the Old Testament, and
Jesus, recognised as a prophet, is also mentioned many
times, along with Mary and John the Baptist. This is quite
natural for Muslims regard Islam as the last and purest
version of the world's three monotheistic religions.
Jehovah, God and Allah are all one and the same, but the
Jews and Christians have corrupted the original divine
word. Muhammad was therefore sent as God's messenger, as the 'seal' of the prophets to give the final word.
Because the Quran is God's actual utterance as transmit-
ted through Muhammad, every believer must submit to
it. Muslim literally means 'he who submits' and Islam,
taken from the same root word, means 'submission'.

---

cursed and abandoned it, and for the next three centuries
it served as the city's rubbish dump. When the Caliph
Omar arrived in the seventh century, he helped clear the
site with his own hands and had a simple wooden mosque
built there. Some 50 years later, in 691, the Caliph Abd al-
Malik erected the famous Dome of the Rock. The dome
itself was constructed to be directly over the rock from
which, according to Muslim tradition, the Prophet
Muhammad, in the twelfth year of his mission, made his
ascent to heaven mounted on his celestial steed Buraq,
having first been led to Jerusalem from Mecca in a single
night by the Archangel Gabriel. According to some
Muslim traditions, the rock is also the spot where
Abraham was said to have been about to sacrifice his son
Isaac. Islam's major annual festival, the Feast of the
Sacrifice, Id al-Adha, commemorates this event. Abraham
is mentioned many times in the Quran, and is claimed as a
direct ancestor of Muhammad.

Jerualem, known in Arabic as Al-Quds (The Holy One),
is never mentioned by name in the Quran, and indeed
Muhammad never visited it in his lifetime. The tradition
of his ascent to heaven from here has grown up from
what is claimed to be an indirect reference to Jerusalem in
the first verse of Chapter 17 of the Quran: '*Glory be to Him,
who carried his servant by night from the Holy Mosque* [of
Mecca] *to the Aqsa Mosque* [literally, the 'furthest'
mosque]'. Since the Aqsa mosque was not built till more
than half a century after Muhammad's death, there is
obviously scope for other interpretations of this verse, and
in fact, the term Al Aqsa here is generally taken to refer to
the whole area of the rock, rather than to the mosque

**Muhammad's
ascent to
heaven**

alone. The rock was said to have come from Paradise and
to be the foundation stone of the world. Next to the
Ka'aba in Mecca (the holy cube round which all pilgrims
circumambulate), it was held to be the most sacred spot in
the universe. On the Day of Judgement, it is believed, God
will change the rock into white coral, enlarging it to
extend over heaven and earth. *'Then shall men go from that
Rock to heaven or hell, according to that great word.'* (Jalal ed-
Din as Suyuti).

**Foundation
stone of the
world**

One picturesque account of Muhammad's nocturnal
journey to heaven from the Rock is given by an early
Islamic theologian:

**Picturesque
account**

Whilst I was sleeping upon my side, he [Gabriel] *came to me,
and cut me open from my breast to below my navel, and took
out my heart, and washed the cavity with Zamzam water, and
then filled my heart with Faith and Science. After this, a white
animal was brought for me to ride upon. Its size was between
that of a mule and an ass, and it stretched as far as the eye could
see. The name of the animal was Buraq. Then I mounted the
animal and ascended until we arrived at the lowest heaven, and
Gabriel demanded that the door should be opened. And it was
asked 'Who is it?' and he said, 'I am Gabriel'. And they then
said, 'Who is with you?' and he answered, 'It is Muhammad'.
They said, 'Has Muhammad been called to the office of a
prophet?' He said 'Yes.' They said, 'Welcome Muhammad; his
coming is well.'*

Whilst he was wooing the Jews of the Hejaz,
Muhammad did for a time order that his followers should
turn to face Jerusalem for their prayers. When he failed to
win converts from among them however, he reinstructed
the faithful in 623 to turn to Mecca as the *Qibla* or direction
of prayer.

**Change of
direction**

The Caliph Omar made Jerusalem his headquarters for a
time, while Mecca and Medina were in the hands of a rival.

Al Walid, son of Abd al-Malik and greatest of the
Umayyad builders, removed the dome of gilded brass
from a church in Baalbek, Lebanon, and set it on the dome
of his father's mosque in Jerusalem. Some hundred years
later, the Dome of the Rock was restored by the Abbasid
Caliph Al Ma'mun (813–833), who crammed his own
name into the space left by erasing the name of Abd al-
Malik in the Kufic inscription round the dome, but inadvertently forgot to change the date, thereby exposing himself to posterity. In the early 1960s the Jordanian government carried out extensive restorations and the gilded
dome was removed and replaced by a new one made of
gold coloured aluminium. The sixteenth-century Ottoman

A trick exposed

tiles on the exterior were also replaced with copies, which explains their somewhat crass appearance today. Jordan has since 1950 had custodianship of all Jerusalem's Muslim sites. The 1300-year-old structure of the Dome now needs repair and a new layer of gold after some harsh winters. Since his country was short of the necessary funds, King Hussein sold his London house to raise $8.5 million for the repairs.

The King's gesture

As you approach the Dome of the Rock, you must remove your shoes and leave them in pigeon holes outside the entrance; and inside, the smell of sweaty feet rising from the rather garish modern carpet is unpleasantly pervasive. It is forbidden to sit down on the floor and most people are therefore forced into a slow circumambulation of the huge fenced-off rock in the centre of the mosque. Dubious guides can be heard telling stories of how everything in the mosque is still original, with the exception of the wooden railing put up round the stone by the Ottoman Turks to stop pilgrims hacking off pieces of holy rock souvenirs. Fortunately the pilgrims could not reach the interior of the dome, where the mosaics still have considerable amounts of real gold. The 3m thickness of the dome has protected these mosaics and their colours from any signs of age and weathering, and their condition still looks pristine.

Real gold mosaics

The holiest place

Underneath the central rock, steps lead down into a grotto which is seen as the holiest of all places. Veiled and shrouded women prostrated in prayer tend to monopolise the limited space available. One Muslim tradition says that souls will reunite here in waiting their turn for the Last Judgement, while another says that the rock tried to follow Muhammad on his ascent to heaven and the Angel Gabriel had to stop it, leaving his handprint visible on the rock. Muhammad's footprint is sometimes also pointed out on it. Of the 36 stained glass windows, 20 date back to Suleyman the Magnificent.

Also within the Haram Esh-Sherif is the **Al Aqsa Mosque**. Again, no bags, cameras or shoes are allowed inside, so you need to take it in turns to go in, while one of you guards your possessions outside. The interior of the mosque has a more noble and dignified air to it than the slightly meretricious Dome of the Rock. A beautifully painted wooden ceiling over the main roof has mainly blues, golds and browns, while the mosaics are in exquisite greens and golds. The atmosphere is less reverential too, with many of the faithful lying asleep on the ample window seats. It was while entering this mosque that King Abdullah, the first king of Jordan and grandfather of King

Hussein, was assassinated in July 1951. The young Hussein was at his grandfather's side and witnessed the whole event, only escaping death himself by virtue of the medal he was wearing on his chest: the assassin's bullet ricocheted off it. His grandfather had that morning insisted on Hussein wearing the uniform with the medal to attend Friday prayers, and Hussein's obedience, even though he had to send for the uniform specially, saved his life.

Dramatic assassination

Underneath the mosque are the so-called Stables of Solomon, approached by a long ramp descending beside the main mosque entrance. Dating from Crusader times, these subterranean vaults are now kept locked. Outside, in front of the mosque, are two pillars close together, and a tradition holds that those who can squeeze between them will also be able to pass through the gates of heaven. Many a corpulent believer will be disappointed.

Too fat for heaven

Nearby, signs point to the **Museum**, once the Mosque of the Moors or Moroccans, where a collection of medieval Quranic manuscripts are displayed along with architectural fragments of the glazed faience from the Dome of the Rock.

Leaving the Haram Esh-Sherif by the Moor's Gate, you have a good view down over the famous **Wailing Wall**, Judaism's most holy shrine. King Solomon had built his temple on the mount where the Dome of the Rock now

The Wailing Wall in Jerusalem (Darke).

stands, with the Ark of the Covenant in the Holy of Holies vault beneath it. King Herod enlarged it in Roman times, but the wall, 20m high and built of huge limestone blocks, is now all that remains of it: in 70 AD it was destroyed at the hands of the Romans, as prophesied by Jesus. The Jews were driven into exile and the wall became for them the focus of their lost Jerusalem, the **Object of** object of intense longing and veneration. In the fourth **longing** century AD Constantine allowed the Jews an annual pilgrimage to return to the wall, an event at which they would weep and tear their robes.

Men and women pray at separate sections of the wall, as laid down by Jewish orthodox custom. Recently Jewish feminists in prayer shawls and skull caps carrying a Torah scroll came to pray at the wall, chanting prayers and singing hymns. The orthodox men were outraged and clambered on chairs to hurl abuse at the women over the wooden partition. The rabbi in charge of the site pro-**Women and** claimed in disgust *'A woman carrying a Torah is like a pig at* **pigs** *the Wailing Wall'*.

From 1948 to 1967 when Jordan ruled the Old City, the Jews were forbidden access to the wall, and in 1967 when the Israelis took over the city, they cleared the courtyard in front of it, an area that had been full of Arab homes. A group of orthodox Jews recently stirred up tremendous unrest among the Muslim population by starting to excavate in a secret tunnel leading under the temple mount itself. The Jewish archaeologists believed the excavations might lead to traces of King Solomon's temple beneath the Dome of the Rock and possibly even to the Ark of the Covenant itself. Amid storms of protest the excavations were finally stopped and the tunnel walled up.

The afternoon excursion takes you to **Christian Jerusalem**. Despite the supreme importance to Christianity of many monuments in Jerusalem, the Christian population today constitutes less than a third of the total and has more than halved since 1948, to approximately 11,000. During the wars between Muslims and Jews, many Christians (mainly Arabs) began to leave, settling in the United States, the Gulf and Jordan. Some fear that in another 50 years there will scarcely be a Christian community in the Holy Land.

Relations within the Christian community, between the 30-odd different denominations, have hardly been a model **Squabbling** of Christian unity. The Greeks, the earliest Christians in **Christians** Jerusalem, began by pushing out the Latins. Both were then hostile to the Syrian and Armenian Christians, and all in turn were unpleasant to the Protestants. The Egyptian

Coptic Christians are in perpetual dispute with the Orthodox Ethiopians over possession of the mud huts that clutter the roof of the St Helena Chapel at the Church of the Holy Sepulchre, and the White Russians on the Mount of Olives call the Red Russians on the other side of the city 'Soviet atheists'. The Greek Orthodox congregation is now the most powerful of all and the competitive cult of relics, tombs and other mementoes has been a prominent feature of Christian Jerusalem.

The first Christian buildings were erected in the fourth century by the Emperor Constantine and his mother Helena, when Rome proclaimed Christianity to be the state religion. For the next three centuries, under Christian Byzantine rule, further churches were added. With the Muslim conquest of the city, the Christian community was, with just a few lapses, permitted to continue its religion unpersecuted, adhering on the whole to the special tolerance exhorted by the Quran to be shown to what it calls the 'People of the Book', i.e. Jews and Christians.

The conquest of Jerusalem by the Seljuk Turks in the eleventh century was the spur that led to the Crusades, another appalling advertisement for Christianity. Crusader rule is generally recognised as one of Jerusalem's blackest periods, characterised by wholesale massacres of the city's Jews and Muslims. *'Heaps of heads and hands and feet were to be seen throughout the streets and squares of the city,'* wrote the historian Ibn al Athir, and over 70,000 were said to have been slaughtered at Al Aqsa Mosque by the Crusader knights. Christian belief held that the Holy Land, 'bought' by Jesus' blood, had been polluted by the presence of Muslims and Jews, and the population of Jerusalem under Christian rule dropped to about 3,000, the lowest since the Romans razed the city to the ground in the first century.

Crusader massacres

The arrival of the three Western European orders of Crusader knights also established in Jerusalem for the first time the Western Latin Church, which instantly became a rival to the Greek Orthodox community who had until then been the city's most powerful Christians. Eight centuries of bickering and squabbling between the Eastern and Western churches was the result. The Latin Crusaders renamed the Dome of the Rock the Temple of the Lord and placed a large golden cross on the dome. They also converted many other mosques to churches. Their rule lasted less than a century, and ended when Saladin retook the city for the Muslims.

Eight centuries of bickering

Today, one of the loveliest and best preserved of Crusader churches is the **Church of St Anne**, close to St

Lovely Church of St Anne

Stephen's (Lion's) Gate. The small modest entrance, bearing a sign saying simply 'Open, push', leads into an attractive open courtyard of trees and flowers, a haven of peace. The church is built on a site venerated as the birthplace of Mary, for it was where the house of her parents, Anne and Joachim, is thought to have stood. The beautiful simplicity of this church contrasts strongly with the catholic clutter you will see later at the Golgotha Chapel in the Holy Sepulchre Church.

Pool of Bethsaida

Beyond the church, the courtyard opens up to reveal the extraordinary **Pool of Bethsaida**, the scene of Christ's miracle of the healing of the man who had been paralysed for 38 years.

Now there is at Jerusalem by the sheep market a pool, which is called in the Hebrew tongue Bethesda, having five porches. In these lay a great multitude of impotent folk, of blind, halt, withered, waiting for the moving of the water. For an angel went down at a certain season into the pool and troubled the water: whosoever then first after the troubling of the water stepped in was made whole of whatsoever disease he had.
(John 5: 2–4).

The deep vaults and arches today are still an emotive place, and steps lead down for you to explore them. The pools would collect rain, which was then used as sacred water. One set of steps still goes down so deep that it reaches water.

Jesus' path to the crucifixion

Walking in a straight line from St Stephen's Gate to the west, you can now follow the **Via Dolorosa**, which has been established by tradition as the path Jesus took from the site where he was condemned by Herod to Golgotha, the place of crucifixion. Along this way are 14 so-called 'stations of the cross', points where Jesus is supposed to have paused, and these are marked by plaques set in the walls or by shrines. The fourteenth station is the tomb of Christ in the Church of the Holy Sepulchre. The first is some 200m beyond the Church of St Anne, in the courtyard where Pilate judged Jesus and presented him to the people with the words *Ecce Homo*, 'behold the man'.

But they cried out, Away with him, away with him, crucify him. Pilate saith unto them, Shall I crucify your King? The chief priests answered, We have no king but Caesar.
(John 19: 15).

Of the 14 stations, the final five are within the Church of the Holy Sepulchre, a site which, in Christ's time, lay outside the city walls, since the entire city was then located slightly to the south. The way is followed every Friday by bands of pilgrims led by Franciscan monks, retracing Christ's steps to Calvary.

The **Holy Sepulchre**, Christianity's holiest shrine, stands on the spot where tradition holds that Calvary or Golgotha and the tomb of Christ lay, and so here, under one roof, we have the site of Christ's crucifixion, his burial and his resurrection. It is in fact an immensely confusing building, a succession of edifices built one on top of the other from the fourth to the twelfth century and it is impossible to view it clearly from the outside because of the clutter of buildings pressing up against it on all sides. Heavily restored by the Orthodox Greeks in the nineteenth century, it is not a single church, but a whole cluster of some 30 chapels, holy places and historic buildings, maintained by six Christian denominations, in accordance with an eighteenth century decree; the Abyssinians, Greek Orthodox, Franciscan (for the Roman Catholic Church), Syrians, Copts and Armenians. No Protestant sect is allowed to use the sanctuary.

Christianity's holiest shrine

The greater part of the building today dates from the Crusader period, the first half of the twelfth century. It is built on the site of the original sanctuary which Constantine's mother, Helena, had erected in 335. The influential Helena also fixed many of the places associated with the life of Christ, based on the advice of her bishops and revelations in her dreams. These places are still the objects of pilgrimage today, even though many are in dispute, not least because the level of present day Jerusalem is 7m higher than it was at the time of Christ.

Helena's dreams

The confusion is compounded by the fact that the church was destroyed by the Persians in 614, and then again by the deranged blue-eyed caliph, the Egyptian Al-Hakim (996–1021), one of the few rulers in Islam to persecute Christians. His edict in 1009 to destroy the Holy Sepulchre (amongst other churches), was one of the contributory causes of the Crusades. The main dome, rising above the tomb of Christ itself, to the far left as you enter the oppressive gloom of the church, has recently been undergoing restoration as part of the colossal restoration project which began in 1960. You can enter into the tiny cramped grotto of the tomb itself, in the antechamber on which an angel is said to have sat during the Resurrection. As you walk round the outside of it, a crouching priest will summon you over to touch the 'Head of Christ', the headstone of his tomb. Over the centuries, the various Christian sects and denominations have divided up the holy site among themselves, so that you have today Greek and Coptic convents and Armenian, Coptic, Jacobite

Mad caliph

The tomb of Jesus

(Monophysites of the Syrian Church), Franciscan and Ethiopian chapels. Different embodiments of these sects in their different uniforms can be seen in the building, jealously guarding their patches.

To the right of the entrance, stairs lead up to Golgotha, the symbolic place of the crucifixion. The array of glitter and statues here is somewhat meretricious, but the medieval mosaics on the chapel walls are quite exquisite.

The Stone of Unction

In the entrance hall, a plaque marks the Stone of Unction, a slab of reddish limestone where the Latins believe the body of Christ was embalmed, and where the Greek Orthodox believe that Christ was unnailed from the cross and wept for by his mother. At the Orthodox Easter, this stone is the scene of extraordinary acts of devotion, with old women prostrating themselves, arms out in the shape of a cross, weeping for the death of the Lord.

The remainder of the Christian quarter can be seen by heading in the direction of the New Gate (new in 1889, when the Sultan Abdul Hamid II permitted a hole to be punched through to allow Christians easier access to their holy places), where you will find such places as the Casa Nova, the Latin Patriarchate and the College of Franciscan Brothers, mainly dating from Crusader times. One of these Crusader buildings has now been converted into a modest hotel, the Knights Palace.

You can now pass into the Armenian and Jewish Quarters, where there is less in the way of visitable monuments, but which are well worth having a stroll round to sample their different flavours.

Walking due south from the Jaffa Gate along the edge of David's Tower, you soon come to a strong gateway where the street narrows. This marks the beginning of the **Armenian Quarter** which, with its thick walls and gateway that is still locked and bolted every night from 10.00 pm to 6.00 am, is like a small city within a city where Armenians have lived since the fourth century AD, still using their own language and with their own separate schools. Their

Beautiful cathedral

Cathedral of St James (the body of James the brother of Jesus and first Bishop of Jerusalem, lies under the main altar), is one of the most beautiful and most authentic buildings in old Jerusalem. It and the tiny quarter around it represent for Armenians the spiritual capital of their stateless nation. The cathedral itself is only open from 3.00 to 3.30 pm daily except Sundays, but it is usually possible to stroll in from the street into the complex around it.

Today all Armenians in Jerusalem hold Jordanian nationality. The Israelis treat them fairly well, but take an excessive amount in taxes from them, in the words of one

Armenian resident , *'on the pretext of socialism, an excuse to take more money for the government'*. The minimum tax band in Israel starts at 40 per cent. The main Armenian complaint therefore, is that their natural mercantile flair is thwarted and their businesses can never grow beyond a certain size. Loyalties in this quarter are still to Jordan: when they say *'We would like the King to return'*, they are talking about Hussein rather the Messiah. The Armenian Art Centre and various other craft shops offer an interesting range of Armenian goods for sale.

Loyal Armenians

Under Jordanian control, the **Jewish Quarter** fell into a severe state of disrepair, but hardly surprisingly, since 1967 a great deal of money has been spent on it, rebuilding and restoring synagogues, Jewish schools and *yeshivas*, orthodox Jewish rabbinical seminaries. The resulting modern architecture here, like that of the settlements, has a distinctly fortress-like, defensive quality, and most of the modern inhabitants are practising orthodox Jews. The main street of the quarter, called the Cardo, has recently been excavated and restored, and now boasts many shops and galleries.

In recent years the number of orthodox Hassidic Jews, in their black suits, top hats, earlocks and long beards, has been steadily increasing and all over Jerusalem are *yeshivas* financed by wealthy American Jews. Inside, they wait for the Messiah's second coming to redeem mankind, occupying themselves in the meantime with the study of the *halakha*, a code of religious instructions on such weighty matters as how to brush the teeth and in which direction, or the correct way to sleep with your wife. Opting out of military service (a badge of pride for most Israelis), and obsessed with their orthodox beliefs, they create many problems for the Israeli government by insisting on such things as a total ban on public transport on the Sabbath (Saturday). They have forced cinemas to close on the Sabbath, and many young Israelis feel that Jerusalem's once bohemian fun-loving spirit has been killed by these lugubrious black-attired devotees, so they now flock out to Tel Aviv on a Friday afternoon for their 'day of rest'. The earnest Hassidim do not of course see themselves as unreasonable: 'We never force people to turn off their videos. There is no coercion'. Because they hold the vital balance of power between the two main political parties of Likud and Labour, they wield a disproportionate amount of power in relation to their numbers and are in a position to demand new religious laws in return for lending their support to more mundane state issues such as economic reforms.

On the increase

Jerusalem's dull Sabbath

DIVISIONS WITHIN JUDAISM

Within the Jewish population, the main division is between the Central European and Russian Jews, known as Ashkenazi Jews, and the Oriental Jews known as Sephardi Jews. The founders of Zionism were Ashkenazi Jews, as were the survivors of the Holocaust. With the founding of the Israeli state in 1948 the doors were thrown open, and many oriental Sephardi Jews began to arrive from Iraq, Yemen, Morocco and Tunisia. Frequently illiterate, unskilled and impoverished, they flocked to the new state, expecting to have wealth and education bestowed on them. Because of their higher birth rate , they now form around 60 per cent of the Jewish population of Israel, whilst still being only scantily represented in the Knesset. The social frictions are considerable, and one Ashkenazi Jew voiced a concern which many share: 'If we ever get peace, we'll have a civil struggle around here that will make us wish we had the Arabs back as enemies'. The latest twist in the in-house Jewish wrangles has been the 'Who's a Jew' issue, with the minority religious parties proclaiming that only orthodox conversions to Judaism should be allowed. American Jews are furious at such restrictive proposals, since 90 per cent of them belong to the Reform and Conservative movements and are unaffiliated. The orthodox policy would therefore make them into second-class Jews, and the result would be a withdrawal of support by American Jews, financial suicide for the Israeli state.

The importance of keeping things within the Jewish family can still be seen by a glance at the personal columns of the Jerusalem Post, where such adverts as the following still abound: *'Exciting, personable, sensitive, aware, emotional, warm, spiritual, intellectual, professional, traditional, Zionistically oriented single Jewish male, 37, seeks very attractive, slim, aware, spiritual, warm and affectionate, traditional, Jewishly orientated female.'*

Probably the best way to see the **Citadel** is at one of the evening *son et lumière* performances. The **Tower of David**, the tallest and most powerful of the five towers of the Citadel is what the Israelis call the whole ensemble now. It is *open daily from 8.30 am to 4.00 pm*, and also contains the Jerusalem City Museum (*10.00 am–5.00 pm Sunday to Thursday, 10.00 am–2.00pm Friday and Saturday*), with exhibits and a video on the city's history. The original building on the site was Herod's Palace, built in 24 BC, and it served then as the residence for the Roman Governor of Palestine for the next few centuries, until Hadrian had it destroyed. The Crusaders rebuilt it in the twelfth century as the residence of the King of Jerusalem, but it was again demolished in 1239 by the Muslim Prince of Kerak, and lay in ruins till 1335. The Ottoman Turks then had the walls and towers built as we see them today, higher and more powerful than ever before. Unfortunately, the two architects omitted to include David's tomb within the walls, forgetting that David was sacred to the Muslims as well as to the Jews and Christians: they were killed by Suleyman for their oversight.

Powerful Ottoman walls

The *son et lumière* performances are daily, after dark, in French, German, English and Hebrew: Arabic is not on offer. You might do well to go to a performance in a language you do not understand so as not to subject yourself to the dreadful script. Israel, a long-time expert at public relations, has wasted its opportunity here, and it is very heavy-handed. Jerusalem is proclaimed as the centre of the world, and the catalogue of rulers is given. Jesus Christ is passed over quickly, then the advent of the Arabs is illustrated by a wailing call to prayer from one tower, while Christian church bells continue ringing from the opposite corner. After the 1967 war, the smug voice boasts, Jerusalem's chequered history is over, and 'all is united now'. The audience is predominantly American Jews on visits with their children.

Sound and Light

Outside the Walls
Because of the mistake of the Turkish architects, the area of Mount Zion, with the Room of the Last Supper and the Tomb of David, now lies outside the walls. At the time of Christ, they were of course inside.

Walking out through the Zion Gate, signs will guide you past the Harp of David Restaurant to the **Cenacle**, the place of the Last Supper. Outside the building itself, a board announces 'COENACULUM – House of Prayer for All People. Welcome !!!' Immediately to the left, steps lead up to the unspectacular empty room. If you go too far on beyond the building, you will realise your mistake, as you inadvertently enter the Diaspora Yeshiva.

Scene of the Last Supper

On the ground floor of the same building as the Cenacle, through a vaulted room with pillars, lies the reputed **Tomb of King David**, a huge impressive sarcophagus. The Jewish and Christian origins of the building are obscure and confused. In 1447 the Franciscan monks who tended the site were dispossessed of it by the Turks, and from then until 1948, it was held as exclusive to Muslims, David being revered as a prophet in the Quran. Jews and Christians were forbidden entry. The Room of the Last Supper was converted into a mosque and endowed with a *mihrab* or prayer niche.

King David's tomb

From the outside you will glimpse to the right (west) the impressive dome of the **Dormition Abbey**, built on the site where Mary was said to have fallen into 'eternal sleep'. The high dome, with six mosaic side domes, was completed in 1910 and has a pleasant light and airy feel. *Open from 8.00 am to 12.00 noon and from 2.00 pm to 6.00 pm*, it is equipped with a modern shop, cafeteria and toilets.

Dormition Abbey

From this area of Mount Zion you can now begin a

walk eastwards down round the edge of the walls to
Mount Ophel, a steep rocky outcrop just south of the city
walls where archaeologists have uncovered the remains of
the Canaanite city that David conquered and Solomon
adorned. Shortly after passing the romantically named
Dung Gate, (from the days when the city's rubbish was
carried through it, to be dumped in the Valley of Kidron),
a steep road plunges to the right downhill for some 500m
to reach the impressive water supply system which irri-
gated the Valley of Kidron. Steps go down into the **Pool
of Siloam** from which **Hezekiah's tunnel**, 540m long and
built by King Hezekiah in 700 BC, is cut into the rock to
reach the Gihon Spring. Wading along the metre-wide
tunnel in the knee-high water is a popular pastime among
local and visiting families. It was to this Pool of Siloam
that Christ, according to St John, sent the man born blind
to go and wash: *'He went his way, therefore, and washed, and
came seeing'.* (John 9: 7)

**Water-filled
tunnel**

From the Pool of Siloam, you can continue downhill
for another 100m or so before turning left to walk back
up the **Valley of Kidron** towards the Garden of
Gethsemane. On the way, you will pass on your left the
Fountain of the Virgin, which gushes out from a grotto
where the Virgin Mary is said to have washed the clothes
of Christ. Next, 100m further on your right, you will
come to the necropolis area at the foot of the cliff, where
the notable monument is the Tomb of the Daughter of
Pharoah, a rare example of the architecture of the kings of
Judea. Some 400m beyond it, again on your right, you
come to another cluster of tombs, this time in Hellenistic
style, the first being the Pyramid of Zachariah on its Ionic
base. A grotto cave with Doric columns is the vestibule
entrance to a series of funeral chambers, thought to date
from the fourth century. The final tomb, partly hewn
from the rock, is the 20m high so-called Pillar of
Absalom, David's rebellious son. It was restored in 1925.

**Valley of
Kidron**

The road now joins the main Jericho road and you continue just another 100m north along it before forking off
into **Gethsemane**. This walk from Mount Zion right round
to Gethsemane is long, some 3km in all, and if you are
short of time and the weather is hot, you may prefer
instead to skirt round the walls and content yourself with
fine views down into the Valley of Kidron. You can then
visit Gethsemane from St Stephen's (Lion's) Gate, the walk
from here takes just 5 or 10 minutes, and from the foot the
1km climb up to the Mount of Olives takes about 30 minutes, allowing for pauses for views and photographs. You
can of course also get a bus (from the Damascus Gate) or

taxi to the cafés and restaurants at the summit of the Mount of Olives. Sometimes there is even a camel waiting, with owner, at the start of the ascent.

At Gethsemane you come first, on your left, to the steps leading down to what has come to be called the **Tomb of Mary**. In practice it is the crypt of a church built in the fifth century by the Byzantines, demolished in 614 by the Persians, then rebuilt by the Crusaders, only to be demolished again by Saladin in 1187. A further candidate for the Tomb of the Virgin, and generally better credited, is in Galilee, and another, also well credited, is in Turkey in the hills near Ephesus, where Mary is said to have been taken by John on his preachings after the death of Christ.

Mary's tomb

A little further on, to the right, is the modern **Basilica of Agony** or Church of All Nations (since many countries contributed funds for it), designed by the Italian architect Antonio Berluzzi and completed in 1924, on the site of an earlier fourth century church. There are mosaics all over the domes and the floor. In the centre Christ is shown alone in the garden; to the left is Judas's kiss, to the right is Christ reappearing after his crucifixion. In the central courtyard, eight venerable olive trees, considered very old even in the fifteenth century, are said to be, if not the very trees that witnessed Christ's agony of doubt, then at least their descendants. Knowing what was to happen the following day, he turned to his disciples and said:

Basilica of Agony

My soul is exceedingly sorrowful, even unto death: tarry ye here, and watch with me.
And he went a little further, and fell on his face, and prayed, saying, O my Father, if it be possible, let this cup pass from me: nevertheless not as I will, but as thou wilt.
(Matthew 26: 38—39)

Near the Basilica of Agony, just before a café resthouse, a little tarred road forks off to the right, leading up the hill towards the Russian Convent of St Mary Magdalene (*open only on Tuesdays and Thursdays, 9.00 am–12.00 noon and 2.00 pm–4.00 pm*). This lovely golden onion-domed convent was built in the 1880s by Tsar Alexander III.

Russian convent

To the right of the road is the huge and ever-expanding Jewish cemetery. Since 1967 prices for grave plots have shot up, as orthodox Jews believe that on the Day of Judgement, those buried nearest the Temple will be called first. The spot also affords an excellent view of the Golden Gate beneath the Temple Mount, closed in 1530 by a Turkish governor. It was through this gate that Jesus was said to have ridden on Palm Sunday, and through which the Messiah is prophesied to return. Here too, the first trumpet

Popular burial spot

Tombs of the prophets

will be sounded on the Day of Judgement: the governor who closed the gate, it is said, wanted to postpone the day.

Higher on up the hill, on the right, are the **Tombs of the Prophets** which Jews claim as the burial places of the prophets Haggai, Zachariah and Malachi. The guardian shows you round the bare dark grottos, now mainly visited by Hassidic Jews.

To the right is the superbly sited 5-star 7 Arches Hotel (formerly the Intercontinental) and to the left the road leads off to a cluster of cafés beyond which are the **Basilica of the Sacred Heart** and the **Sanctuary of the Ascension**. The former is built on the site where Christ was said to have initiated his disciples into the secrets of the end of the world. Nearby, the **Church of Pater Noster** marks the spot where Christ is said to have taught his disciples the Lord's Prayer. Inside are tablets with the prayer written in 44 languages, donated from all over the world.

Beyond the churches, a road leads off to the villages of Bethpagé and Bethany, 1 and 2 km respectively from the Sanctuary of the Ascension. In Bethpagé a little church lies over the traditional site of the tomb of Lazarus. From Bethany it is 5km by road back to Jerusalem.

The afternoon excursion takes you to the **Rockefeller Museum** (*10.00 am–5.00 pm Sunday to Thursday, 10.00 am–2.00 pm Saturday*). This is the major archaeological museum on the West Bank and one of the finest museums anywhere in the Middle East. It is set just outside the walls at the north-east corner, near Herod's Gate. Built in the 1930s, it was a gift from John D. Rockefeller Jr. Well designed and extremely well laid out, it is arranged around an attractive open central courtyard, its oblong pool covered in water liles. Among the outdoor exhibits here by the pond is the huge foot of a statue, at least ten times the size of a human foot.

Excellent layout

Relics of Ummayad palace

The museum boasts the best exhibits, chronologically arranged, from each period of excavation in the Holy Land, from the Stone Age through to Ottoman times. One of the major exhibits, particularly relevant for visitors from Jordan who have seen and enjoyed the Umayyad desert palaces, is the superb collection of decorative plaster friezes taken from Hisham's Palace, Khirbet el-Mafjar, near Jericho, the only one of the Umayyad palaces on the West Bank. Highly elaborate, these friezes are full of animals, such as winged horses and partridges. Fragments of the friezes still bear some colour. The palace was built at the time of Walid II (743–744), but was destroyed by an earthquake before completion. At the entrance to the reconstructed baths a rather squat topless dancing girl some

The Rockefeller Museum (Darke).

1.2m tall, grins from within the frieze to greet you. From the navel down she is wearing a draped skirt. The style of decoration shows Persian (Sassanid), Byzantine and Coptic influences, but is essentially rather crude and primitive. Among the foliage of the plaster, monkeys and people are intertwined, their faces peering out like gargoyles.

Some 500m north of the Damascus Gate up the Nablus Road you can walk to the **Garden Tomb**, set in a garden (*open 8.00 am–12.00 noon and 2.00 pm–5.00 pm*) which is believed by some traditions to be the true site of Golgotha and the tomb where Christ was buried.

A further 1km north up the road you come to the **Tombs of the Kings** (*open 8.00 am–12.30 pm and 2.00 am–5.00 pm*), where the kings of Judea were thought to be buried. A huge staircase leads down into a courtyard, and the tombs all have stones which were rolled across the entrance.

THE SOUTHERN CIRCUIT

Southern Circuit Facts

The circuit can easily be done in a day returning to Jerusalem for the night, but if you want to spend a night on the way the following accommodation is recommended:

*** **Ein Gedi Hotel** (*tel: 84757*). Attached to a kibbutz on the Dead Sea 18 km north of Massada. 91 rooms. Pool and beach.

** **Taylor** (*tel: 84349*). Massada. A youth hostel with 200 beds.

* **The Palace Hotel** (*tel: 742798*). Bethlehem. Set in a garden off Manger Square. A simple but attractive place to stay.

The ruins at Qumran (Darke).

Qumran

The site of **Qumran**, raised up on its platform overlooking the Dead Sea, is a 35-minute (44km) drive from Jerusalem, and the route is clearly signposted. *Open from 8.00 am to 6.00 pm (5.00 pm in winter)*, the site is well laid out, with arrows indicating the best circuit, and is also provided with a modern café/restaurant built in the early 1980s, along with a shop selling Dead Sea mud cosmetics, like face packs and cleansing lotions.

Dominated by the cliffs above, the site was originally an Iron-Age fort, but was chosen in the second century BC as a centre by the Essenes, a Jewish sect who had broken away from the orthodox clergy of Jerusalem. Living in a sort of exile, they made themselves into a totally self-contained community, growing their own crops and designing their own water supply. They also had their own bakery, pottery, blacksmith and furnace. Here the community lived peaceably studying and writing until the settlement was sacked and destroyed by the Roman legions around 68 AD, after the first Jewish revolt. The Essenes had warning of the Romans' approach, and hurriedly hid their most precious possession, their library of scrolls, in caves in the nearby cliffs. Most of the inhabitants were massacred, and those that survived never returned to retrieve the scrolls.

The Dead Sea Scrolls

So far, some 4000 of these Dead Sea Scrolls have been found in total, either in caves or buried under the floors of houses. You can scramble across to the caves from the ruined settlement, notably the one where the two shepherd boys discovered the first scrolls in 1947. Among the most significant of the scrolls were manuscripts of the Bible which predated by some 1000 years the earliest known Hebrew text of the Old Testament. They were therefore of vital importance in verifying the biblical text and for the study of biblical history. The scrolls found so far cover a period of about 300 years before and after the birth of Christ, shedding much light on the background of the earliest Christian period. An international group of scholars has been given responsibility for the huge task of cataloguing and studying the scrolls and all the fragments. So far, most of the books of the Old Testament have been identified among them.

Nature reserve and waterfall

From Qumran, the good new road follows the western shore of the Dead Sea southwards, passing, after 35km, through **Ein Gedi**. Created in 1953, this kibbutz runs a hotel, a youth hostel, a camp site, a thermal spa and a restaurant. There is also a beautiful nature reserve, an oasis of springs and lush vegetation under the escarpment, which can be visited from *8.00 am to 3.00 pm except Saturdays*. One spring falls from a height of 185m into a natural pool where you can swim.

Massada

The ultimate Jewish site. Massada lies within Israel proper, not on the West Bank. It would be perverse, however, to omit it here, since it not only lies on the southern circuit, but it is also one of the most impressive sights in Israel, brought alive in many peoples' imaginations through TV and cinema productions. 18km beyond Ein Gedi, the colossal 300m high block plateau looms into view unmistakably and the road forks up to the right to reach the

Cable car ascent or backpackers climb

cable-car station and ticket booths. The 45 minute to one hour climb up the steep Snake Path in the middle of the night, arriving at the summit in time for the dawn is *de rigeur* for backpackers. The experience is often not very pleasant, however, quite apart from the exertion, as you tend to find yourself among 500 others all tripping noisily over each other in the dark.

The Swiss-built cable car functions *between 8.00 am and 4.00 pm*, with *departures every half hour. The last ascent is at 3.30 pm, and the last descent is at 4.00 pm.* If you want to make both journeys by cable car, the latest possible ascent you should catch is therefore at 2.30 pm, allowing an hour (the absolute minimum) at the top before the final descent. Best of all in many ways, is to make the ascent by cable car, spend as long as you like on the summit (probably around two hours), then make the descent on foot at your leisure (usually a further hour). The Snake Path is mildly vertiginous but quite wide. Underfoot, the surface is loose rock, so wear comfortable shoes.

Herod's fortress

The name Massada comes, appropriately enough, from the Hebrew for fortress, and the naturally defensive spot was chosen by King Herod in around 40 AD for the construction of a huge and magnificent palace-cum-fortress. He was intent on making it virtually impregnable, first against the Jewish people who hated him so, and secondly against a feared attack by Cleopatra, queen of Egypt. In scarcely six years, an army of slaves had completed the elaborate structure, together with the complex water network of cisterns and channels.

During the Jewish Revolt against the Romans in 66 AD, a band of Jewish rebels were, ironically, to benefit from Herod's thoroughness, seizing the fortress in a surprise attack. Once installed, they were able to take advantage of all the stored provisions of food and live comfortably for several years on the summit, defending themselves with

Roman arms and even making the occasional guerilla attack on Jerusalem and other targets.

The Roman legate Flavius Silva finally decided that Rome had suffered enough embarrassment at the hands of a few hundred Jews, and taking 10,000 troops with him, he camped at the foot of Massada and began a siege, also making a series of attacks with flaming torches and rock catapaults. The rubble walls of the Roman camps, eight of them in all, can still be seen from the summit, forming large squares around the base of the mountain. When, after two years, there was still no sign of an end to the siege, Silva devised the ingenious scheme of having a huge ramp built up to the summit, which would enable his troops to storm the fort *en masse*. Watching the ramp nearing completion, the 900 Jews realised that defeat was inevitable. They agreed, at the instigation of their leader Eleazar, to commit mass suicide – women, children and all – rather than accept slavery under Roman masters. When the Romans stormed in the next day, bristling with arms and setting fire to everything in sight, they were staggered at the silence that greeted them.

The famous ramp

Extensive excavations on the summit have laid bare all the elaborate parts of the fortress, and the Roman ramp can still be seen on the western side. As in all Israeli sites, everything is extremely well laid out, with drinking water supplies and toilet facilities at regular intervals. The flat plateau summit is surprisingly extensive, and an excellent chart, also on sale as a map from the stalls down below by the cable car station, marks a range of three circuits for you to choose from: short (two hours), intermediate (three or four hours) and extensive (over five hours). Not to be missed are the Southern Citadel (35 on the map) and its cistern (34), the Western Palace (3) near the Roman ramp, and the spectacular three-level palace on the northern edge (14, 15 and 16). The bulk of the excavation work took place in 1963, 1964 and 1965, when thousands of volunteers from over 20 different countries answered adverts to come and help a handful of professional archaeologists.

Well laid-out

There are no café or refreshment facilities other than water available on the summit, but there is a café for light snacks at the foot by the cable car station. There is also a large youth hostel for the backpackers' dawn assault.

A Detour to Sodom
As you drive further south along the Dead Sea, the shoreline becomes ever whiter and saltier, and those who feel so inclined can continue to the very southernmost point, where the Israelis claim their own site of **Sodom**.

Lot's wife

As on the Jordanian side, nothing whatever remains of any ancient town, and the area is heavily industrialised with potash and phosphate factories. Claimed, at -396m to be the lowest inhabited place on earth, signs lead to the pillars of salt, one of which is claimed to be Lot's wife. The whole area is desolate, with a smell of sulphur in the air. Not long ago, an enterprising body proposed the construction of a gambling casino at Sodom. The imaginative scheme was vetoed by religious authorities as too dangerous – history might repeat itself.

Hebron

North of Sodom, the road forks right to Arad, then climbs quite quickly out of the Dead Sea valley and up into the barren hillsides which form the edge of the Wilderness of Judea. It then sweeps round north again, passing through the Palestinian town of **Hebron**. One of the oldest cities in the world, Hebron is noted today for the cluster of tombs where Abraham and Sarah, Isaac and Rebecca, and Jacob are said to be buried, in another fortress built by Herod (*open 8.00 am–12.00 noon and 2.00 pm–4.00 pm daily, except Fridays*). Within the walls, a mosque has been built around the tombs and the whole area is called Haram el-Khalil (el-Khalil is Arabic for Hebron, meaning Friend of God, the epithet for Abraham).

Abraham's tomb

On the main road between Bethlehem and Hebron, Solomon's Pools make a pleasant shady spot for lunch at a restaurant next to one of the three pools.

The Herodium

Another of Herod's palaces

Continuing the route north to Jerusalem, a small detour not to be missed is the **Herodium**, Herod's palace in the hills some 10km south of Bethlehem. The distinctive shape of the hill of the palace, a flattened cone, is visible from a long way off. It is *open daily from 8.00 am to 5.00 pm*, and the visit involves a short but steep walk up from the car park to the summit of the mound. At the ticket kiosk is a monument to a Jew killed in 1982 'by terrorists while doing his duties for the National Parks Authorities'.

Arriving at the rim of the cone, it becomes apparent for the first time that the mound is hollow, and the palace buildings are set down inside it, as if in the cone of a volcano. The site is impressive for this and for the magnificent view it offers eastwards towards the Dead Sea, rather than for the extent of the buildings themselves. Traces of the piped water system hint at the luxurious style in which the palace rooms were once appointed. It was built by Herod the Great in 37–34 BC, and at the foot of the mound, the remains of an unexcavated town, known as Herodia, can be distinguished.

Bethlehem
Having made the detour to the Herodium, you can now stay on this smaller road to drive north for 9km to reach **Bethlehem**, then rejoining the main road shortly before Jerusalem.

Bethlehem is today a half Christian, half Muslim town of 35,000. Set on a hill, it is largely modern and not especially attractive, but it is visited by tourists and pilgrims for its **Church of the Nativity**, set in the central Manger Square, near the highest point of the town. The church, the oldest one in the country, is built above the grotto where tradition has it that Jesus was born, and it is approached today across a large paved courtyard. Constantine the Great built the first church on this spot which his mother Queen Helena had sought out on the basis of the advice of local people. It was destroyed by an earthquake and rebuilt by Justinian some 200 years later. These two early churches were then restored by the Crusaders in the twelfth century. The very low entrance door, called the Door of Humility, is said to have been made to prevent Turkish soldiers riding into the church on horseback. The door leads into a huge and impressive nave with a wooden-raftered roof and a strange quadruple row of pinkish brown Corinthian marble pillars: this section still dates from Constantine's reign in the fourth century. The atmosphere in the church, if you are fortunate enough not to meet up with a group, is evocative. In the central aisle, wooden trapdoors are left open to reveal sections of the original mosaic flooring below. The church was unusual in being spared destruction at the hands of the Persians: they saw the Magi as their ancestors, because of their Persian dress in one of the front mosaics. High up on the walls above the columns are further gilded mosaics.

Towards the altar, steps lead down from either side into the grotto of the Nativity itself, with an altar where the crib is thought to have stood. The floor is marble and the walls are covered in icons, together with an old leather tapestry. The care of the church is divided out between Greek Orthodox (in long black robes), Armenian (in purple and cream robes), and Franciscan priests (in simple brown habits).

Christmas is obviously the time of year when most pilgrims visit Bethlehem, and on Christmas Eve thousands of Christians have traditionally packed the church and square for a carol service followed by the celebration of

Christ's birth place

Impressive interiors

midnight mass. Since the Intifada began in 1987 however, it has been a rather different picture, with armed Israeli soldiers outnumbering the few hundred visitors who venture into the rainswept streets. The town's special Christmas decorations are not put up, and shops and restaurants stay closed. Admission to the church and square at Christmas is strictly controlled, and all tourists wishing to enter must have obtained special tickets in advance from the Franciscan Pilgrims Office at the Jaffa Gate, Jerusalem.

Tourism in Israel as a whole dropped by 15 per cent from 1987 to 1988, but in Bethlehem and Jerusalem custom has dropped by nearly three times that much.

Rachel's tomb

At the roadside on the northern outskirts of Bethlehem on the main highway to Jerusalem is **Rachel's Tomb**, a spot where pilgrims come to pray for fertility and sons. Rachel, wife of Jacob, bore 11 sons before dying in childbirth with Benjamin. It is closed on Saturdays.

Shepherds' Fields

From Bethlehem, a more picturesque alternative to the main road back to Jerusalem is the small scenic road that loops to the east, starting from just before Manger Square then going on to **Beit Sahur**, the traditional site of 'where shepherds watched their flock by night', and bringing you some 10km later, to the Mount of Olives. The road winds through the Hebron valley and after some 7km, a bad road forks off to the right for about 7km to the spectacular **Monastery of Mar Saba**. Clinging to the edge of a deep ravine, this monastery was built in 486 by Saba of Cappadocia in Central Turkey, and at its height boasted a total of 5000 monks. Only a few remain today, and so as not to disturb them unnecessarily, no women are permitted to enter, although they may view the monastery from a special tower. For men, the large, five-storey monastery is well worth a visit.

Mar Saba Monastery

On the remaining stretch of road into Jerusalem you will notice many caves cut into the sides of the valleys, many of them still inhabited. They were originally dug out by Christian hermits and monks.

THE NORTHERN CIRCUIT

Northern Circuit Facts

Nazareth
There are two good hotels:

*** **Hotel Galilee** (*tel: 71311*). A modern 90-room hotel on Paul VI Street in the centre of town near the Basilica of the Annunciation.

*** **Grand New Hotel** (*tel: 73020*). Another 90-room modern hotel but with better views and baths rather than showers.

Nof Ginossar
A kibbutz on the western shore of Lake Galilee, 9km north of Tiberias with a 4-star hotel (*tel: 22163*). The hotel has 170 air-conditioned rooms. It is expensive but worth it, with an excellent private beach and water sports facilities, and limitless good-quality food on a self-service basis. The lake fish, St Peter, is a speciality to be tried. There are tours of the kibbutz for the curious. A museum in the grounds houses the remains of a fishing boat thought to date from the time of Christ.

Tiberias
There are numerous hotels here, the best of which are:

***** **Galei Kinnereth** (*tel: 92331*). 127 rooms.

***** **Plaza** (*tel: 92233*). 272 rooms.

***** **Tiberias Club Hotel** (*tel: 91888*). 310 rooms.

**** **Ganei Hammut** (*tel: 92890*). 190 rooms.

The lakeside at Capernaum (Darke).

The Road North

The main road north out of Jerusalem towards Ramallah
follows the crest of a range of hills which are covered in
the concrete jungle of new Israeli settlements. All the
signposts to them are in Hebrew only, and their fortress-
like walls underline their dual purpose both as housing
for Jewish settlers in former Arab areas, and as quasi-mil-
itary structures to dominate the strategic heights above
the Palestinian villages below. Most of the land for these
settlements was confiscated by the Israeli government:
the seizures were declared legal under Israeli law because
they were 'for a public purpose'.

**Jewish
settlements**

Some 10km out of Jerusalem, a road forks west towards
the village of **El-Jib** where excavations a little to the south
mark the spot where *'the sun stood still'* at Gibeon
(Joshua 10: 12–13). This is also the 'Road to Emmaus'
where Christ appeared to his disciples after his resurrection. Just 2km after the village of Emmaus itself is
Latroun, still just within the West Bank, where the
Trappist monks of the modern monastery produce the
Latroun wines which are widely available in Jordan. On
the summit of the hill above the monastery is a heavily
ruined Crusader fort, adapted with trenches and used by
the Israelis in twentieth century wars to guard the pass to
Jerusalem from Tel Aviv.

Latroun wines

Sebastea

Back on the main road, the landscape as you continue
northwards is pleasantly treed with green hillsides. This
is the biblical region of Samaria, and though the main
towns of Nablus and Jenin offer little to the visitor, one
interesting short diversion is to the ruins of **Sebastea**,
ancient capital of Samaria, picturesquely situated on a
hilltop.

Hilltop ruins

A narrow tarred road is signposted right, leading you
after 2km to the rather scruffy little village. The road
passes a mosque on the right, and behind it you will
notice some old Roman tombs. The mosque is on the site
of the former church of John the Baptist, built by the
Crusaders in the twelfth century, for local tradition held
that the Baptist's body was buried here at Sebastea. At the
site entrance by the vast open forum, is a small refreshments and souvenir stall, but it is best to take a picnic and
walk on up through the site, climbing above the theatre to
the temple on the highest point, from where the views
over the rolling Samarian landscape are very attractive.
Most of the extant ruins are of Roman date.

Nazareth

As you continue northwards, passing through Jenin, the road to Galilee brings you close to **Nazareth**, which is in Israel itself. Though not actually on the circuit, many may wish to make the short detour, if only to feel they have set foot in Jesus' childhood town. Just a small village at that time, Nazareth today has Irael's largest Arab community outside Jerusalem. About half the population is Christian, and as a result, many shops are closed on Sundays but open on Saturdays.

Half Arab, half Christian

The main religious monument is the **Basilica of the Annunciation**, whose vast modern cupola serves as a useful landmark. Inside, the walls are covered in contemporary murals from all around the world, and the Japanese Madonna and Child is especially striking. The church is built over earlier sites, all set above the cave, now the church's crypt, where the Angel Gabriel is said to have announced to Mary: *'Hail, thou that art highly favoured, the Lord is with thee: blessed art thou among women…behold, thou shalt conceive in thy womb, and bring forth a son, and shalt call his name Jesus'.* (Luke 1: 28 and 31).

The Annunciation

For local colour, the best part of Nazareth is the old Arab market, an exciting district of narrow winding streets which may not have been very different in Christ's time, except that as well as selling herbs and spices, it now also sells chandeliers and plastic buckets. Make sure you bargain for everything.

The Sea of Galilee

Distances in Israel are short and the Sea of Galilee is just 157km north of Jerusalem. The route from the south brings you in at **Tiberias**, with a population of 30,000 the largest town by far on the lakeshore.

Resort of Tiberias

Violent earthquakes in the past have destroyed most of Tiberias's old monuments, although the famous hot sulphurous springs still survive. The town today is a modern flourishing resort and makes a good base for a circuit of the lake. Even better, you could stay in one of the luxurious kibbutzim on the lakeshore, such as the four-star Nof Ginossar, some 9km to the north.

The tranquil lake, 210m below sea-level, makes excellent year-round swimming, and at weekends and on holidays is crowded with picnicking families equipped with barbecues and mountains of food. The women, often fully clothed, splash in the shallow water, then come out to sit in deckchairs in transparent wet dresses, smoking cigarettes. Along the shoreline north from Tiberias at Magdelena is a fine public beach lined with pretty eucalyptus trees.

Swimming parties

Feeding of the five thousand

Just 3km to the north of Nof Ginossar is a left fork which brings you after another kilometre to the **Church of the Beatitudes** at a peaceful spot right on the lake shore. The basilica is modern and was rebuilt in 1980–82 on the original foundations, over the rock where Christ is said to have put the bread and fishes for the feeding of the five thousand. The ruins of the ancient basilica here were not discovered until 1932, after being hidden for 1300 years. A temporary church was built over them in 1936, which the modern basilica has now replaced. The mosaic floor with colourful motifs of birds, fishes, snakes and foliage is from the original basilica, and has been dated to 480 AD. The atmosphere of the church is rather marred by such crassnesses as plastic door hangings, labelled entry and exit signs for the one-way flow of coach parties, and audiovisual shows.

Capernaum

At the northernmost tip of the lake is **Capernaum**, the scene of numerous biblical episodes, where the apostles Peter and Andrew lived, and where Jesus spent much time. Excavations here have uncovered a large ruined temple and synagogue foundations in white limestone, an octagonal church of the fifth century built on 'the house of Peter', and various ordinary houses which date back to the time of Christ. Restorations were carried out in 1921 by Franciscan monks, who had bought the site in the nineteenth century and built a monastery beside it. An entry fee is charged, since it is not a church, and the site is *open from 8.30 am to 4.15 pm*. Many people make the approach by boat from Tiberias, which moors up at the quay in front of the site.

A circuit of the 19-km long lake takes only an hour by car without stops. Along the eastern shore you have views towards the Golan Heights to the north-east. It is generally less built up than the western shore, just having a series of campsites rather than fully blown hotels.

Where John the Baptist baptised Christ

Arriving at the Deganya crossroads at the south, where the Jordan flows out of the lake, you can drive on for 2km until an orange sign points off to the left saying 'Pilgrims Baptismal Point'. This is where John the Baptist is said to have baptised Christ. Swimming in any area other than this is forbidden by signs all along the road from Deganya. Parking at the official baptismal point is organised and fenced in, with souvenir shops and postcard stalls. The approach to the river is down steps which wind to and fro between railings. Pilgrims are allowed to walk in and submerge themselves, though not to swim. In practice most visitors simply take off their shoes and paddle a little. The spot is still pretty, with lots of greenery and tall eucalyptus trees, though the atmosphere and view are to some extent marred by a large concrete road bridge in the background. Coach tours are processed down the steps and into the water in about 20 minutes, and if you have rather more time than this, you can sit on a bench and be entertained by the spectacle.

The Jordan Valley
The road south through the valley skirts alongside extensive agricultural. Tobacco, cucumbers, oranges, bananas and date palms cover the land between the road and the river, and the river itself is never visible throughout the whole drive south. In parts the road almost leaves the valley entirely, passing through bleak shadeless hillsides.

Belvoir Castle
A worthwhile detour of 5km can be made to the Crusader castle of **Belvoir**, perched 500m above the Jordan with excellent views over the valley. Built in 1140, the vast fortress is still well preserved. Now set in a national park, it is *open from 8.00 am to 5.00 pm in summer and 8.00 am to 4.00 pm in winter,* and has a restaurant.

Fine castle

Beit She'an
12km from Belvoir is the town of Beit She'an, set 120m below sea level. A half-hour detour will suffice to see the Roman theatre, the best in Israel, now set in a national park and *open from 8.00 am to 5.00 pm (8.00 am to 4.00 pm on Fridays and in winter).* Built in around 200 AD the basalt rows of seats can hold 5000 spectators. Also worth seeing are the floor mosaics in the Byzantine monastery of the Virgin Mary to the north of the town.

The best theatre

Hisham's Palace
A visit not to be missed, and of particular interest to those who have seen the desert palaces in Jordan, is **Hisham's Palace**, also known as Khirbet al-Mafjar, the only one of the Umayyad palaces that lies west of the Jordan river, and originally one of the most ornate and extensive.

Ornate palace

The site is signposted off to the left just a few kilometres to the north of Jericho. At the entrance is a simple refreshments stand (*open 8.00 am–5.00 pm*). Inscriptions found on the site show that the palace was begun by the Caliph Hisham, son of Abd el-Malik, in 724, and the building work continued until 743. Only four years after its completion it was destroyed by a severe earthquake, which is why the walls do not rise to any great height today. Most interesting and unusual of all is the superb mosaic of a tree bursting with fruit and gazelles. Of Byzantine inspiration, it decorates the floor of the bathhouse, now reconstructed and roofed-in for protection.

Jericho

The stop at **Jericho** is generally considered compulsory, although in fact there is little to see and much has to be left to the imagination. The large artificial mound, **Tell es-Sultan**, marks the site identified with the biblical Jericho whose walls came tumbling down around 1230 BC as a result of Joshua's trumpets. More interesting in some ways, and certainly more current, are the Palestinian refugee camps which line the roadsides, some just ghost towns, others still occupied.

To the west, there is a fine view of the Hills of Judea, with the **Monastery of The Temptation** clinging to the steep hillside – best seen with binoculars. The Greek Orthodox monks who built the monastery in the nineteenth century regard the summit of this mountain as the

The Devil's temptation of Christ

spot where the Devil tempted Christ after his 40 days and 40 nights in the wilderness.

And the devil, taking him up into an high mountain, shewed unto him all the kingdoms of the world in a moment of time.
And the devil said unto him, All this will I give thee, and the glory of them: for that is delivered unto me; and to whomsoever I will give it.
If thou therefore wilt worship me, all shall be thine.
And Jesus answered and said unto him, Get thee behind me, Satan: for it is written, Thou shalt worship the Lord thy God, and him only shalt thou serve.
(Luke 4: 5–8)

Valley of the Shadow of Death

A spectacular and little used route from Jericho back to Jerusalem is via the **Wadi Qelt,** a deep and dramatic ravine where Herod the Great had his winter palace, and identified by many as the Valley of the Shadow of Death of the 23rd Psalm. A small tarred road forks off to the right (west) about half a kilometre south of Jericho and climbs up along the southern rim of the wadi, offering occasional glimpses into the dizzy gorge below. If you have an hour to spare, leave the car in the parking area at the road edge, and walk down the steep path to visit the **Monastery of St George of Khoziba**, founded around 450 by an Egyptian from Thebes. It clings to the vertical side of the ravine, suspended just above the lush vegetation of the valley bottom. The silence is broken only by the murmuring of the plentiful springs. The two old churches have icons and frescoes from the sixth and

seventh centuries. Outside, a few hermits' caves have
been built into the cliff, and can be approached by precarious ladders. Tea can be taken with the monks.

The small tarmac road continues for a further 6km
before rejoining the main Jerusalem highway.

**Tea with the
monks**

APPENDIX

USEFUL ARABIC WORDS AND PHRASES

Everyday Arabic

hello, welcome	*marhaba* or *ahlan*
goodbye	*ma'a as-salaama*
yes	*aiwa* or *na'am*
no	*la*
please	*min fadlak*
thank you	*shukran*
sorry, excuse me	*muta'assif*
hurry up, let's go	*yallah*
more, again, also	*kamaan*
is it possible? may I?	*mumkin?*
how much (does it cost?)	*bikaam?* or *adaysh?*
cheap	*rakhees*
expensive	*ghaali*
money	*fuluus*
a lot, much, very	*kateer*
no problem	*mish mushkila*
never mind	*ma'a laysh*
shop	*dukkaan*
open	*maftuuh*
closed	*musakkar* or *mughlaq*
bank	*bank* or *masraf*
post office	*maktab bareed*
chemist	*saydalia*
diarrhoea	*ishaal*
market	*souq*
museum	*mathaf*
hospital	*mustashfa*
police	*shurta*
airport	*mataar*
ticket	*tadhkara*
suitcase	*shanta*
hotel	*otel, funduq*
room	*ghurfa*
toilet, bathroom	*hammam, bait moi*
towel	*manshafa* or *bashkir*
soap	*saabuun*
gents	*rijaal*
ladies	*sayyidaat*
the bill	*el-hisaab*

restaurant	*mat'am*	**Eating out**
breakfast	*futoor*	
lunch	*ghada*	
dinner	*'asha*	
glass	*kubbayeh*	
wine	*nabeed*	**Food and drink**
red wine, white wine	*nabeed ahmar, nabeed abyad*	
rosé	*rosé*	
beer	*bira*	
mineral water	*moi ma'daniyeh*	
tea	*shay*	
coffee	*gahwa*	
eggs	*bayd*	
fish	*samak*	
meat	*lahma*	
fruit	*fawakeh*	
milk	*haleeb*	
butter	*zibda*	
cheese	*jibneh*	
yogurt	*laban*	
jam	*murabba*	
honey	*'asl*	
bread	*khubz*	
sugar	*sukkar*	
vegetables	*khudra*	
today	*al-youm*	
tomorrow	*bukra*	
shared taxi	*servees*	
car	*sayyara*	
right	*yameen*	**Directions**
left	*yasaar* or *shimaal*	
straight on	*dughri* or *ala tool*	
far	*ba'eed*	
near, close by	*gareeb*	
petrol	*benzeen*	
where?	*wayn?*	
bus	*bas*	
forbibben	*mamnuu'*	
good	*kuwwayis*	
bad	*mish kuwwayis*	
hot	*harr*	
cold	*baared*	

In addition to these simple words, there are a few phrases you will hear often and should be aware of, even if you do not have the confidence to use them yourself.

tafaddal: please go ahead, come in

in sha Allah: if God wishes, meaning roughly 'hopefully'. If you say, 'See you tomorrow', an Arab will reply '*In sha Allah*', ie, 'Yes, if God permits it and you don't fall under a bus in the meantime'. Or you can say 'Will it be ready tomorrow?' and he can reply '*In sha Allah*', meaning 'Yes I hope so, but if it isn't I've got a let out.'

al-hamdu lillah: thanks be to God. Said every time something works out the way it should have done. Often has the force of 'Thank God for that!' to express relief.

FURTHER READING

Jordan and the Holy Land

King **Abdullah** of Jordan *My memories completed "Al Takmilah"*,
Longman, 1978

Iain **Browning** *Petra*, Chatto and Windus

Abba **Eban** *My Country: The Story of Modern Israel*,
Weidenfeld and Nicholson, 1972

David **Gilmour** *Dispossessed: The Ordeal of the Palestinians 1917-80*,
Sidgewick and Jackson, 1980

John Bagot **Glubb** *Britain and the Arabs*, Hodder and Stoughton, 1959
(Glubb Pasha) *A Soldier with the Arabs*, Harper and Bros, 1959
The Story of the Arab Region, Da Capo, 1976

G. Lancaster **Harding** *The Antiquities of Jordan*,
Jordan Distribution Agency, 1979

HRH Prince **Hassan** *A Study of Jerusalem*, Longman 1979
Bin Talal

S. W. **Helms** *Jawa: Lost City of the Black Desert*,
Cornell University Press, 1981

David **Hirst** *The Gun and the Olive Branch*, Faber and Faber, 1977

Tony **Howard** *Treks and Climbs in the Mountains of Petra*,
Jordan Distribution Agency, 1987

King **Hussein** Ibn Talal *Uneasy Lies the Head*, Heinemann, 1962
My War with Israel, William Morrow, 1969

Rami **Khouri** *Jerash – a frontier city of the Roman East*,
Jordan Distribution Agency, 1986
Petra – a guide to the capital of the Nabateans,
Jordan Distribution Agency, 1986

Teddy **Kollek** and *Jerusalem: A History of Forty Centuries*,
Mosha Pearlman Steintelky, 1991

T E **Lawrence** *Seven Pillars of Wisdom*, Penguin 1976

Major General James **Lunt** *Hussein of Jordan*, Fontana, 1990

D. S. **Margolionth** *Cairo, Jerusalem and Damascus*,
Chatto and Windus, 1907

H. V. **Morton** *In the Steps of the Master*, Methuen and Co., 1937

Trevor **Mostyn** *Jordan, a MEED Practical Guide*, MEED 1983

Christine **Osborne** *Insights and Guide to Jordan*, Longman 1981

Steven **Runciman** *A History of the Crusades, 3 vols*,
Cambridge University Press, 1953-54

Peter **Snow** *Hussain: A Biography*, Burns and Jenkins, 1972

Gerald **Sparrow** *Hussain of Jordan*, Harrap 1960

Colin **Thubron** *Jerusalem*, Heinemann, 1969

Peter **Vine** *The Heritage of Jordan*, Immel, 1987

Shelagh **Weir** *The Bedouin*, Museum of Mankind, 1966

INDEX

-A-

Abila	83
Accommodation	13
Adasiyeh	78
Air Travel	11, 12, 184
Ajlun	68, 85
Alexander the Great	28, 55
Allenby Bridge	23, 183
Amman	52, 58
Airport	46
Altitude	46
Car hire	51
Citadel	58
Environs	63
Folklore museum	61
Hotels	46
Plan	57
Restaurants	50
Roman theatre	60
Shopping	51
Tour of	58
Umayyad Palace of	59
Aqaba	117, 176
Hotels	117
Plan	178
Travel to	117
Ar-Rabad castle	85
Arabic Language	41, 210
Arab Revolt	179
Aybak	86, 87, 107
Azraq	69

-B-

Bab el-Dhra'a	132
Baha'is	78
Banks	18
Beaches	118
Bedouin	34, 61
Beidha	145, 171
Beit Sahua	216
Beit She'an	221

Belvoir Castle	221
Bethlehem	210, 215
Bibliography	227
Black iris	44
Boat travel	11
Budgeting	15
Burckhardt, James	149
Bus travel	11, 12
Buseira	138

-C-

Calendar of festivals	24
Camels	34, 175
Camping	13
Capernaum	220
Capitolias	83
Car ferries	12, 117
Car hire	13, 184
Carnet de passage	11, 12, 13
Christianity	29
Chronology of historical events	27
Climate	17, 185
Clothing	17, 186
Communications	16
Coral Reefs	177, 178
Credit cards	15
Crossing to West Bank	23, 183
Crusaders' castles	133, 221
Cultural Heritage	25

-D-

Dead Sea	115, 119
Dead Sea Scrolls	211
Deih Alla	73
Desert palaces	102, 221
Desert road	180
Dhat Ra's	136
Dhiban	128
Dibeen	68, 88
Discounted fares	11
Drink	14
Driving	13

-E-

Economy	40
Education	40
Ein Gedi	211
Electricity	16
Es Sabah	146
Exodus	28

-F-

Festivals	24
Fish	177
Flora and fauna	43
Food and drink	14, 184

-G-

Gadara, see Umm Qais	
Gallilee, Sea of	219
Geography	26
Gerasa, see Jerash	
Glubb Pasha	30, 174
Gomorrah	130
Government	37

-H-

Hamman el-Sarakh	105
Hebron	214
Herodinn	214
Himmeh, el-	77
Hisham's Palace	221
History	27, 53, 91, 147, 188
Holy Land	181
Crossing from Jordan	183
History	188
Itineraries	189
Tourist Offices	186

-I-

Iraq el-Amr	64
Irbid	68, 82
Information, where to go for	20, 186
Internal flights	12

Intifada	8, 186
Islam	32, 60

-J-

Jawa	101
Jerash	69, 88
site plan	90
tour of	91
Jebel Haroun	146, 171
Jericho	222
Jerusalem	187, 189
Armenian Quarter	202
Christian Jerusalem	198
Haram Esh Sherif	193
Hotels	187
Holy Sepulchre	201
Itinerary	189
Jewish Quarter	203
Plan	190
Wailing Wall	197
JETT	11, 12
John the Baptist	128, 220
Jordan Valley	72, 221
Judaism	204

-K-

Kerak	115, 133
Khaf, al	63
Khirbet al-Mafjar	221
Khirbet Tannur	137
King Abdallah	37, 62
King Hussein	37
King's Highway	120, 147

-L-

Language	41
Latroun	218
Lawrence, T E, (of Arabia)	30, 173
Lot's wife	131, 214

-M-

Ma'an	180
Machnas, El	146
Madaba	121
Mansaf	14
Marriage customs	36
Mar Saba monastery	216
Massada	212
Media	16
Mezze	14
Money	15, 185
Moses	122
Moses' grave	122
Moses' spring	140
Mt Nebo	121
Mt Sartaba	77
Mu'awiya	103
Mukawir (Herod's Palace)	126
Muhammad	33, 194
Mukhayyat, al-	123
Mukheibeh	77
Museums	18
Mu'tah	136

-N-

Nabateans	29, 55, 100, 137, 148
Nazareth	217, 219
Nuweiba	11
Nof Ginossar	217
Nuweijis, al-	63

-O-

Opening hours	18
Oryx	44

-P-

Pella	68, 75
Petra	140
Background Infromation	146
Hotels	115
Itineraries	144
Plan	142
Tour of	151
Visitors' Centre	116
Petrol	13
Pharoahs Island	178
Pilgrim trail	172
Population	32
Postal service	16
Prehistoric graveyard	119
Prince Hassan	34
Proverbs	150
Public Holidays	24

-Q-

Qasr Amra	108
Qasr Azraq	106
Qasr el-Hallabat	104
Qasr Kharaneh	111
Qasr el-Mushatta	67, 113
Qasr Tuba	112
Queen Nour	39
Qumran	211
Quweisme, al-	63

-R-

Rabad, Ar- castle	85
Rail travel	12
Ramadan	24
Ras el-Naqab	174
Religion	32
Roads	13
Roman rule	28
Rum, Wadi	116, 173

-S-

Sabra	171
Saladin	29, 86, 133, 134, 139, 140
Salt	68, 70
Samaria	218
Sea of Galiliee	219
Sebastea	218
Security and safety	18
Service taxis	12

Shagara ed-Durr	87
Shawbak	138
Shaumari Wildlife Reserve	44, 107
Shawarma	15
Shopping	18, 51
Siq al-Baared	145, 170
Sodom	130, 213
Solomon	54
Swafiyeh	65

-T-

Tafila	138
Taxis	12
Tell es-Saidiyeh	73
Tiberias	217, 219
Time	16
Tipping	15
Tour operators	20
Transjordan	56
Travel to Jordan	11
Travel within Jordan	12

-U-

Umm al-Biyarah	104
Umm al-Jimal	99
Umm ar-Rassas	129
Umm Qais	68, 79
Umayyad palaces	102, 105, 109, 221
Universities	41

-V-

Vaccinations	185
Visas	16, 185

-W-

Wadi el-Hassan	137
Wadi es-Sir	64
Wadi Masa	140
Wadi Mujib	129
Wadi Qelt	222
Wadi Rum	116, 173

Water	15, 17
Watersports	20
Weights and measures	18
West Bank, crossing to	23
Wine	15
Woairah	146, 170

-Z-

Zai National Park	71
Zerqa ma'in	115, 125